Development and Conflict in Community Lending Programs

Development and Conflict in Community Lending Programs: A Socio-Cultural Perspective

BY

NISHI MALHOTRA

Indian Institute of Management, Sambalpur, India

emerald
PUBLISHING

United Kingdom – North America – Japan – India – Malaysia – China

Emerald Publishing Limited
Emerald Publishing, Floor 5, Northspring, 21-23 Wellington Street, Leeds LS1 4DL

First edition 2026

Reprints and permissions service
Contact: www.copyright.com

Printed and bound by CPI Group (UK) Ltd, Croydon, CR0 4YY

British Library Cataloguing in Publication Data
A catalogue record for this book is available from the British Library

ISBN: 978-1-83708-291-9 (Print)
ISBN: 978-1-83708-290-2 (Online)
ISBN: 978-1-83708-292-6 (Epub)

INVESTOR IN PEOPLE

I would like to dedicate this book to my parents, sister, my professors from IIM Kozhikode and to all the mentors, Government of India and self-help groups in India.

Contents

List of Abbreviations

AEPS	Aadhar Enabled Payment System
ATM	Automated teller machine
BC	Business Correspondent
BFS	Board for financial supervision
BMMU	Block mission management unit
CGMTSE	Credit Guarantee Fund Trust for Micro and Small Enterprise
CIDA	Canadian International Development Agency
CIF	Community Investment Fund
CLF	Cluster Level Federations
CM	Chief Minister
CRP	Community resource person
CRP	Community resource person
CSC	Common service center
CSO	Civil Society Organizations
DAY	Deendayal Antodaya Yojana
DMMU	District Mission Management Unit
DRDA	District level with District Rural Development Agencies
DRDA	District Rural Development Agency
GDP	Gross Domestic Product
GOI	Government of India
GP	Gram Panchayat
HRD	Human Resource Development
IIBF	Indian Institute of Banking and Finance
IIT	Indian Institute of Technology
IMF	International monetary fund
ISO	International Standard Organization
MAC	Mutually Aided Corporation
MAIN	Majlis Agama Islam Negeri

MAIM	Melaka Islamic Religious Council
MAIS	Majlis Agama Islam Selangor
MFI	Micro finance institutions
MSME	Micro Small and Medium Enterprises
MYRADA	Mysore Resettlement and Development Agency
MNREGA	Mahatma Gandhi National Rural Employment Guarantee
NABARD	National Bank for Agriculture and Rural Development
NGO	Non Government Organizations
NIT	National institute of technology
NPA	Nonperforming assets
NRLM	National Rural and Livelihood Mission
OCEN	Open Credit Enablement Network
OECD	Organisation for Economic Co-operation and Development
ONDC	Open Network for Digital Commerce
RBI	Reserve Bank of India
RBI	Reserve Bank of India
RBV	Resource Based View
RBV	Resource based view
PMSVA	PM Street Vendor's Atamanirbhar Nidhi.
PPP	Purchasing power parity
PRI	Panchayat Raj Institutes
PRADAN	Professional Assistance for Development Action
P2P	Peer to peer
ROSCAs	Rotating Savings and Credit Association
RSETI	Rural Self Employment Training Institutes
SAKSHAM	Stimulating Advanced Knowledge for Sustainable Health Management
SBLP	Self help group bank linkage program
SDG	Sustainable Development Goals
SEWA	Self Employed Women's Association
SHG	Self-help group
SHPAs	Self help promoting association

SLRM	State livelihood rural mission
SMMU	State mission management unit
SVAMITA	Survey of Villages and Mapping with Improvized Technology in Village Areas
TPB	Theory of Planned Behavior
UN	United Nation
UPI	Unified Payment Interface
VLE	Village level enterprises
VO	Village organizations
WTO	World trade organization

Preface

Community lending initiatives have emerged as panacea for combating the financial woes of more than 1.7 billion people, who are below the poverty line across the globe. The marginalized sections of society not only lack access to collateral, but they also are excluded from the larger social set up called as society. The community lending initiatives provide an opportunity for those at the bottom of the pyramid to become part of the groups. When the social reality of marginalization of these people interacts with the group membership, which comprises of the members from various diverse backgrounds, conflict emerges. The groups which are source of motivation and social capital for the members of the group in lack of effective leadership suffer from various conflicts. A group or community initiative is a mechanism that allows members who are typically marginalized in terms of access to resources to obtain formal finance. However, in reality, these social mechanisms suffer from various inherent conflicts. The complex process of interaction of the social reality of grim poverty, marginalization of the members, and group membership creates conflict of interests. At an empirical level, the group initiatives lead to abuse of power and extreme marginalization of the members, who lack voice within the group. The book aims to explore the negative cases, the instances of abuse of power, and marginalization of the poor members within the group. The resource constrained members get access to resources through aggregation in a social group. But without transformational leadership and financial leadership, the interaction of the individual and the structural factors such as peer mechanism and joint liability leads to violence, making it difficult for the members to achieve their financial objectives. The social cultural imperatives and use of peer pressures within the group without social control can lead to severe conflicts and abuse of power within the group. Financial leadership refers to the democratically appointed chairpersons, who have financial acumen and motivation to ensure the safety of funds and economic interests through proper allocation of resources within the group. Moreover, the co-optation of these initiatives through state intervention to ensure efficient allocation of funds and access to funds has come to play an extremely important role in ensuring development. The book aims to corroborate the role of state intervention and leadership in achieving development through conflict resolution and consensus building in a community lending program. Further, the book aims to develop a comparison between the inclusive and extractive social groups and institutional designs to highlight the factors and role of leadership in achieving financial inclusion of poor.

Acknowledgment

I would like to thank my parents, the Armed forces, the Government of India, IIM Sambalpur, IIM Kozhikode for the immense support and academic inputs, motivation, and encouragement to author this book. I would like to thank Emerald Publishing, Editor Daniel Ridge, Lydia Cutmore, Lucy loveday, Sally Wilson for this opportunity. Without their academic inputs and encouragement, this would not have been possible.

Chapter 1

Conflicts in a Community Lending Program: Interaction of Individual and Structural Factors

Abstract

This chapter will examine the conflicts in a community lending program and explore how the interaction of individual and structural factors leads to conflicts in a group. This chapter will use the theoretical lens of developmental conflict theory to study the real-world cases of failures of community lending programs in Asia. This chapter will use the case study method and hermeneutics to explore the underlying factors that lead to conflicts within the community lending initiatives. It will further differentiate between the good and bad groups through a comparative analysis of the groups using multiple case studies. Inclusive groups will be the groups that are successful and do not have any conflicts and lead to equitable distribution of the resources among the members of the group. The extractive groups are the groups that create inequities and suffer from conflicts among the members of the group. While many studies have explored the success of the community lending model, there is a gap in terms of a study on factors that lead to conflict within the groups. This chapter will provide the reader with a comparative study of good and bad community institutions and how they differ. It will provide a conceptual framework of factors leading to conflict within the group. It will also touch upon the issue of resource constraints and scarce resources within the groups. The scope of the study will be diverse, including India, Nepal, Bangladesh, China, and European countries like Germany, Britain, and Ireland.

Keywords: Conflicts; microfinance; development; community; lending groups

Development and Conflict in Community Lending Programs, 1–21

Published under exclusive licence by Emerald Publishing Limited
doi:10.1108/978-1-83708-290-220251003

Introduction

Community lending is a way to provide finance to the people at the bottom of the pyramid through leveraging social capital and existing network relationships. These people are marginalized sections of society and they do not have access to finance due to the lack of collateral and lack of any information about their creditworthiness. UN Sustainable Development Goals have highlighted the importance of poverty reduction and women's empowerment. The group lending is aimed at promoting financial sustainability, and resilience among the members of society. However, despite maintaining very high repayment rates, the groups often suffer failure in extreme cases due to various reasons. Conflicts among the members of the group are often the reason for the weak institutional sustainability and breaking up of the groups. In the context of the groups, as the social realities of marginalization of the members interact with the social environment, it becomes extremely difficult for the members to raise finance from the formal sector or the banks. Adverse selection and lack of information symmetry regarding the character and creditworthiness of the borrowers are the major reasons for the breaking up of the groups. Generally, the groups are to be formed by people who are of the same risk category, which will help create solidarity and thus reduce the moral hazard or risk of misutilization of loans among the members of the group. Thus, the heterogeneity of the members is one of the most important reasons for the breaking of the groups. Similarly, the social capital among the members of the group is the other reason for the success of the group. Social capital refers to the social relationships and good relationships among the members of the group. This social relationship is generated by the existing professional relationships and personal relationships among the members of the group. Not only social capital but the size of the group also has an important impact on the success and stability of the groups. The study highlights that small groups have higher chances of being successful and generally suffer from fewer conflicts. Thus, various factors lead to issues in lending to these people. There is a lack of studies on what leads to conflict among the members of the group. Previous studies show that socioeconomic factors, or cultural factors, might lead to the breaking of the groups. In this chapter hermeneutics and grounded theory approach have been used to discuss the role of various factors in the success of the groups or community lending programs.

Research Problem

Group lending and collective lending provide loans and credit to the people at the bottom of the pyramid. These people do not have access to physical capital and through the social capital, they can access the loans as part of the members of the self-help groups or community lending programs. In this regard, the groups provide various benefits to the members such as access to finance, credit, and social capital and for banks, it provides benefits such as achieving the objective of financial inclusion for the poor at the bottom of the pyramid. Though the groups are the most viable mechanism for ensuring access to finance to the people at the bottom of the pyramid, various factors impact the success of the groups. Groups are the source of finance and ensure various advantages such as 100% repayment rates and financial viability of the poor. This study will explore the impact of various factors on the economic sustainability of the groups. The case study method will be used for studying the impact of various factors on the financial sustainability of groups. The study mainly classifies the factors responsible for conflict among the group as cognitive factors such as social capital, size of the group, and homogeneity of the members. Besides, affective factors such as the free rider problem, trust erosion due to external influences, lack of trust-building exercises, and lack of interpersonal relationships are cited as the reasons post-formation of the group, responsible for the breakage of the group. The issue of marginalization of the poor refers to first-order cooperative dilemma that refers to a situation in game theory where, for each individual involved, the best course of action based on self-interest is to not cooperate, even though the collective outcome would be significantly better if everyone cooperated; essentially, it describes a scenario where the individual gain from defecting outweighs the benefit of cooperation, leading to a suboptimal outcome for the group as a whole, like the classic *"Prisoner's Dilemma"*. This study also aims to explore the behavioral dimension of group operations and success. The major research problem of the study is to identify the real causes of conflict in a great social innovation like group lending. Most of the communities are subject to conflicts and strife and are often referred to as the fragility contexts. The communities provide various contexts for resilience to combat desolation through social structures and political will. However, the paradox of community is that it can be a source of distress in case of conflict of interest.

Theoretical Lens

A community lending group is predominantly a network of relations among the members. This network could be bonding, which refers to the within-group network relations, or linkages, which refers to the relationship with the banks and other financial institutions in the form of loans and credit relations. In this study, the social capital theory has been used to explore the various reasons for the conflict among the members of the group. Social capital theory highlights the importance of the networks and the existing social relationships on the financial sustainability of the groups. Institutional theory explores the impact of institutional factors such as norms, regulations, practices, and behaviors on the economic sustainability of the groups. The theoretical framework for social conflict theory highlights that social conflicts are largely caused due to various social factors such as gender bias, cultural bias, and network relations in predominantly women-led communities. The impact of these conflicts is that they lead to class struggles, and discrimination of a certain individual, which provides a certain degree of balance. The coping strategies for these are the use of mass media and state intervention. The manifestation of the same is migration.

Table 1 provides details regarding social conflict theory.

Table 1. Social Conflict Theory.

Social conflict theory	Causes: Power, gender, cultural bias and networks Impact: Conflict and class struggles Resolution: Negotiation, intervention and intelligence Manifestation: Migration

Source: Author's work.

Further, in this study, we will be using the conflict theory that highlights that the social order is to be maintained using democratization and participation, rather than using power hierarchies. In any kind of group, the scarcest thing is the access to resources. In this regard, the developmental conflict plays an important role in ensuring access to financial capital for financial inclusion. Hence, often a healthy interplay of conflict and developmental initiatives plays an important role in the peaceful existence of the groups.

Research Methodology

For conducting this study, the qualitative research design has been used to get an understanding of the problem. To conduct this study, the primary data was collected by using the semi-structured interview method. Further hermeneutics method has been used for the analysis of the secondary data collected from the books, journals, and publications. While collecting the data, the ethical considerations were duly taken into consideration, which include taking care of the informed consent and confidentiality.

Discussion and Analysis

Beneath the waters of faith, blue domes pierce the sky, their twins reflected in pools below, each doorway opening to new wisdom, where white marble glows. A white elephant and horse stand guard in this sanctuary, like sentinels from ancient tales in this archipelago of art. Enchantress of the east your beauty spans above, below, an oasis of the spirit where tulips and bougainvillea grow. Based on the vision of Islam namely *zakat*, these flowers brave the desert heat, adapting, thriving, and blooming still where sand and sacred waters meet. A journey of enlightenment, where culture, faith, and beauty blend, in this grand mosque's embrace, where East and West transcend. The enchantress signifies co-adaptation, adaptation, and acculturation, enabling evolution and providing room for newer species and new life forms. Within the prosperous country of Malaysia, a religious practice called Majlis is based on five principles of Islam, namely beliefs, Al Shahada (profession of faith), Solat (the prayer), Sawm (the fast of Ramadan), Zakat (compulsory charity) and Hajj (the pilgrimage). In the holy Quran and hadith, the practice of providing money, goods, and charity to others is mentioned as an act of nobility. Out of all these virtues, Zakat (the practice of Islamic charity) is aimed at providing alms to the marginalized sections of society to improve the quality of life. In the city of Malaysia, the practice of Zakat is institutionalized and the state is involved in raising money through Lembaga Zakat Selangor for the poor rightful beneficiaries (*ansaf*) through Majlis Agama Islam Selangor (MAIS). In Malaysia, the practice of Zakat is a socioeconomic practice that is institutionalized to provide benefits to the lower sections of society. Various state agencies and institutions are involved in raising the funds in the form of Zakat which is distributed applying various principles of donations. There are mainly two different types of Zakat, i.e., zakat on self (Fitrah) and zakat on wealth. *Zakat on Fitrah* is a sacrifice made from own wealth, the main purpose of which is to help the less fortunate. Zakat implies to grow, sacrifice, and to grow. This amount is contributed annually compulsorily. Another form of charity is Zakat on wealth, which is paid from existing wealth out of own wealth. Further, the Zakat is distributed among various sections of needy and marginalized sections of society, which include fakir (below nisab or poverty threshold), masakin, amil (administrator of matters relating to zakat), Muallaf Al-Qulub and riqab (free slaves). Another important category for the receipt of Zakat includes Jumhur ullama defined ibnu sabil as Musafir or wayfarers. One of the major reasons for the success of this practice is the increase in access to technology such as Internet banking and mobile banking. In Islam, Majlis or community meetings are the most common form of meeting together and discussing the issues of importance for the survival of life. In Malaysia, the practice of administration of zakat is handled through Majlis Agama Islam Negeri (MAIN). The main issue in the sustainability of these institutions is the moral hazard and the probability that the funds might be misutilize for ulterior purposes. Thus, the monitoring and supervision of these financial institutions play an important role in the sustainability of these groups. Islamic microfinance is based on the principle of interest-free loans to all. The case in point is Grameen Bank, which charges interest for providing loans to the people at the bottom of the pyramid. Evolution is not a simple process and involves a continuous struggle for survival, which involves strife and conflicts among the various life forms to occupy the space in the mosaic or archipelago of life. Similarly, in Islamic microfinance, terms and covenants of loans have evolved over some time to meet the needs of the beneficiaries. Various group lending practices such as amurabahah (cost-plus financing), qard al-hasan (benevolent loans), and musharakah (partnership) have started to provide financial assistance to the people at the bottom of the pyramid. In the case of these three kinds of microfinance lending practices, the loan is provided to the group based on group and spousal guarantees guided by ethics. One such institution Melaka Islamic Religious Council (MAIM) was established in September 1980 to assist with the distribution of Zakat among the lower sections of society. MAIM provides microfinance and supply of loans, through the funds collected from the monthly contribution made by the contributors. The duration of the contribution is determined with mutual consent and the funds collected are disbursed to the small entrepreneurs. The beneficiaries are selected through a stringent screening process to benefit the Miskin (poor) or the destitute (fakir). MAIM is based on the *Qard al Hassan* contract, which aims to repay the loans that are borrowed. The review of the literature highlighted that the main challenge to this practice is the perception that the zakat is their divine right and that repayment is unnecessary. The nonrepayment of loans often leads to conflicts and strife in a group. This principle also applies to the evolution of groups and communities that exist to ensure access to finance for the people at the bottom of the pyramid. Symbiosis refers to the mutually beneficial relationship between two groups and people. Whereas the parasitic relationship in which the parasite thrives on the body of the host. One of the major problems in the case of a group that is lending money is the problem of free riding. From nature, if we look at the example of a Mistletoe, it signifies that given the diversity in nature, the mistletoe has a parasitic behavior, where it thrives on the nutrients of the host plant. This kind of parasitic behavior leads to the death and demise of the host. Similarly, in a group, the parasitic attributes and properties or free rider problem leads to the emergence of conflicts among the members of the group (Darwin, 2024). Thus, the free rider behavior is the major reason for the conflicts among the members of this group.

Majlis for Women

The emergence of grassroots movements in desert communities, often called "flowers of fire," represents a powerful symbol of resistance and resilience, particularly among women and marginalized groups. Like hardy desert blooms, these social movements flourish in challenging conditions. These movements have attracted the attention of various non-governmental organizations and advocacy groups, which catalyze social change and empowerment. Their involvement helps amplify local voices and supports community-led initiatives. Unlike natural evolutionary processes, the growth of these movements stems from conscious human action and organized responses to systemic inequalities. The "seeds" of change are deliberately planted and nurtured through collective action. The widespread impact of these disparities (the "umbrella effect") between privileged and disadvantaged groups continues to shape social dynamics. These differences manifest in access to resources, opportunities, and representation. However, through established legal frameworks and institutional support systems, these movements have achieved some success in challenging existing power structures. This has created pathways for disadvantaged communities to gain greater agency and voice in societal decisions. Social structures include the avenues to deliberate and reach a mutual consensus through social cooperation and collaboration. In the case of the marginalized sections of society, the people living below the poverty line do not have any access to physical resources. Within the definition of the marginalized section of society is included the definition of the indigenous people. These people are at odds with other sections of society, as they are not allowed access to public places due to their antecedents. These people are vulnerable to the prowess of the higher castes and they need state intervention to secure some basic rights, and struggle to protect economic and social value. When we compare the individuals residing in a country or a nation in terms of diversity, we find that indeed all of them are so diverse and different from each other due to the varied living conditions, climates, genes, education, income, and gender. This brings us to the conclusion that diversity indeed leads to many conflicts and complex dynamics in the group. The homogeneity of the members within the group is the precursor of the group membership and paves the way for development and growth. Thus, the criterion of selection of the members of the group paves the way for institutional sustainability. Homogeneity of the members in terms of color, race, and gender sets the trajectory for the success and financial sustainability of the common lending programs.

Within a group, the shared norms and social relations are dynamic and keep on varying with the change in the circumstances and conditions, both external and internal to the group. To preserve the homogeneity and yet create financial prudence, the state often conducts various social intermediation initiatives to ensure the financial sustainability of groups. Despite the homogeneity of the traits, hardly there is any perfect machine that can ensure behavioral homogeneity and no moral hazard. It is only through continuous monitoring and surveillance that the group leader can identify the deviations and variability of financial behavior. In this regard, the role of financial intermediation and social intermediation cannot be overemphasized. If we look at the living world, we will find instances of conflict emerging due to the struggle for life and the underlying principle of survival of the fittest. This principle is at odds with the principle of solidarity in a group. Even in the natural world, there is a practice of evolution and discrimination and the origin of new species and forms. In a world of marginalization, there is hardly any other remedy than putting in place certain screening criteria for creating homogenous groups that can sustain and can as a group work collaboratively toward the achievement of financial goals. The natural world is diverse and living beings are diverse in terms of genes and genetic makeup across the globe. Darwin's theory cites examples of coexistence and the correlation of growth, and inheritance as the first phase of human evolution. Within this phase, the organisms stay together and fight for survival, during which the weaker species go extinct. Contrary to sexual selection, the rudimentary organs become extinct, which gives way to living independently. Similarly, in the initial phases of the group, the members select each other and then they cooperate and collaborate for the distribution of scarce resources based on sexual selection. Conflict arises due to the unequal distribution of resources and is resolved through sexual selection.

This gives rise to new breeds and new traits and the evolution of new forms and species. In a human species that is more than a million years old, the material and capitalist world order is based on deliberate efforts to select members based on certain predetermined criteria to reduce the chances of adverse selection. In such groups, weaker members are hand-held and nurtured by the other members, which is contrary to the natural theory of survival of the fittest. Through solidarity and cooperation, the members motivate the defaulting members to pay the loans. Within a group, the shared norms and social relations are dynamic and keep on varying with the change in the circumstances and conditions, both external and internal to the group. To preserve the homogeneity and yet create financial prudence, the state often conducts various social intermediation initiatives to ensure the financial sustainability of groups. Despite the homogeneity of the traits, hardly there is any perfect machine that can ensure behavioral homogeneity and no moral hazard. However, the homogeneity of the members is the ultimate defense against adverse selection. For marginalized that gain financial traction, it becomes viable to exercise constitutional remedies for the dignity of the human species. The objective of this study is to analyze the influence of the dominance style, and social power on conflicts within a group or community. The group lending programs are aimed at providing access to finance for the people at the bottom of the pyramid. Society and culture refer to the relational system of interaction among individuals. In his study, the author draws an analogy between the Macaque world and the communities that thrive within the society. The literature highlights that the social relationships among the rhesus macaque are characterized by agnostic asymmetries, whereas Tonkean macaques are characterized by no asymmetries (Thierry et al., 2004). Conflicts among the members of a group are propagated by the dominance of a single individual or refer to egalitarian rule, while in the case of the more tolerant group, are characterized by the sharing of power and hierarchies among the members of the group. The groups characterized by the power concentrated in the single individual are often termed despotic, which leads to strife among the members of the group. The outcomes of the conflict and the strives among the members of the group are characterized by the social contract and understanding among the members of the group. It depends upon the alliances and relationships among the members of the group and the social knowledge about the group among the members. The literature highlights the importance of the distribution of social power among the individual as the reason for the conflicts among the members of the group. Self-help groups are community lending programs that are aimed at providing access to finance for the people at the bottom of the pyramid. These are the people who lack the physical resources and collateral to access finance. Thus, these are the people whose social realities when interacting with the environment, lead to friction and conflicts. The factors that lead to conflict among the members of the group include the exogenous factors and the endogenous factors. The exogenous factors are the factors that exist in the external factors and impact the sustainability of the groups. Besides, the endogenous factors refer to the internal factors that impact the solidarity and harmony in the group. Endogenous factors refer to group dynamics such as unequal participation, free rider problem, and conflict resolution, which lead to conflicts and friction within the group, (Magambo, 2024). Various other external factors include macroeconomic conditions, and regulations to name a few. The external regulatory environment exerts immense influence on the success of community lending programs. The financial institutions should exercise conflict resolution mechanisms to ensure the sustainability of the group lending programs. In their 2020 study, N. Sabin and F. Reed-Tsochas point out that a group's social structure often encourages its members to informally enforce loan repayment. Non ability to punish the noncooperators often leads to the disintegration of the groups and the breaking up of the groups. The paper mentions the first-order cooperative dilemma, which propagates that it refers to internal motivation to share the collective benefits, without cooperating. Most of the literature cites that the groups fail because of the first-order cooperative dilemma, people not contributing and sharing the benefits. And the second-order cooperative dilemma refers to the people not contributing to the enforcement of norms, without personally contributing to enforcement, (Oliver, 1980). Further literature highlights that both reasons can lead to conflicts in a group. However, the existence of the second-order cooperative dilemma can exaggerate the existence of the first-order cooperative dilemma. Due to the homogeneity of members and existing social relationships, the members who exaggerate sharing in collective benefits without contributing can accentuate the problem of the second-order cooperative dilemma. The members hence in the group face two dilemmas, whether they should sanction the member who does not contribute to the group and whether the members should at all pay back their loans taken from the group. There are two reasons for the breaking up of the group, i.e., the first-order cooperative dilemma and the second-order cooperative dilemma.

First-Order and Second-Order Cooperative Dilemmas Among Group Members

The first-order cooperative dilemma, where they do not pay back the loans taken from the group is due to the nonhomogenous members who do not know each other. A first-order cooperative dilemma refers to a situation in game theory where, for each individual involved, the best course of action based on self-interest is to not cooperate, even though the collective outcome would be significantly better if everyone cooperated. Each participant is incentivized to choose noncooperation, even if it means a worse outcome for the entire group. In this kind of scenario, the members do not cooperate. A second-order cooperative dilemma exists when the members are homogenous, they know each other and hence will not punish each other, considering they plan to stay together. The issues and challenges concerning first-order and second-order cooperative dilemmas also arise because of the social structure and the position of the members in the social structure. This further leads to the risk of strategic default among the members of the group.

Fig. 1 provides details regarding factors impacting conflict in the group.

The ability and willingness to cooperate depend on the structural embeddedness of the social norms and the structural covenants. Cassar and Wydick (2010) in his research study highlights the importance of social capital in promoting financial sustainability and peer influence can have positive and negative impacts on the sustainability of a group Bonacich et al. (1976) in his research study highlights that the size of the groups has an impact on the financial sustainability of groups. Avruch (2022) and Bell and Song (2005) in their research study highlighted the role of emotions in the resolution of the conflict process. There are various emotions that include hostility or a self-focused approach,

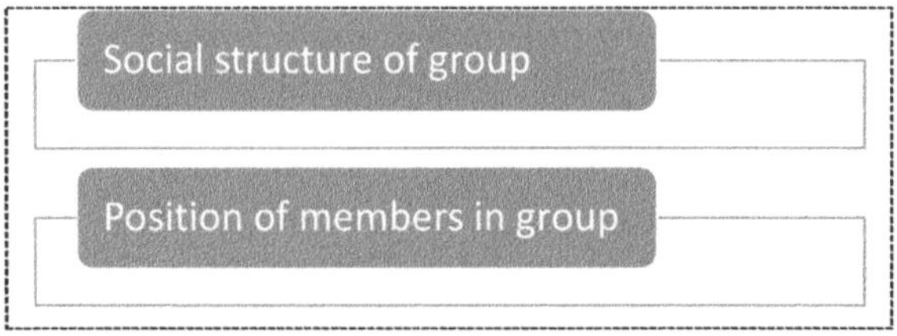

Fig. 1. Factors Impacting Conflict in the Group. *Source:* Author's work.

self-conscious emotions or avoidance approach, relational positivity or another focused approach, fear approach, or self-blame approach. Tse et al., (1994) in their research study highlighted that in China, the suggested strategies to avoid conflicts are negotiation, and withdrawal negotiation, with person-related conflict generating more negative responses. Rajeev et al. (2019) highlight the presence of high transaction costs as the reason for breaking up and discontinuance of the groups. Venittelli (2022) highlights that the group mechanism leads to reduced agency costs and higher incentives for lending to the poor. Ahlin, and Townsend (2007) highlight that the repayment is impacted negatively by joint liability and social ties and positively by the correlation of output and the borrower's ability to act cooperatively. Haldar and Stiglitz's (2016) research study highlights that social capital and trust are the major factors that impact the well-being the group lending program in India. Chatterjee and Sarangi (2004) highlight that the social identity and sociocultural norms greatly impact the success of the group lending programs. Ralston and Wright (2003) in their study highlighted that loan monitoring and social objectivities have a deep impact on the conflicts within an organization. According to research by Anon (2003) and Haldar and Stiglitz (2016), implementing stronger Know Your Customer (KYC) norms and screening processes can be highly effective in minimizing disputes among group members. N. Sabin and F. Reed-Tsochas (2018) in their research study highlights that peer lending without peer sanctioning is not the right pathway to achieving financial resilience and could give rise to more conflicts in the group lending mechanism. Existing studies highlight that at the heart of the issue is the resource-based view, which includes access to capital and financial resources. Due to the existing power hierarchies and structures, the conflict among the members of the group increases drastically. Boone (1992) in his study draws an analogy as Hawk–the Dove contest as a competition for scarce resources. As per the various studies, resources at the disposal of the organizations are distributed according to the hierarchal positions and power hierarchies. Within the organization, there are two kinds of roles, the subordinate role, which is characterized by the rights of the individuals, and the superior role that are characterized by the hierarchy of superior-subordinate relationships.

Generally, the higher responsibility and power-centric roles are associated with the superior ranks and hierarchies.

Stereotyping and Halo Effect

One of the major reasons for conflict among the group members is the stereotyping of the members. This stereotyping and the halo around the roles lead to discrimination among the members of the group. The conflicts are mainly perpetuated when the self-image of the members of marginalized sections interact with the perception and biases of others and the social realities. Cognitive stability often is determined by the match between the reality and self-image of the members. And the mismatch between reality and self-image leads to underdevelopment and skull fractures. In a group, the subordinate often tries to reduce tensions through the submission to the demands of the superior rank. The role relations between the superior and subordinate are created in a way that there is no extant limit to the expansion of the prestige of the superior at the expense of the poor and subordinates (Thompson, 1961). In a social lending group, the membership comprises people from different backgrounds. Generally, the members in a group are nonhomogenous, which leads to increased conflicts and thus the second-grade cooperative dilemma among the members of the group (Schouten et al., 2024). Highlights the importance of the hierarchy conflict, which refers to the dispute that arises among the members due to the difference in ranks and social positions. Professional dignity and the dignity of work is the important thing in a workplace or community lending. The self-interest of the individuals. Based on the research of Ralston and Wright (2003), when individuals act in their own self-interest, it can cause social objectives to interfere with economic goals. This often leads to conflicts and disputes within a group. Various studies highlight that social identity and group formation can lead to failure in the group and can also lead to conflict within the group, which propagates various social problems and issues for the group. Dusuki (2008) in his research study highlights the importance of the concept of social solidarity as propagated by Ibn Khaldun.

Teinemaa (2013) in his study highlights that intragroup conflicts increase when the members of a village live near each other and these emotions lead to severe peer pressure and further conflicts among the group of people. Ba-Tri et al. (2024) in his research paper highlights that various sanctions hurt the financial sustainability of the groups. Binns (2020) in his research study has highlighted that the conflict within the group is the outcome of the blunt application of principles of conflict resolution. Mishra and Ongena (2019) highlight that location and geographical diversity have a major impact on the conflicts in a group. Leidner and Kayworth (2006) in his research study highlights the increasing instances of conflicts due to the implementation of the technology. Colletta and Cullen (2000) in his research study highlights that social capital, social cohesion, and violent conflict lead to conflict and strives between civil society, government, and international actors. In general, the groups exist to facilitate savings among the members of the group and to circulate loans among the members. Thus, from the analysis of the data, the loans taken in an organization harm the group environment. The loan taken often leads to conflict in the group. Moreover, for the groups that are taking the loan the group efficacy or the confidence in the capability to repay the loans has a significant impact on the intention of the groups to indulge in deliberate and constructive engagement for the diffusion of conflicts (Syna Desivilya & Eizen, 2005). In various phases of group evolution (1) Forming (2) Norming (3) Storming (4) Performing, the group undergoes conflict zone. While forming a group it is important to assess the conflict appetite of members to optimize their welfare or seek redistribution of resources over group welfare. Homogeneity of risk appetite and common vision leads to peaceful coexistence and mutual maneuverability. Further, there should be a top-down approach to conflict management through corporate governance, control, and communication to control. Once experts who can quantify and assess the conflicts are selected, the next step is to design the strategies which include. Further, select a range of strategies as acceptance and mitigation of conflict rather than acceptance to create a congenial environment. Higher self-efficacy in a group, results in a more collaborative approach rather than an avoidance approach to create transformational leaders. Individuals with high self-efficacy approach conflicts proactively, often leading to better outcomes. They tend to prefer collaborative resolution strategies that benefit all parties. Strong self-efficacy across team members creates an environment of open communication. Self-efficacy can be improved through the practice of empowering leadership, providing consistent, constructive feedback, investing in conflict resolution training, and building psychological safety and trust. When team members believe in their ability to handle conflicts, they are more likely to address challenges head-on rather than avoid them. This creates stronger, more resilient teams. What strategies have you used to build self-efficacy in your teams? In the case of a community lending initiative, the stability of the group is based upon the homogeneity of the members or the members who are the same in terms of traits and classification. The heterogeneity of the members in the group leads to conflict among the members of the group. As the members belong to different categories and classes in terms of profession, demographics, and gender the crisis and conflict among the members increase manifold. With prior knowledge about the member's riskiness, the group is better suited to combat the challenges. Class cleavages that exist in society are the precursors of the violent strife between the various ethnic groups (Conteh-Morgan, 2004). The problem of inequality in terms of the unequal distribution of resources gives rise to various social problems such as poverty, economic deprivation, unemployment, and discrimination of all forms. Conflicts are prevalent in all kinds of societies and civilizations and intermediation has come to play an important role in the group scenario. The complexity of relations and ignorance of understanding mutual relations in the archipelago of financial life called a group will lead to conflicts and disputes. The crystal of life is unified because of the molecular forces called complex relations. If we look at the analogy from the animal kingdom, the most popular of the animals thrive in variety due to geometric progression. In the phenomenon of life, rare species will be modified or improved and beaten in life by improved versions. Popular ones will be diverse (varying in a correlated fashion in a Fibonacci Risky with higher variation—Yes, there's a strong correlation between components in the Fibonacci sequence. Each number is the sum of the two preceding numbers) and occupies places in the polity of nature. Thus, though the homogeneity of the group members is the panacea to the existence of humankind, yet homogeneity can be a challenge for the existence of the group. A plot with the same species will not grow at the same pace as a plot with diverse cross-breeds. Thus, we conclude groups with diversity and network relations thrive better and face fewer conflicts.

Discussion and Analysis

True solidarity isn't about surface-level connections—it's built on shared values, trust, and meaningful contribution. Social capital drives sustainable relationships, authentic participation builds lasting networks, clear accountability prevents free riding and mutual support creates tangible value. Traditional practices like *Kharchi* demonstrate timeless principles of consistent contribution, and real relationships that provide fortune and community trust. Thus, to maximize returns, what matters is how the members of the group *build networks* based on genuine value rather than status alone. Often *gender* comes in the way of the financial sustainability of the groups. Ivory towers of gender and power, often come in the way of real change and productivity if it's not motivated with self-participation and laden with hollow beliefs and taboos like shadow management. Consensus to the mission is the result of common issues and goals and in any ivory tower of a superior caste, antecedents often block the way. Theories on women's empowerment need a lot of critical analysis to filter out opportunism by women who just want to free ride and get away with moral hazard by supporting men or passing on community funds for nonproductive purposes. Innumerable women in marginalized sections complain of stripping demands by women of upper caste in the name of camaraderie. These upper caste women free ride and thanks to state laws many are met with punishments. During interviews, we have come across cases where monthly menstruations are touted as afflictions of upper-caste women and littering marginalized women and abusing them are exercised to get access to power in the name of committed and bestowed leadership. Thanks to state intervention, human rights and sustainability are often given higher priority over the power of upper-caste women. In such cases, intermediation through technology comes as an aid to this form of punitive negative reinforcements that come in the way of women who want to get into the groove of saving (that might not come naturally). In the case of a large number of women, they are not in the habit of saving regularly and a slight distraction is enough to derail the path of financial development. Intermediation through technology comes as an aid to this form of punitive negative reinforcements that come in the way of women who want to get into the groove of saving (that might not come naturally). Acculturation should not be followed by bouts of competitive rounds with women from upper caste or influential women to maintain

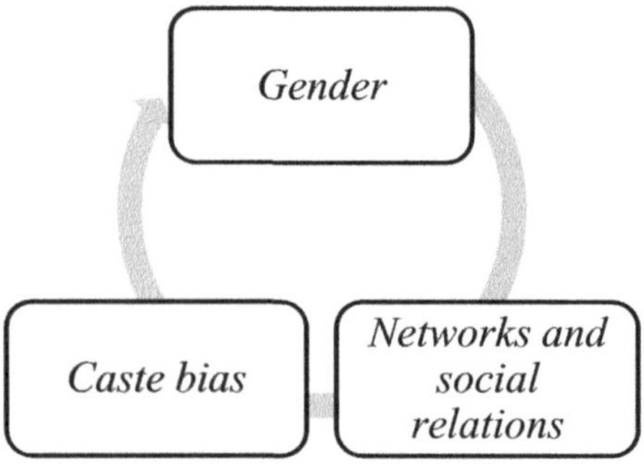

Fig. 2. Causes of Conflict Among Female Groups.

the continuity of a separate world that sets the tone for a better tomorrow. Women often feel demeaned as their social realities interact with the ivory towers of *upper-caste women*. Thus, the conflict is often the result of the way the social realities of the marginalized interact with the given social structures in the country. Thus, in brief, gender, caste bias, and network bias often lead to conflict among the members of the group.

Fig. 2 provides the causes of conflict among groups.

Power and Conflict Among Groups

Power and conflict are inherent elements of social relations and the volume of social capital possessed by an agent depends on the size of the network of connections that can effectively be mobilized. From various literature and studies, it is established that power and conflict are inherent elements of social relations and the volume of social capital possessed by agents depends on the size of the network. Within the group, the members have different levels of power and authority which leads to unequal distribution and conflicts among the members of the group.

Fig. 3 provides reasons for conflicts in the group.

Self-Help Groups

Self-help group (SHG) is a small group of 10–12 people. SHG formation is not homogenous and non-activity-based. Guidelines allow the coverage of houses on the same lane; some houses are doing pottery, some are doing weaving, and the next household is doing petty businesses. These non-homogenous groups take loans under the Self-help group Bank Loan Disbursement (SHGBLP) and one member utilizes the loan for pottery and one is utilizing it for weaving. This leads to non-repayment of loans. In a SHG which is homogenous, members can monitor each other. However, the non-homogeneity or the constitution of the groups by the members from different income groups leads to a severe conflict of

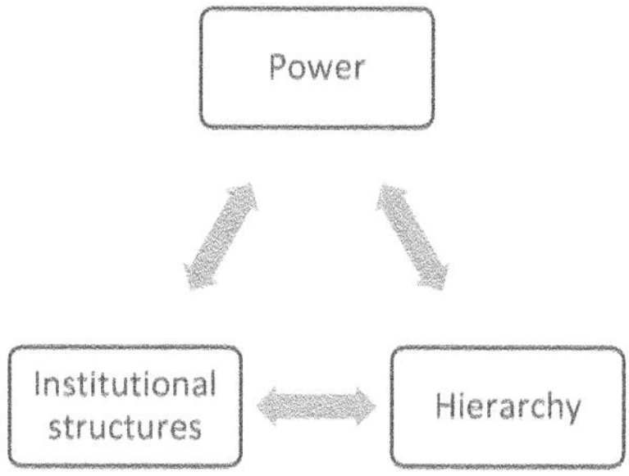

Fig. 3. Reason for Conflicts in Group. *Source:* Author's work.

interest. In an interview with the members of the group, even if somebody leaves loan is paid. If a member defaults in payment to the bank, the members get blacklisted from the group. Members are also blacklisted and this leads to further conflicts and polarization in the group. Polarization further leads to collusion and strategic default in the group. From the interview:

> Absolutely, members of a group are trusted by the bank and if an individual member approaches the bank from the group the bank remains skeptical that they might not pay. Banks are further motivated by the regular monthly meetings. Our group conducts weekly meetings in which we decide the amount of loan to be taken and the savings amount to be collected. One member of the meeting is selected as the leader of the group. In our group, there are no instances of loan default. If the member does not pay, he is expelled from the group. Peer monitoring and social sanction help in reinforcement and better repayment of loans. As all the members take the loan for productive activities and are aware of the Joint liability, they peer monitor and individual members know that they might need the loan and in case of default might be expelled from the group.

From the analysis of the interview, it becomes apparent that defaulting members are expelled from the group. This kind of negative reinforcement leads to better discipline in the group and helps to resolve the conflicts within the group.

Leadership and Conflict

The president and the co-ordinations of the panchayat Community Development Society (CDS) helped many groups in getting the maximum financial benefit, in solving conflicts, and in initiating social activities. Thus, leadership aids the resolution of conflicts and social activities. This paper uses the naturalist paradigm and within this research framework, he defines that beyond everything evolution is defined by natural selection. Thus, living beings continuously strive for the survival of the fittest and leadership plays an important role in building a favorable disposition and attitude to save among themselves. One of the major factors that leads to success in a group is the literacy of the group. Lack of financial literacy is the main reason for the non-maintenance of the books of account. Book account maintenance is not easy and minimum education is required for maintenance of the books of account. Digital literacy is extremely important for the people at the bottom of the pyramid. The members can monitor each other, as these SHGs are located in the area-specific clusters. Each unit has responsibility for the utilization of loans and also for providing loans for the setting up of the showrooms. These showrooms take responsibility for the payment of loans. Joint Liability Groups are not registered groups, but the group head can take responsibility for the payment of loans. If any of the members are not paying on time, the Joint Liability Group monitors only the group leader. In the cluster 10 to 15 members are operational. Masters' craftsmen are responsible for monitoring the craftsmanship. All the master craftsmen are formed into an apex body and the master craftsmen can exercise the pressure in his group and the other group. This craftsman is responsible for covering all the groups and the craftsmen are brought from all over the world including Banaras and West Bengal. Mutually Aided Co-operative (MAC) society and Ministry of Micro, Small & Medium Enterprises (MSME) have a lot of benefits as they can be registered under the company's act. Schedule banks can provide loans to the banks and MAC members know the banks.

Working with artisans is a very rewarding experience; it feels incredibly good to know you've helped someone earn a living. As far as a federation as things as changed, whoever they want to help, they do not do so, it is a good experience. Twenty women are chosen to form a group. Once an account is opened, your membership becomes permanent, and you can then register if you choose. Training is done for 6 months and a stipend is given to the trainer. The Directorate of Handicrafts provides a good market. The purpose of selecting the members is so that they can group and meet nearby. Thus, most of the women selected should be within 2 km. This will lead to problems. These people meet regularly and once in a month. In Orissa, banks, do not do anything, the bank gives them a loan and they distribute this loan between them and on time they pay back the loan with interest and increase their loan. In some places, the women do not need these loans. But if they get a chance to form self-help groups and our government is based on Self-help group linkage, why they would leave it? They take loans and do not pay them back and consume or utilize it. The group will not be disrupted in those cases, where the group members invest that amount. Many of the groups break away. The government gives money to SHG so that they can do some work, so that they will keep some money and they will not sit idly. In a group, if one of the members does not pay back the money, then the rest of the 19 women go back to his door and pressurize on him. The government makes schemes for the common good, but beyond a point, money gets into the hands of the wrong people. The people remain poor because still people are poor. After all, the moment money goes ahead of the government, middlemen keep their share, and all the things are not rightly managed and followed up.

This interview highlights that the bad leadership and power structures within a group lead to conflict in the group. This is to further justify that if wrong people get the authority to distribute resources, this will lead to bias and moral hazard. Thus, the bad character of leaders and dishonesty lead to the misutilization of funds and resources in a group. Thus, to increase productivity and efficiency in a group it is important to select a person as leader, only if he or she has sufficient experience in conflict handling. And to mitigate conflicts in a group the leader must be from the same socio-cultural background.

Interview regarding conflict in a group with highly marginalized members.

We are going through a crisis period. The handicraft sector during the COVID period has been highly affected. Our Self Help Promoting Institutions (SHPI) specializes in Dhokra art. They make daily utility items such as bottles, and cycles, but they do not have any tools. They go to the art center, they need tool kits, and market linkages. We make clusters and SHGs are formed only through artisans in the handicraft sector and then these are clubbed into the SHG Federation. Rest is not allowed and these groups are linked to Self-help group Bank Linkage Programme (SBLP) and other government schemes such as insurance, medical activities, pension, and senior citizen pension scheme. Due to corruption, most artisans are unable to benefit.

Thus, the interview highlights that corruption and theft also lead to conflict within the group. Discrimination and exploitation also lead to conflict in the group.

> There is a need for the behavioral change of the artisans. In the initial period, the SBLP loan granted for a particular handicraft is utilized for their purpose e.g., they buy assets for their children. Most of the members are all kind. They regularly follow SHG meetings, accounts, and bookkeeping. This is an organized sector but it will take time to organize them. The artisans live in one geography. These people live outside the bank periphery. Bank officers come and they take us to the field. We have helped them to make the groups but after the formation of the group they changed. The male members are addicted to drink. They are less interested in monitoring.

Thus, the interview highlights that behavioral changes in an artisan are of utmost importance to reduce the conflict among the people. Through intermediation and attitude change, artisans can be motivated to adopt the best financial practices.

Fig. 4 provides issues that lead to conflict in the group.

The government officers under National Rural Livelihood Mission (NRLM) also monitor them. The government only implements the program but they do not follow up. We also have limited resources and hence we cannot follow them. We do not have money to go to the field again and again. The members regularly submit accounts, they tell them and we do proceedings and then we conduct meetings. There was an artisan Ram, who was already a defaulter from the loan and Ram's wife was included in the SHG.

Fig. 4. Issues That Lead to Conflict Among Groups.
Source: Author's work.

Thus further analysis of the interview highlights, that in case of lack of resources, the limited oversight and supervision also leads to conflict in the groups. Moreover, in a financial environment fraught with challenges for the disadvantaged, the struggle among the existing group members for survival and access to resources leads to conflicts. Not only this migrant labor and members also leads to conflict within the group. And because of this bank denied the loan. The members do not know about the loan paying capacity or loan history of the members. Only when the bank denies the loan do we get to know about them. These people want short term benefits and do not look at the long-term benefit and it has become their habit. They go for product verification training and they do not get any skill but look at their immediate benefit. They are concerned about the stipend and their tour and do not care about the organization. At the time of formation of group even members do not know about each other creditworthiness. For example, at the time when they form group, members do not reveal about their prior loans. They work only for immediate benefit and bank only looks at the credit worthiness of the spouses of the members and denies the loan. We have 120 SHG and 55 SHG work well and repay loan in time and they follow up. More than 50% SHG are working well and the artisans have been given the karigars card. If somebody is unable to pay the loans and artisans all of them do not have the card. There was an exhibition to be conducted in Pragati Maidan and in this, the state government identifies the artisan and sends them to the fair. But the middlemen, gives money to the government department and unjustified people are allowed loan. The monitoring of artisans is difficult for us and we can follow up. Follow up, mobilizing the human resource, and training them are important. Most of the artisans are not financially literate. We conduct the financial literacy training for leaders and he should be responsible for interaction. However, the leaders of the groups do not interact with them. The artisans are bank defaulters and are afraid of going to the bank. When they realize that the person who visits bank is a bank officer, he hides as he is afraid of bank. There is TV and they spend time in entertainment and they also do not have opportunity. Bank loans for product orders misuse that amount. These people are poor and do not have WhatsApp. Some of them have T.V. and we are exploring opportunities to conduct meetings at the Common Services center. We have trained 15 people to be master trainer, so that they can give training outside. The artisans are not professionally networked and they do not share business formation. In each cluster, one common services center IT facilities such as WhatsApp should be developed for training and capacity building. There is one leader, the treasurer.

These people conduct meeting under the trees, cottage office of village. These members should be trained to be more regular and trained to make Minutes of Meetings. The members pressurize the defaulting members, they abuse the members and they fight. We are an NGO, the State and Government are the stakeholders and members trust NGOs more. There is a need for financial literacy and capacity building for members. Financial literacy, women empowerment, and product verification are important. They can sell the product in the market but there is no demand for their product. Technology development and prototype development will help strengthen the project.

Conclusion

In a group involved in lending money, conflict is an evolutionary process, that arises because of the sacrifice an individual has to make for the betterment of other individuals. In a group, the members have joint liability, where they are required to pay for the defaults of the other members of the group. Generally, the groups are driven by the commonality of goal and purpose. If a particular member fails to pay the money, the other members are responsible for the payment of the loans. This leads to conflict among the members of the group. As per the study there are various reasons for conflict among the group members, which include gender, caste bias, network relations, corruption, moral hazard, and behavioral issues.

References

Ahlin, C., & Townsend, R. M. (2007). Using repayment data to test across models of joint liability lending. *The Economic Journal*, *117*(517), F11–F51.

Anon. (2003). Lending procedures and the viability of social objectives conflict in credit unions. *International Journal of Bank Marketing*, *21*(6/7), 304–311.

Avruch, K. (2022). Culture and conflict resolution. In O. P. Richmond & G. Visoka (Eds.), *The Palgrave encyclopedia of peace and conflict studies*.

Ba-Tri, T., Truong, L. D., Friday, H. S., & Pham, T. P. (2024). The effects of monitoring activities on loan defaults in group-based lending program: Evidence from Vietnam. *Journal of Risk and Financial Management*, *17*(8), 357.

Bell, C., & Song, F. (2005). Emotions in the conflict process: AN application of the cognitive appraisal model of emotions to conflict management. *International Journal of Conflict Management*, *16*(1), 30–54.

Binns, R. (2020). On the apparent conflict between individual and group fairness. In *FAT* '20: Proceedings of the 2020 conference on fairness, accountability, and transparency, New York*.

Bonacich, P., Shure, G. H., Kahan, J. P., & Meeker, R. J. (1976). Cooperation and group size in the N-person prisoners' dilemma. *Journal of Conflict Resolution*, *20*(4), 687–706.

Boone, J. L. (1992). Competition, conflict, and the development of social hierarchies. In *Evolutionary ecology and human behavior*. Routledge.

Cassar, A., & Wydick, B. (2010). Does social capital matter? Evidence from a five-country group lending experiment. *Oxford Economic Papers*, *62*(4), 715–739.

Chatterjee, P., & Sarangi, S. (2004). *Social identity and group lending*. Deutsches Institut für Wirtschaftsforschung (DIW). DIW Discussion Papers No. 405.

Colletta, N. J., & Cullen, M. L. (2000). *Violent conflict and the transformation of social capital: Lessons from Cambodia, Rwanda, Guatemala, and Somalia*. World Bank Publications.

Conteh-Morgan, E., (2004). *Collective political violence: An introduction to the theories and cases of violent conflicts*. Psychology Press.

Darwin, C. (2024). *On the origin of species*. Fingerprint.

Dusuki, A. W. (2008). Lifting barriers in financing the small and poor entrepreneurs: Lessons from group-based lending scheme and Ibn Khaldun's social solidarity. In *Islamic finance for micro and medium enterprises*, (p. 15).

Haldar, A., & Stiglitz, J. E. (2016). Group lending, joint liability, and social capital: Insights from the Indian microfinance crisis. *Politics & Society*, *44*(4), 459–497.

Leidner, D. E., & Kayworth, T. (2006). Review: A review of culture in information systems research: Toward a theory of information technology culture conflict. *MIS Quarterly*, *30*(2), 357–399.

Magambo, E. F. (2024). An assessment of group lending challenges facing microfinance Institutions in Mwanza, Tanzania. *International Journal of Advanced Business Studies*, *3*(1), 18–30.

Mishra, M., & Ongena, S. (2019). *The effect of conflict on lending: Empirical evidence from Indian border areas*. CEPR.

Oliver, P. (1980). Rewards and punishments as selective incentives for collective action. *American Journal of Sociology*, *85*(6), 1356–1375.

Rajeev, M., Vani, B. P., & Veerashekharappa, A. (2019). Group lending through an SHG bank-linkage programme in India: Transaction costs and social benefits. *Development in Practice*, *30*(2), 168–181.

Ralston, D., & Wright, A. (2003). Lending procedures and the viability-social objectives conflict in credit unions. *International Journal of Bank Marketing*, *21*(6/7), 304–311.

Sabin, N., & Reed-Tsochas, F. (2018). *Able but unwilling to enforce: Cooperative dilemmas in group lending*. Centre Emile Bernheim.

Sabin, N., & Reed-Tsochas, F. (2020). Able but unwilling to enforce: Cooperative dilemmas in group lending. *American Journal of Sociology*, *125*(6), 1602–1667.

Schouten, M. E., van Knippenberg, D., & Greer, L. L. (2024). Hierarchy conflict: Causes, expressions, and consequences. *Organization Science*, *35*(4), 1535–1551.

Syna Desivilya, H., & Eizen, D. (2005). Conflict management in work teams: The role of social self-efficacy and group identification. *International Journal of Conflict Management*, *16*(2), 183–208.

Teinemaa, T. (2013). *The impact of group lending on participants' entrepreneurial resources*.

Thierry, B., Singh, M., & Kaumanns, W. (2004). *Macaque societies: A model for the study of social organization*. Cambridge University Press.

Thompson, V. A. (1961). Hierarchy, specialization, and organizational conflict. *Administrative Science Quarterly*, *5*(4), 485–521.

Tse, D. K., Francis, J., & Walls, J. (1994). Cultural differences in conducting intra- and inter-cultural negotiations: A sino-Canadian comparison. *Journal of International Business Studies*, *25*, 537–555.

Venittelli, T. (2022). Is group lending a collateral for informal credit? *Progress in Development Studies*, *22*(4), 392–407.

Chapter 2

Literature Review: Lack of Financial Literacy as the Main Cause of Conflict in Community Lending Groups[1]

Abstract

Community lending has emerged as a panacea to the financial woes of the people at the bottom of the pyramid. Most rural micro borrowers do not have formal finance due to a lack of collateral and information asymmetry. Formal financial institutions do not have any access to information about the creditworthiness of the micro borrowers. The literature celebrates the high repayment rates and financial success of the group. Yet a large number of groups suffer from financial instability due to the lack of financial literacy and transformational leadership. Various studies cite that the lack of financial literacy and lack of consensus on goals and objectives of community lending due to the lack of a good leader are the main reasons for the conflicts among the members of the group. These conflicts further lead to the breaking up of the groups. More than often, cultural background and religion of women in a community define the level of discrimination and stereotyping they face in a group. Thus, defaulting members often misutilize the funds and finances for nonproductive purposes. Despite all efforts and various financial literacy and intermediation initiatives, the groups remain nonviable. Heterogeneity of caste and classes leads to conflict among the group members. There is not much literature on what financial illiteracy is and how a lack of financial literacy leads to the breaking up of groups. This study provides a discussion on the literature on financial literacy.

[1]Parts of this chapter have been republished from the original article, Malhotra, N., & Baag, P. K. (2022). How social capital impacts the sustainability of group lending programmes - A grounded theory approach. *International Journal of Business & Economics* (IJBE), *6*(2), 327–352. https://doi.org/10.58885/ijbe.v06i2.327.nm

Development and Conflict in Community Lending Programs, 23–45

Published under exclusive licence by Emerald Publishing Limited
doi:10.1108/978-1-83708-290-220251006

Keywords: Financial knowledge; financial literacy; financial attitude; microfinance; intermediation

Introduction

The rural finance system suffers from financial exclusion. As a result of the absence of collateral and knowledge asymmetry, most economically disadvantaged micro-borrowers are excluded from the financial system. And they can't process the financial data required to use these services. In the 15th and 16th centuries, merchant banks began offering grain loans to farmers, and modern banking, which serves citizens' financial requirements, migrated from northern Italy to northern Europe. Emerging economies have realized the value of banking in fostering economic growth. Developing economies have accepted the UN Sustainable Development Goal 2030 to enhance financial inclusion and eliminate poverty. The existing studies highlight that in the case of group gender bias, cultural bias, and caste discrimination often lead to conflict among the group members. Moreover, the lack of homogeneity among the members of the group further leads to conflicts. The free rider problem often leads to the exploitation of the working members in a group and leads to conflict among the members of the group. Thus, the free-riding and moral hazard also lead to conflicts among the members of the group. Conflicts among the members of a group are propagated by the dominance of a single individual or refer to egalitarian rule, while in the case of the more tolerant group, they are characterized by the sharing of power and hierarchies among the members of the group. Lack of financial literacy often leads to conflict among the members of the group. Money management has become more challenging as financial services and products have become more complicated. However, the lack of social intermediation and training prevents the marginalized poor from accessing financial services, jeopardizing universal banking. And financially illiterate persons experience increased debt levels due to a lack of financial abilities, leading to a vicious debt cycle (Cole & Shastry, 2008). Although experts disagree on the skills and abilities required, financial literacy has emerged as a significant factor impacting the universalization of banking and financial services. Financial literacy is defined as knowledge, skills, confidence, and willingness to save money. The researchers can't agree on a definition of financial literacy or the characteristics that influence it. Financial inclusion is a concept without a universally accepted definition and lacks standardized tools for measurement. Marcolin and Abraham (2006) and Remund (2010) defined financial literacy as a combination of conceptual and operational components. Taking cognizance of all the review studies undertaken to date, the author defined financial literacy as (1) knowledge of financial concepts, (2) ability to communicate financial concepts, (3) aptitude to manage personal finances, (4) skillset required to make appropriate financial concepts, and (5) confidence required to plan effectively. Globally, scholars have identified the importance of financial knowledge, and literature emphasizes that to manage money effectively, there is a need to attain a certain degree of knowledge about money (Braunstein & Welch,

2002). There are various reasons for the conflict among the members of the group, which include excessive stereotyping and the halo effect witnessed by the members of the group.

Definition of Stereotyping and Halo Effect

Stereotyping and the halo effect are cognitive biases that significantly influence group dynamics and interactions. Stereotyping involves categorizing individuals based on perceived group characteristics, leading to oversimplified and often inaccurate assumptions. In a group, the members may hold prejudices and preconceived notions about an individual that might lead to conflict among the members of the group. These stereotypes can further lead to conflicts and bias among the members of the group, leading to conflict among the group. Members often stereotype and pigeonhole them into specific expectations. A self-fulfilling prophecy often leads to discriminatory behavior, leading to conflicts among the members of the group. Mitigating the negative effects of stereotypes requires fostering awareness, valuing individuality, and adopting competency-based assessments. Thus, through a culture of inclusivity, conflicts can be resolved in a group. Thus, financial literacy and lack of awareness are possibly the reasons for the conflicts among the group.

Definitions and Concept of Financial Literacy

In the extant literature, the ability or aptitude to manage personal finances has been identified as the most critical factor impacting financial inclusion, and many researchers define financial literacy as the ability or aptitude to manage personal finances (Volpe et al., 1996). Financial literacy has been characterized as managing cash and payment commitments and understanding essential financial and banking services, such as bank accounts and insurance products, using a holistic concept of inclusion and universal financial services (Emmons, 2005). Financial literacy is defined as the capacity to handle one's finances successfully and confidently and understand and communicate financial ideas. Financial literacy increasingly includes financial abilities. Mortgage ownership or retirement savings are considered markers of financing ability. Budgeting, saving, borrowing, and investing are the most commonly mentioned financial literacy operational definitions. To make the measures comparable, include risk management, asset transfer, and financial management variables. Banks and governments are among those interested in financial literacy. Consumers who lack financial literacy are less able to save and manage money, which negatively impacts markets. High interest rates have increased the likelihood of bankruptcy... It's tough to measure the success of financial literacy initiatives, and the primary goal of financial literacy is to raise financial awareness. Literacy in financial matters is defined as the capacity to read, evaluate, manage, and communicate about personal financial matters. Borden et al. (2008) and Hogarth and Hilgert (2002) assume financial literacy to be synonymous with financial knowledge. Financial literacy is defined as

> knowledge and understanding of financial concepts and risks, as well as the skills, motivation, and confidence to apply such knowledge and understanding to make effective decisions across a range of financial contexts, to improve individuals' and society's financial wellbeing, and to enable participation in economic life. (OECD, 2013)

The OECD concentrated on three key aspects of financial literacy: financial knowledge, financial behavior, and financial attitude. Researchers have different opinions on financial literacy. Lusardi and Mitchell (2011) defined financial literacy as the capacity to understand fundamental financial concepts and perform simple computations. Financial literacy is defined as "the capacity to analyze new and sophisticated financial products and make informed decisions about which instruments to use and how much of them to use" (Mandell & Klein, 2007). Debt literacy is an essential part of financial literacy, and it includes the capacity to make simple debt decisions and apply interest compounding knowledge to real-life circumstances. Individuals with high financial literacy are more likely to perform better in terms of numeracy. There is a lack of unanimity among the researchers regarding the definition of financial literacy and the skills required to use financial services. As per Herd (2012), financial literacy is defined as a person's understanding of their financial circumstances, and different kinds of literature have attempted to develop variables to facilitate the measurement of financial literacy. According to existing literature, financial literacy encompasses an understanding of the time value of money, the implications of inflation and risk (Lusardi & Mitchell, 2011), and investment returns (Lusardi & Tufano, 2015). Financial literacy is further defined as knowledge of debt products, debt literacy, the relationship between risk and return, the role of diversification in risk reduction, the functioning of credit, and individuals' self-perceived financial knowledge. According to the extant literature, Asian economies like Indonesia lag behind in terms of financial literacy and the ability of the citizens of the country to deal with the everyday routine savings, borrowings, budgeting, and investment activities. The literature defines financial literacy as an outcome of financial knowledge, financial behavior, and financial attitude (FINRA, 2003). As per Moore (2004), financial literacy is defined as the ability of an individual to understand financial concepts and is acquired through the experience and integration of knowledge. On a conceptual plane, financial literacy has been defined as the familiarity with the basic economic principles and knowledge about the economy, with the understanding of the key economic terms and principles (NCFE, 2005). The conceptual definition of financial literacy is a point of contention among policymakers, economists, and financial specialists, and there is also a lack of unanimity among researchers regarding the impact of financial literacy on financial self-efficacy. The problem of financial literacy is two-dimensional, as there is (1) no conceptual definition of financial literacy and

(2) no measurement tool to measure the impact of financial literacy on self-efficacy (Remund, 2010). This study aims to provide a discussion on the different dimensions and categories of the concept of financial literacy. There is a lack of comprehensive literature regarding the standardized instrument to measure financial literacy, and this study provides a discussion on the development of a standardized measurement scale to measure the level of financial literacy. Most of the previous definitions of financial literacy have been limited to the construct's definition, validation of the construct, and measurement of the construct through the scoring procedure. In most literature, the operationalization of the construct has been a significant issue (Huston, 2010). Despite multiple conceptual definitions of financial literacy, methods used to measure financial literacy vary drastically.

Definition of Transformational Leadership

Women in rural India are deprived of the access to the finance due to the societal roles and obligations, including the cultural norms. Leadership is the process of social influence, which helps to encourage the solidarity and financial behavior among the members of the group. Transformational leadership refers to the inspirational and motivational stimulation that enables the women at the bottom of the pyramid to achieve financial autonomy through access and inclusion. Transformational leaders are the individuals who nurture motivational leadership on the basis of trust, capability, commitment, and entrepreneurial zeal and prowess. Across the globe, community lending and group lending have emerged as the panacea to the woes of the people at the bottom of the pyramid. Under the National Rural Livelihood Mission (Aajeevika), the Government of India has launched initiatives such as the *Drone Didi* and *Bank Sakhi* programs to enhance financial literacy and provide greater access to finance for people at the bottom of the pyramid. The literature emphasizes that transformational leaders adopt a democratic and participative style, fostering mutual decision-making through shared leadership. Moreover, transformational leaders lead to higher creativity, innovation, and entrepreneurial ability and higher levels of transformational leadership.

Fig. 5 provides traits of transformational leadership.

Various studies highlight that transformational leadership in a group takes the form of entrepreneurial zeal and prowess. According to the diverse literature, the transformational leadership qualities among the members lead to Human Resource Development (HRD)-related outcomes such as higher income for the members of the community lending groups and success of the microfinance enterprises. Through transformational leadership, leaders can create a compelling vision among the members of the group. Through dynamic leadership, microfinance institutions can achieve higher organizational effectiveness in the form of higher customer satisfaction, operational effectiveness, and corporate social responsibility. A great leader with good financial knowledge and entrepreneurial

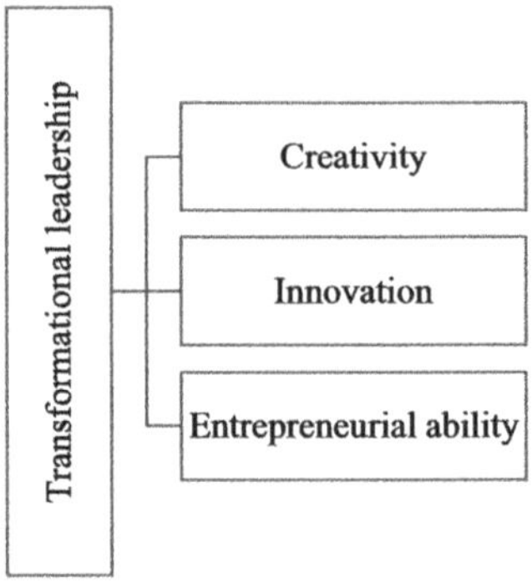

Fig. 5. Traits of Transformational Leadership. *Source:* Author's own source.

zeal can provide direction and pave the way for the financial sustainability of the community lending groups.

Research Problem

There is a lack of financial literacy and education among the marginalized poor, but the current financial education programs cannot result in financial behavior among the poor sections of society. Literature has recognized the lack of motivation as the key factor responsible for the lack of financial usage among the poor and the breaking up of the groups (Mandell & Klein, 2007). This directly implies that financial literacy is not sufficient to promote financial behavior in the form of savings and credit among the rural poor; there is a need for improving the poor's financial efficacy. This study will provide a repository of academic research in the domain of measurement of financial knowledge, attitude, and behavior and evaluation of existing tools for measuring financial literacy. And this study will further the cause of financial literacy in reducing the conflicts among the members of the group.

Theoretical Lens

Through extant literature, the issue of dormant learning without effective results in terms of behavior has been discussed through the theoretical lens of expectancy theory, also called the force model, and the utility model. Further, some of the strand literature also mentions the integration of goal setting (Hollenbeck, 1987). The outcome of the performance of the task, as per Locke (1990), is dependent on the efficacy of individual goals and objectives. In this paper, we have adopted the theoretical lens of expectancy theory. Expectancy refers to the expectation of the individual regarding what individuals are capable of achieving or their capability, and according to the capability, the need for training or supervision is decided, and instrumentality refers to the relation between the performance and rewards, and valency refers to the utility of the outcomes. This study will analyze the efficiency and effectiveness of various measurement models proposed by different researchers in measuring the efficacy of financial literacy measurement tools. Behavioral models have been in vogue for some time in the extant literature to measure the financial literacy among individuals. The model argues that people's use of financial services is influenced by their proclivity to use them, factors that facilitate or obstruct their usage, and their need for care. The model is a simple model that comprises predisposition, enabling use, need, and use of characteristics. The psychological theory of Self-efficacy—Toward a Unifying Theory of Behavioral Change states that an individual's psychological makeup alters the strength of self-efficacy, and these expectations of personal efficacy determine whether appropriate financial behavior will be initiated. According to the Theory of Planned Behavior (TPB), an individual's intention to engage in a behavior is influenced by subjective norms or social capital, personal attitudes, and perceived behavioral control. Besides, there is some literature about financial literacy through the lens of crystallized intelligence and fluid intelligence. Fluid intelligence refers to the use of critical reasoning and thinking innovatively. It is more closely related to Intelligence Quotient (IQ), and crystallized intelligence refers to the accumulated knowledge, which refers to the individual's investment in acquiring knowledge through course curriculum and concept building. There are empirical papers that discuss the impact of various measurement tools designed based on fluid and crystallized knowledge on financial literacy. Fluid intelligence comprises applying the skills and reasoning to solve problems relating to numbers, comprehension, and perceiving complex relationships. Crystallized intelligence is the ability to recall past experiences based on accumulated knowledge. Combined, crystallized intelligence and fluid intelligence were called a theory of generalized intelligence (Cattell, 1905–1998). In finance, researchers have applied this theoretical lens to measure the impact of demographic factors such as age on outcomes of financial decision-making.

Theoretical Lens for the Study

For this research study, we have adopted the theoretical lens of TPB, which states that financial behavior is impacted by subjective norms, financial attitudes, and financial knowledge.

Fig. 6 provides a cognitive theory of financial literacy.

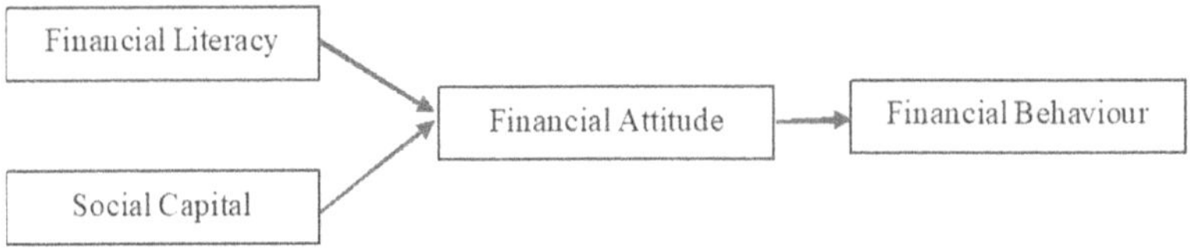

Fig. 6. Cognitive Theory of Financial Literacy. *Source:* Author's own source.

Discussion and Analysis

Financial Knowledge

No comprehensive definition of financial literacy exists, nor do the variables and constructions that make it up. Initially, financial literacy was defined as financial knowledge. This was called theoretical financial literacy understanding. There are also two types of financial literacy studies: (1) effect evaluation of individual financial literacy programs and (2) population-based financial literacy tests. According to the report, for the measurement of financial literacy (ANZ, 2008), socio-demographic factors influence financial literacy. According to the survey, financial literacy is higher among males, older adults with college degrees, white-collar workers, and residents of a certain region. Variables included in this study included numeracy, financial literacy (understanding risk and return), insurance products and superannuation funds, financial planning, and budgeting, as well as consumer rights and duties. This study does not consider that financial knowledge is the same as financial literacy and emphasizes the conceptual definition (Hira & Loibl, 2005). Their study has identified four financial literacy areas: retirement planning, investing, future planning, and credit management. Compared to the previous study by ANZ (2008), this study also includes numeracy and consumer rights and responsibilities. This study adopts fluid as well as crystallized intelligence to measure financial literacy. Beal and Delpachitra (2003) developed a survey to assess financial literacy by examining individuals' understanding of basic financial concepts, financial markets and instruments, financial planning, financial analysis, and insurance and risk management tools. The study was aimed at testing the proficiency of individual persons regarding basic financial concepts. Hogarth and Hilgert (2002), in their study, have designed an instrument to test the proficiency of individuals regarding personal finance. Financial knowledge comprises measures such as cash flow management, general credit management, savings, investment, mortgages, and other financial management topics. Income, income management, saving and investing, and spending and debt are all highlighted as indicators of financial understanding (Tennyson & Nguyen, 2001). Their research study tested the individuals regarding their proficiency in personal finance topics including income, savings/investment, spending/debt, and money management. The researchers in this study have drawn a relationship between the state curriculum and financial literacy. Volpe et al. (1996), in their paper, have highlighted the importance of poor investment knowledge, poor knowledge about personal loans, credit cards, insurance, and investments, lack of money management as the indicators of financial literacy. They have designed the survey instrument to test the individuals with regard to risk, diversification, financial advisor, tax planning, financial market instruments, global investing, and interest rate charges. This paper specifically deals with crystallized intelligence regarding personal investing. The study by Godsted and Mccormick (2007) describes financial knowledge as knowledge about basic concepts in personal finance, which includes banking, regulation, consumer rights, credit, financial planning, homeownership financing, taxes, insurance, investing, lending/borrowing, money management, retirement planning, saving money, and spending money. Xiao and O'Neill (2016), in their study, measured individuals' knowledge regarding financial education and its relationship with financial capability, which comprised variables regarding financial literacy, financial behavior, and financial self-efficacy. In this study, the author measured the financial capability index using Z scores of the respective variables. Danes and Haberman (2007), in their study, aim to highlight the gender differences in the effect size of financial knowledge on self-efficacy and behavior among high school students after studying the financial planning curriculum. In addition, the study highlights the gender difference in social roles performed by people within the family to facilitate financial learning. According to the study, males are more proficient in financial decision-making than females in budgeting and planning. This study discusses the concept of financial literacy within the social context of a family, where learning is a social experience. Curriculum and study materials have become a key source of imparting formal education on finance. The variables identified for measuring financial self-efficacy, knowledge, and behavior include financial planning, income level, financial statement, compound interest, tax deductions, knowledge about money market instruments, equity, savings, retirement planning, insurance, and debt have emerged as the major variables to measure financial literacy. Eventually, Oanea and Dornean (2013), in their study, have propagated a much wider definition of financial literacy, which includes financial knowledge as well as abilities and skills. Financial markets and instruments are measured in the survey design. It assesses financial understanding of asset liquidity, nonspending instruments, and interest rate calculation. Some of the other competencies covered in the poll are: comprehending inflation; investing; using personal finance products like checking accounts, savings; credit cards; foreign exchange; insurance; and pensions. Few questions in survey are regarding the risk awareness, behavior and money management and planning. Moore (2004) has tried to draw a relationship between financial experience, financial knowledge, and financial behavior. The study's goal was to assess the participants' participation in generating financial behavior. The first group used focus groups to assess the impact of financial education on borrowers who had complained about predatory lending. The second group was chosen at random from the general public. A test was also conducted to assess the two groups' financial literacy. The study revealed that victims of predatory lending had much worse financial literacy than the general population. Complex financial themes like compound interest, bonds, mortgages, fees, savings, investments, loan repayment, and the time value of money were utilized to test financial literacy. However, the report did not distinguish between financial knowledge and financial literacy. The scholar operationalizes the concept of financial knowledge through action and ability. According to Chen and Volpe, financial knowledge is essential for promoting financial literacy. This financial knowledge construct includes savings and borrowing, insurance, and investing information. The author defines savings and borrowings as creditworthiness, consumer credit reports, deposit insurance, checking account overdraft, compound interest, certificate of deposit terms, loan co-sign implications, annual percentage rate, and credit card use. Investments include mutual fund selection, retirement planning, exchange rates, foreign currency rates, etc. With the advent of technology and the changing nature of business, banking expertise has become vital. Servon and Kaestner (2008), in this research study, have recognized digital technology and ICT proficiency as a significant variable for measuring financial understanding. Hence, according to this survey, financial literacy is defined as the ability to use financial ideas and electronic banking. Faulcon Bowen, (2002) examined financial knowledge with a focus on how the effect of financial literacy varies across different age groups. The study has mentioned understanding key concepts and financial terms as the source of financial knowledge. Savings, auto life health insurance, house owner insurance, credit cards, taxes, and investments are among the topics included in the research study. The article's knowledge was tested with questions about taxes, retirement, insurance, credit use, inflation, and budgeting. It also affects how people think about money. The study also considers human social capital, including family discussions about money, family members teaching about life insurance, and financial record keeping. Robb and Sharpe (2009) have specifically differentiated between financial knowledge and financial literacy. In a sample of more than 20,000 college students, the scholar aimed to identify the impact of financial knowledge on revolving credit balance. He measured financial knowledge using six questions regarding debt literacy. Questions were adapted from the Jump$tart Survey used in prior research, which measured parents' perceptions and self-reflections on money management, as well as their concerns regarding the financial attitudes and behaviors of teenage children in their households. In this study, financial knowledge is measured through questions about money management and financial attitude, and behavior in terms of savings, spending, earnings, and financial independence. Money management proficiency has been measured through budgeting, credit card management, investing, retirement planning, insurance, mortgages, retirement, and taxes. Personal finance has been given separate weightage by including questions regarding saving, investing, budgeting, and cashbook. The CFPB (2015) defined financial literacy as a set of financial abilities and conducted research to assess its impact on financial capability. In this paper, financial capability has been defined as financial well-being and financial outcomes. The research study has identified financial behavior as managing money, research and knowledge-seeking, planning and goal-setting, and following through. Further study highlights the gap between financial knowledge or crystallized intelligence and financial decision-making. It propagates that factual knowledge in itself is not sufficient. There is a need for behavior change or attitude change. Financial ability is defined as the set of skills that strengthen behavior. And financial attitude mediates the relationship between knowledge and behavior or ability. Courchane and Zorn (2005), in their paper, have measured the impact of financial literacy on creditworthiness. In the context of the mortgage markets, the authors argue that consumer literacy and experience help to reduce the level of delinquency among the borrowers. Lusardi and Mitchelli (2007), in their paper, have measured the financial knowledge through conceptual questions regarding inflation, interest rate, risk diversification, retirement planning, and savings. Bernheim and Garrett (2003), in their research study, have measured the impact of workplace or employer-assisted financial education and asset accumulation. Further, the survey instrument to measure the impact of financial knowledge was based on conceptual questions regarding saving, earnings, income, pension coverage, retirement education in the workplace, and economic and financial knowledge. Borden et al. (2008) examined financial knowledge by focusing on credit and debit literacy, using variables such as awareness of credit card APR, payment due dates, credit limits, and payment methods through checks. The study measured the impact of the seminar on participants' financial behavior. Baron-Donovan et al. (2005) have designed an instrument to measure the impact of financial knowledge on the effectiveness of trainers or instructors. This study pertains to the knowledge of the trainers and their proficiency to instruct. Financial concepts included in the financial knowledge construct are awareness of successful strategies for making more thoughtful spending, saving, and credit use decisions. In its 2018 survey, the NFCC measured financial literacy using constructs such as budgeting, spending, saving, retirement planning, credit card debt, and homeownership. In this survey, there is no distinction between financial literacy and financial knowledge. Volpe, in their research study, measured the financial knowledge of the employees in US companies pertaining to personal finance, including insurance plans, planning and budgeting, inflation, time value of money, investment through capital markets, tax planning, and estate planning. The research study established that the employees are deficient in retirement planning, personal finance, investment and estate planning. Lyons et al. (2007) use credit literacy indicated through readability and comprehension of credit literacy reports and understanding of credit scores as an indicator of financial knowledge. Lusardi (2008) assessed individuals' financial literacy based on their conceptual knowledge of interest rates, inflation, and risk diversification. Lusardi and Mitchelli (2007), in their earlier study, devised questions to measure the financial knowledge of the consumers regarding the saving decisions, abilities, and skills to make informed decisions and method of collecting information about decision-making. Salisbury et al. (2001), in their EBRI Retirement Customer Survey 2001, have discussed the basic conceptual knowledge about the retirement concepts.

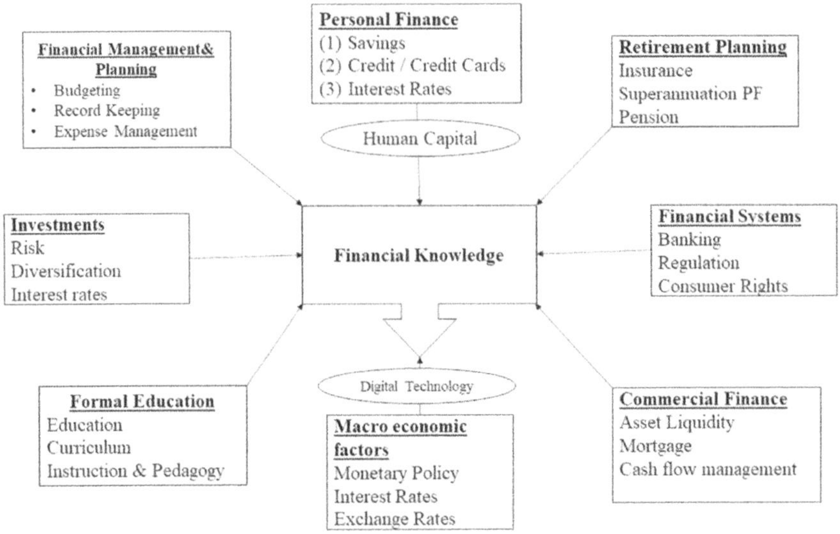

Fig. 7. Themes in Financial Knowledge.

Fig. 7 provides themes in financial leadership.

Financial Attitude

Huston (2010), in his study, argues that financial knowledge is not equal to financial literacy. As per the author, financial knowledge is an endogenous concept, and unless and until it results in financial self-efficacy, it will not lead to financial behavior. Financial literacy, as per the author, is a combination of financial literacy and financial behavior. Financial self-efficacy refers to the set of skills and attitudes.

Fig. 8 provides a theoretical lens for financial self-efficacy or attitude.

Financial attitude has not been discussed explicitly in the literature. However, there is a mediating role of self-efficacy, which might be impacted by the skills, personal and social factors, family, culture, experiences, and training. Therefore, financial knowledge is part of a subset of financial literacy.

Fig. 9 provides a relationship between financial knowledge and financial behavior.

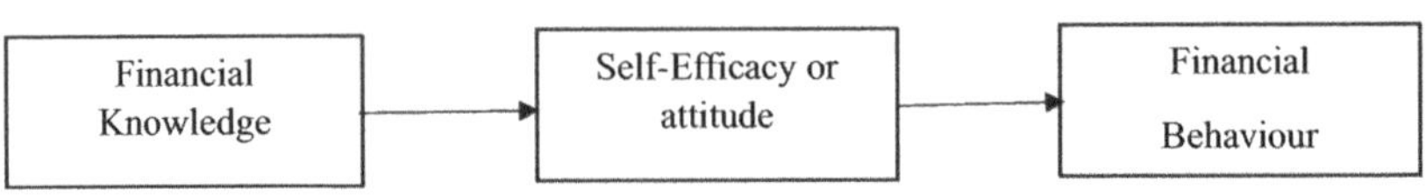

Fig. 8. Theoretical Lens for Financial Self-Efficacy or Attitude.

Fig. 9. Relationship Between Financial Knowledge and Financial Behavior.

Hung et al. (2009), in their research paper, have discussed financial knowledge as a broader concept that comprises financial education and skills, and abilities. Many of the tests used numeracy to measure financial literacy, a concept of crystallized intelligence. The authors believe that financial attitude is distinct from capacity or skills, and abilities. Besides the financial mentality, the authors note the gap between perceived and actual knowledge. However, the financial attitude is defined to be different from the abilities and skills. Mandell and Klein (2009), in their research study, highlight the paradox that financial education does not directly lead to financial literacy. Further scholars argue that it is the self-efficacy of the individual that transforms financial knowledge into financial literacy. Mandell (2008), in his research article, propounds that financial education does not lead to financial literacy. He cites the difference in resources as the main reason behind the difference in outcomes of financial education. Also, Jump $tart surveys highlighted that financial education might not lead to financial behavior. Mandell (2008) clarifies this issue by arguing that financial education gained through curriculum might be dormant, and individuals might not be able to use this education due to the lack of skills and abilities. Remund (2010), in his research study, has highlighted the complexity in defining the concept of financial literacy. The scholar argues that financial literacy has been defined as operationalized and conceptual financial literacy within extant literature.

Self-efficacy of the individual borrower is operationalized to transform financial education into financial literacy. As per the author, financial literacy is much beyond financial education or knowledge, and it can be divided into five categories. These categories include (1) knowledge of financial concepts, (2) ability to communicate about financial concepts, (3) aptitude in managing personal finances, (4) skill in making appropriate financial decisions, and (5) confidence in planning effectively. Mandell and Klein (2007) argue that motivation has a significant role to play in transforming financial education or knowledge into financial behavior. Lewin, in his theory, has furthered the perspective on motivation. Vroom explains the underlying motivations behind human behavior in terms of instrumentality, expectancy, valence, or utility. This theory, through instrumentality, defines the difference in performance or outcomes through instrumentality or valence, i.e., through reward and utility. Repository (2016) has established the difference between financial literacy and financial knowledge. By citing various examples, the report highlights that financial knowledge cannot be equated with financial literacy in the lack of skills and abilities. Beyond personal factors, motivation levels also impact the level of financial literacy. Individuals with better achievement orientation are generally more financially literate. Burnet, in his book, argues that financial literacy is not simply knowing about the financial concepts but also includes other personal and psychological dispositions, including achievement orientation, making choices, and pursuing leisure pursuits, to name a few. Repository (2016) propagates that individuals make sense of information utilizing a combination of skills and technology, resources, and contextual knowledge to make informed decisions.

Fig. 10 provides details of financial literacy as sense-making.

In the above diagram, financial literacy is a sense-making process driven by resources, skills, and knowledge. The level of self-efficacy determines understanding and sense-making to enable informed decisions and desired outcomes.

Measuring Financial Attitude

The extant literature demarcates research studies in the domain of financial literacy as (1) different forms, and types of financial literacy (Mandell & Klein, 2007) (2) studies aimed at evaluating the efficacy of individuals Huddleston-Casas et al. (1999) and Shockey (2002), in their study, have defined attitude as the ability of a learner to integrate concepts, facts, and emotions to respond positively is referred to as attitude. It's a psychological technique that helps people make better decisions.

In most research studies for measuring financial literacy, separate questions are included regarding financial attitude, and most of these questions are in the form of expectations and propensity drivers. OECD (2013), in the report on

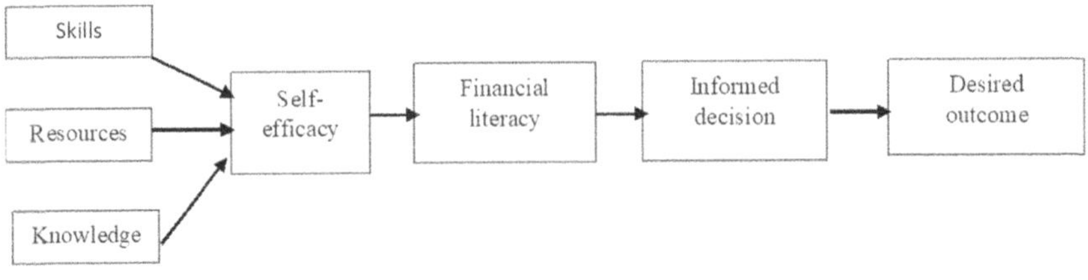

Fig. 10. Financial Literacy as Sense-Making.

financial literacy, has defined financial literacy as an outcome of financial behavior and financial attitude. And financial attitude has been defined as preferences and dispositions. In the questionnaire for measuring financial literacy, three separate questions are included for measuring financial attitude. These are questions relating to the expectations and attitudes of the individuals toward money and planning. Lusardi (2008) emphasized the distinction between subjective and objective knowledge, highlighting the role of planning in operationalizing conceptual financial knowledge. Similarly, van Rooij underscored the importance of individual attitudes, particularly perceptions of risk and return. Fernandes et al. (2014), in their research study, have highlighted that financial literacy is not the same as financial behavior. Highlighting the problem of endogeneity and omitted variable bias, the author argues that psychological traits that have been omitted from the relational equation between financial behavior and education impact the outcomes of financial knowledge. The author recommends taking cognizance of psychological factors impacting financial literacy. Lusardi and Mitchell, (2011), in their research study, highlight the importance of planning retirement and financial services to reap the benefits of financial knowledge. It also highlights the importance of psychological factors. Taft et al. (2013), in their research study, have discussed the importance of psychological factors on financial well-being, financial literacy, and financial concern. Bay et al. (2014), in their paper, have discussed the concept of the situated model of financial literacy that highlights the importance of context. The authors argue that financial education supported by the individual level traits and characteristics, which could be the level of self-confidence or personality that is embedded within the social setting, impacts the outcome of financial literacy. Further, Wagland and Taylor (2009) have discussed the concept of skills and capability in measuring financial literacy. Worthington (2006), in their research paper, have highlighted the impact of socioeconomic factors, skills, and personal chrematistics on the outcome of financial literacy. ANZ (2008) or the ANZ survey was designed to evaluate knowledge and comprehension, behavior, attitudes, perspectives, and awareness, rather than merely skills. Even this study negates the notion that financial knowledge is the same as financial literacy and highlights financial attitude and psychological traits. Mandell (2008), in his study, finds that financial education does not necessarily lead to financial literacy. Financial literacy is also an outcome of attitudinal changes, or a financial course leads to attitudinal changes, which leads to behavioral changes. Lyons et al. (2007), in their research paper, highlight the importance of attitudes of individuals in promoting financial behavior. This survey was conducted among high school students, and the study finds that socialization of the students helps in developing desired dispositions to result in behavior. Atkinson et al. (2006), in their research study, highlight the importance of financial capability, which comprises managing money, planning, choosing products, and staying ahead as the main factors that impact financial capability. The authors argue that the ability to plan also impacts the financial attitude of the borrowers, which further impacts the outcome of financial literacy. Choice of financial products is also impacted by the confidence level of the individuals and their attitude toward the risk. Bhuvana and Vasantha (2016) and Kumari (2021), in their research, highlight that financial literacy combines financial attitudes, knowledge, skill, decision-making, and planning about finances as per the Bank of Ceylon. The authors discuss the Family resource management theory, highlighting the importance of values, attitudes, knowledge, and personal characteristics in financial planning and literacy. Kadoya and Rahim Khan (2020), in their research study, have highlighted the importance of socio-demographic factors in promoting financial behavior and financial attitudes. The authors argue that age and gender have a vast impact on financial attitude, which impacts the financial behavior.

Scales for Measurement of Financial Attitudes

Shockey (2002) developed a scale that has been used extensively for the measurement of financial attitudes. This scale includes questions regarding income goals, intention to do other work, planning for significant expenses, father's education, and money management. This scale has been used extensively across different studies. Xiao et al. (1995), in their research study, have designed a scale to measure the overall attitude of the students toward credit cards using the 5-point Likert scale. This scale provided a ranking for Cognitive, Affective, Behavioral, and Overall attitude. Furnham and Lester developed a scale to measure money attitudes, which was constructed using factor analysis. The first factor measures money as security, exemplified by statements such as 'I worry about my finances much of the time.' The second factor reflects money as a source of power and status, for instance, 'I sometimes feel superior to those who have less money than I do, regardless of ability or achievement.' The third factor captures conservative yet anxious saving behavior, while the fourth factor assesses anxiety about spending, illustrated by the statement 'I often say I can't afford it, whether I actually can or not.' Jorgensen (2007) designed a new scale to measure financial literacy using the questions in two domains. The first was financial capability, including financial literacy, behavior, skills, self-efficacy, and confidence. Financial capability included 17 questions, and financial planning, control, and bookkeeping included four questions. Templer, in their seminal study on money, identified five factors, power/prestige, retention time, distrust, quality, and anxiety, as the most critical factors impacting money management. Tokunaga (1993), in his study, has identified five significant factors that impact the financial attitude of the participants. These factors include locus of control, self-efficacy, self-attitude, attitude toward money and decision-making under risk, sensation seeking, and background characteristics. Reknes et al. (2019), in their study, have mentioned a measurement scale to measure the impact of internal or external locus of control. This scale mentions internal locus of control, external locus of control, and psychological strain items. Mitchell et al. in their seminal paper, have identified seven factors, namely, value importance of money, personal involvement with money, time spent thinking about financial affairs, knowledge of financial affairs, comfort in taking financial risks, skill in

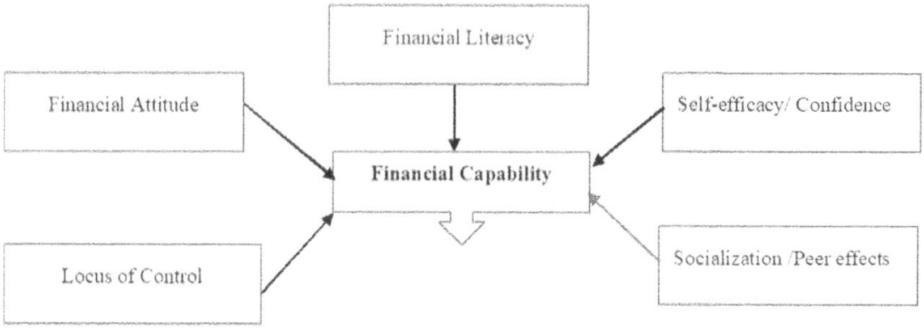

Fig. 11. Financial Capability. *Source:* Author's own work.

handling money, and money as a source of power and status. Rubinstein developed a survey named the Money and Life survey that was published in Psychology Today. Tang, in his research study, has developed an ethic scale to measure attitude toward money as good, evil, achievement, respect, budget freedom, and power.

Fig. 11 provides details of financial capability as a driver of financial literacy.

Financial capability is a broader concept than financial literacy. It also includes socialization effects, which refer to the effect of socializing with the family; financial attitude, i.e., psychological dispositions and expectations; self-efficacy of the individuals; and the individual's locus of control.

Fig. 12 provides details of financial capability as a function of personality traits, locus of control, emotions, and self-efficacy.

Financial Behavior

Most studies state that financial education leads to financial literacy, which leads to financial conduct and financial contentment. The primary measures performed to promote savings, borrowing, and financial inclusion among micro borrowers are called financial behavior. Scheresberg identified three key financial behaviors linked to financial well-being: reliance on high-cost borrowing, maintaining precautionary savings and planning, and preparing for retirement. Menkhoff, in his research paper, mentions that financial literacy leads to financial behavior. Financial behavior comprises financial decisions such as borrowing and debt management, budgeting and planning behavior, saving and retirement saving, insurance and risk mitigation, remittance behavior, and bank account behavior. Bruhn et al. (2013), in their research study, have mentioned that financial literacy leads to financial behavior in saving, spending money, tracking recurring expenditure, and negotiating payment methods. Yahaya et al. (2019) found that financial knowledge enhances financial attitudes, which in turn improve financial behavior. Financial behavior, as defined in their study, includes understanding and managing credit cards, savings, life insurance, investment loans, retirement and superannuation funds, as well as emergency funds. Nghia discussed how

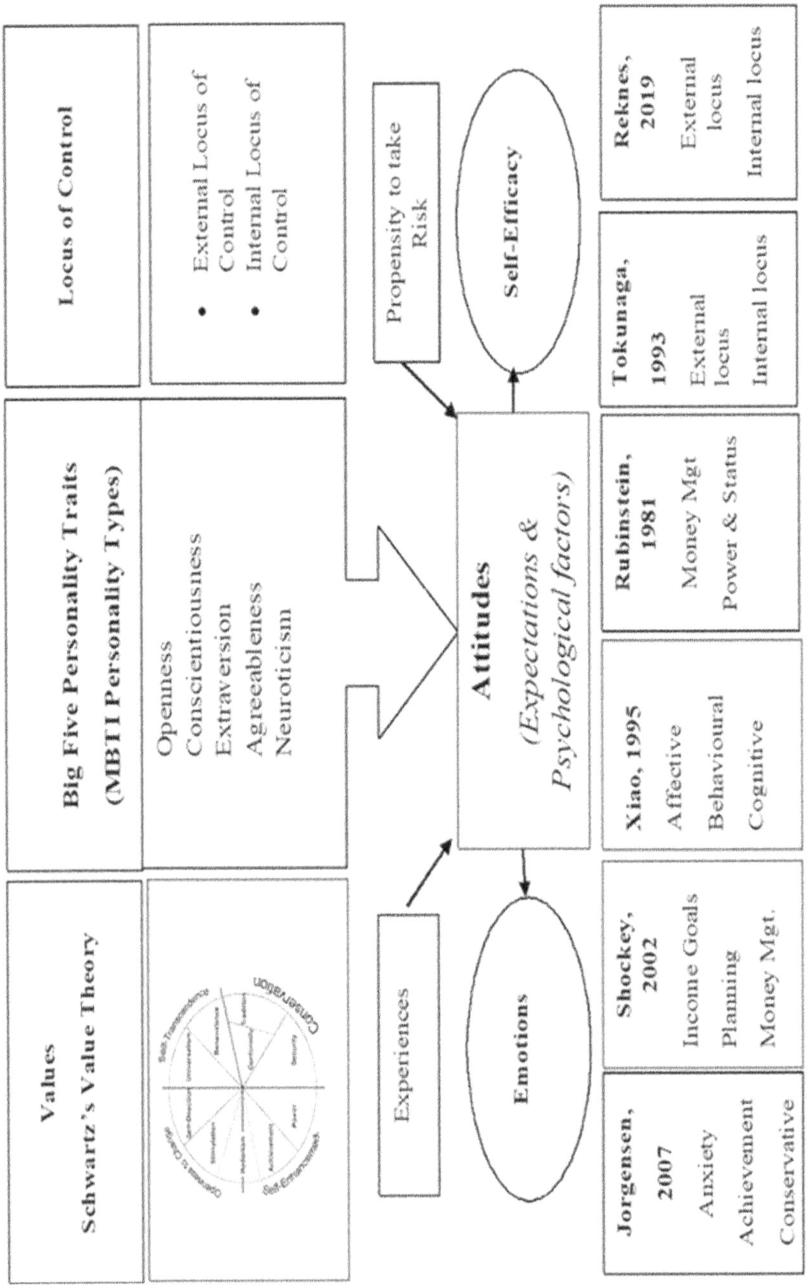

Fig. 12. Financial Capability.

financial literacy fosters appropriate financial behavior, encompassing areas such as debt management, saving, investing, insurance, tax planning, budgeting, and seeking financial advice. Chaulagain highlighted that financial literacy drives changes in financial behavior. Further financial behavior comprises of consumption and financing. The author argues that in addition to financial knowledge, financial skills, and perceived knowledge are also important Efrata, in his research paper, states that financial knowledge impacts financial behavior in the form of budget management, investing, and emergency funds, and characterized by a habit of doing financial planning, paying the bills, and managing finances. Watung discussed that financial literacy is composed of three dimensions: financial attitude, financial knowledge, and financial behavior. As per the study, financial literature positively and significantly influences financial behavior. Financial behavior refers to credit management, cash management, and saving management. This study further propagates that positive financial behavior is related to financial well-being.

Conclusion

Financial literacy is one of the major causes for the lack of financial inclusion in the rural world. A transformational leader is capable of promoting better dissemination of financial skills among the members of the group. Despite good education, micro borrowers are unable to access finance due to a lack of financial literacy. Thus, literature argues that financial attitude is an essential factor that impacts financial literacy. In a group, all the members are not literate and heterogeneity of the members further leads to conflicts within the group. Thus, financial literacy and homogeneity of the members lead to the stability and financial sustainability of the groups. This study mainly aims to discuss all research done to date in financial education and literacy and highlights the lack of a comprehensive definition of financial literacy and which various factors basically lead to the conflict among the members of the group. Financial literacy comprises financial knowledge, which comprises financial planning and control, retirement benefits, personal finance, investment, and commercial finance. Financial capability is the primary concept that leads to financial literacy, and financial capability comprises financial attitude, self-efficacy, and locus of control. Financial capability comprises financial attitude, which comprises various scales for measurement, including measurement of various types of dispositions toward finance impacted by the personality traits. This study will be of great importance in highlighting the role of financial literacy in ensuring financial inclusion. More research can be conducted in the domain of the impact of socio-demographic factors on financial literacy and inclusion in rural parts of the emerging world.

References

ANZ. (2008, October). *ANZ survey of adult financial literacy in Australia*. http://www.anz.com/Documents/AU/Aboutanz/AN_5654_Adult_Fin_Lit_Report_08_Web_Report_full.pdf

Atkinson, A., McKay, S., Kempson, E., & Collard, S. (2006, March). *Levels of financial capability in the UK: Results of a baseline survey*. Financial Services Authority.

Baron-Donovan, C., Wiener, R. L., Gross, K., & Block-Lieb, S. (2005). Financial literacy teacher training: A multiple-measure evaluation. *Journal of Financial Counseling and Planning*, *16*(2), 63–75.

Bay, C., Catasús, B., & Johed, G. (2014). Situating financial literacy. *Critical Perspectives on Accounting*, *25*(1), 36–45. https://doi.org/10.1016/j.cpa.2012.11.011

Beal, D. J., & Delpachitra, S. B. (2003). Financial literacy among Australian university students. *Economic Papers*, *22*(1), 65–78. https://doi.org/10.1111/j.1759-3441.2003.tb00337.x

Bernheim, B. D., & Garrett, D. M. (2003). The effects of financial education in the workplace: Evidence from a survey of households. *Journal of Public Economics*, *87* (7–8), 1487–1519. https://doi.org/10.1016/S0047-2727(01)00184-0

Bhuvana, M., & Vasantha, S. (2016). Drivers of financial inclusion to reach out poor. *Arabian Journal of Business and Management Review*, *6*(4). https://doi.org/10.4172/2223-5833.1000235

Borden, L. M., Lee, S. A., Serido, J., & Collins, D. (2008). Changing college students' financial knowledge, attitudes, and behavior through seminar participation. *Journal of Family and Economic Issues*, *29*(1), 23–40. https://doi.org/10.1007/s10834-007-9087-2

Braunstein, S., & Welch, C. (2002). Financial literacy: An overview of practice, research, and policy. *Federal Reserve Bulletin*, *88*(11), 0. https://doi.org/10.17016/bulletin.2002.88-11

Bruhn, M., Leao, L. S., Legovini, A., Marchetti, R., & Zia, B. (2013). Financial education and behavior formation: Large scale experimental evidence from Brazil. *Finance & PSD Impact Evaluation Note; No. 26*. World Bank Group, *1*, 1–67. http://siteresources.worldbank.org/NEWSLETTERS/Resources/442941-1360884692016/Financial_Education_IE_Feb_7_2013t.pdf

CFPB. (2015, January). *Financial well being: The goal of financial education* (p. 48). Consumer Financial Protection Bureau. http://files.consumerfinance.gov/f/201501_cfpb_report_financial-well-being.pdf

Cole, S., & Shastry, G. K. (2008). *If you are so smart, why aren't you rich? The effects of education, financial literacy and cognitive ability on financial market participation* (pp. 1–49). Harvard Business School and Department of Economics. http://www.afi.es/EO/FinancialLiteracy.pdf

Courchane, M., & Zorn, P. (2005, February). *Consumer literacy and creditworthiness and pitfalls: As consumer options multiply, Who Is* (pp. 1–33). http://www.wdfi.org/_resources/indexed/site/ymm/govcouncilfinlit/presentations/ConsumerLiteracyCreditWorthinessWI-DataWIDFI.pdf

Danes, S. M., & Haberman, H. R. (2007). Teen financial knowledge, self-efficacy, and behavior: A gendered view. *Journal of Financial Counseling and Planning*, *18*(2), 48–60.

Emmons, W. R. (2005). Consumer-finance myths and other obstacles to financial literacy. *Saint Louis University Public Law Review*, *24*(2).

Faulcon Bowen, C. (2002). Financial knowledge of teens and their parents. *Journal of Financial Counseling and Planning*, *13*(2), 93–102.

Fernandes, D., Lynch, J. G., & Netemeyer, R. G. (2014). Financial literacy, financial education, and downstream financial behaviors. *Management Science*, *60*(8), 1861–1883. https://doi.org/10.1287/mnsc.2013.1849

FINRA. (2003). *NASD investor literacy research: Executive summary*. http://www.finra.org/web/groups/investors/@inv/@protect/documents/investors/p011459.pdf

Godsted, D., & Mccormick, M. H. (2007, August). National adult financial literacy research Overview. *Network Financial Institute*, 1–20.

Hira, T. K., & Loibl, C. (2005). Understanding the impact of employer-provided financial education on workplace satisfaction. *Journal of Consumer Affairs*, *39*(1), 173–194. https://doi.org/10.1111/j.1745-6606.2005.00008.x

Hogarth, J. M., & Hilgert, M. A. (2002). Financial knowledge, experience and learning preference: Preliminary results from a survey on financial literacy. *Journal of Family and Consumer Sciences*, *48*, 1–7.

Huddleston-Casas, C. A., Danes, S. M., & Boyce, L. (1999). Impact evaluation of literacy program: Evidence for needed educational policy changes. *Consumers Interest Annual*, 109–114.

Hung, A. A., Parker, A. M., & Yoong, J. K. (2009). *Defining and measuring financial literacy*. http://doi.org/10.2139/ssrn.1498674

Huston, S. J. (2010). Measuring financial literacy. *The Journal of Consumer Affairs*. *44*(2), 296–316. https://www.jstor.org/stable/23859793

Jorgensen, B. L. (2007). Financial literacy of college students: Parental and peer influences. *Journal of Chemical Information and Modeling*, *53*(9), 1689–1699.

Kadoya, Y., & Rahim Khan, M. S. (2020). Financial literacy in Japan: New evidence using financial knowledge, behavior, and attitude. *Sustainability*, *12*(9). https://doi.org/10.3390/su12093683

Kumari, P. (2021, May). Factor affecting for personal financial literacy of Undergraduates. *International Journal of Research and Innovation in Social Science*, *5*(5).

Lusardi, A. (2008). *Financial literacy: An essential tool for informed consumer choice?* Nber Working Paper Series. http://www.nber.org/papers/w14084

Lusardi, A., & Mitchell, O. S. (2011). *Financial literacy: Implication for retirement wellbeing. Financial Literacy: Implications for Retirement Security and the Financial Marketplace* (pp. 17–39). http://www.nber.org/papers/w17078

Lusardi, A., & Mitchelli, O. (2007). Financial literacy and retirement preparedness: Evidence and implications for financial education. *Business Economics*, *42*(1), 35–44. https://doi.org/10.2145/20070104

Lusardi, A., & Tufano, P. (2015). Debt literacy, financial experiences, and over-indebtedness. *Journal of Pension Economics and Finance*, *14*(4), 332–368. https://doi.org/10.1017/S1474747215000232

Lyons, A., Rachlis, M., & Scherpf, E. (2007, January). *Working paper quantile regressions* (pp. 1–36).

Mandell, L., & Klein, L. S. (2007). Motivation and financial literacy. *Financial Services Review*, *16*, 105–116.

Mandell, L. (2008). *Financial literacy of high school students* (pp. 163–164). https://doi.org/10.1007/978-0-387-75734-6_10

Mandell, L., & Klein, L. S. (2009). *The impact of financial literacy education on subsequent financial behavior* (Vol. 206, pp. 15–24). https://files.eric.ed.gov/fulltext/EJ859556.pdf

Marcolin, S., & Abraham, A. (2006). Financial literacy research: Current literature and future opportunities. *Proceedings of the 3rd International Conference on Contemporary Business*, Australia, September, 21–22.

Moore, D. (2004). *Survey of financial literacy in Washington state*. https://doi.org/10.13140/2.1.4729.4722

Oanea, D.-C., & Dornean, A. (2013). Defining and measuring financial literacy. New evidence from Romanian' students of the master in finance. *Annals of the Alexandru Ioan Cuza University – Economics*, *59*(2). https://doi.org/10.2478/v10316-012-0036-3

OECD. (2013, June). Financial literacy and inclusion: Results of OECD/INPE survey across countries and by gender. *Financial Literacy & Education: Russia Trust Fund*, 1–175. https://www.oecd.org/daf/fin/financial-education/TrustFund2013_OECD_INFE_Fin_Lit_and_Incl_SurveyResults_by_Country_and_Gender.pdf

Reknes, I., Visockaite, G., Liefooghe, A., Lovakov, A., & Einarsen, S. V. (2019). Locus of control moderates the relationship between exposure to bullying behaviors and psychological strain. *Frontiers in Psychology*, *10*(June), 1–12. https://doi.org/10.3389/fpsyg.2019.01323

Remund, D. L. (2010). Financial literacy explicated: The case for a clearer definition in an increasingly complex economy. *Journal of Consumer Affairs*, *44*(2), 276–295. https://doi.org/10.1111/j.1745-6606.2010.01169.x

Repository, I. (2016). *Conceptualising financial literacy*. https://hdl.handle.net/2134/2016

Robb, C. A., & Sharpe, D. L. (2009). Effect of personal financial knowledge on college students' credit card behavior. *Journal of Financial Counseling and Planning*, *20*(1), 25–43.

Salisbury, D., Turyn, T., Helman, R., & Greenwald, M. (2001). EBRI 2001 retirement survey: Retirement confidence retirement survey (RCS), minority RCS, and small employer retirement survey (SERS). *EBRI Issue Brief/Employee Benefit Research Institute*, *234*, 1–26.

Servon, L. J., & Kaestner, R. (2008). Consumer financial literacy and the impact of online banking on the financial behavior of lower-income bank customers. *Journal of Consumer Affairs*, *42*(2), 271–305. https://doi.org/10.1111/j.1745-6606.2008.00108.x

Shockey, S. S. (2002). *Low-wealth adults financial literacy, money management behavior and associates factors, including critical thinking* (p. 370). ProQuest Dissertations and Theses 3039524. http://rave.ohiolink.edu/etdc/view?acc_num=osu1486402544590666

Taft, M. K., Hosein, Z. Z., & Mehrizi, S. M. T. (2013). The relation between financial literacy, financial wellbeing and financial concerns. *International Journal of Business and Management*, *8*(11). https://doi.org/10.5539/ijbm.v8n11p63

Tennyson, S., & Nguyen, C. (2001). State curriculum mandates and student knowledge of personal finance. *Journal of Consumer Affairs*, *35*(2), 241–262. https://doi.org/10.1111/j.1745-6606.2001.tb00112.x

Tokunaga, H. (1993). The use and abuse of consumer credit: Application of psychological theory and research. *Journal of Economic Psychology*, *14*(2), 285–316. https://doi.org/10.1016/0167-4870(93)90004-5

Volpe, R., Chen, H., & Pavlicko, J. (1996). Personal investment literacy among college students: A survey. *Financial Practice & Education*, *6*(2), 86–94.

Wagland, S. P., & Taylor, S. (2009). When it comes to financial literacy, is gender really an issue? *Australasian Accounting, Business and Finance Journal*, *3*(1), 13–25. http://ro.uow.edu.au/aabfj/vol3/iss1/3

Worthington, A. (2006). Predicting financial literacy in Australia. *Financial Services Review*, *15*(1), 59–79. http://ro.uow.edu.au/cgi/viewcontent.cgi?article=1124&context=commpapers

Xiao, J. J., Noring, F. E., & Anderson, J. G. (1995). College students' attitudes towards credit cards. *Journal of Consumer Studies & Home Economics*, *19*(2), 155–174. https://doi.org/10.1111/j.1470-6431.1995.tb00540.x

Xiao, J. J., & O'Neill, B. (2016). Consumer financial education and financial capability. *International Journal of Consumer Studies*, *40*(6), 712–721. https://doi.org/10.1111/ijcs.12285

Yahaya, R., Zainol, Z., Abidin, J. H. O. @ Z., & Ismail, R. (2019). The effect of financial knowledge and financial attitudes on financial behavior among university students. *International Journal of Academic Research in Business and Social Sciences*, *9*(8), 22–32. https://doi.org/10.6007/ijarbss/v9-i8/6205

Chapter 3

Conflicts in Community Lending Programs: A Sociocultural Perspective

Abstract

Social finance primarily aims to cater to the people at the bottom of the pyramid. These people do not have access to finance and lack collateral. Due to the lack of collateral banks, formal financial institutions are unwilling to provide microfinance to these people. Hence, social finance and microfinance, in the form of community lending programs, play a crucial role in providing access to finance for the people at the bottom of the pyramid. Yet there is a presence of inherent conflict among the members of the groups. Generally, in a group, the selected members are homogenous but vary in terms of their habits and traits, including demographics. When in a group, all the members converge and contribute to the defaulting loan. Yet this temporary convergence leads to wide faults if the member becomes habitual to not making the payment in time due to a moral hazard and false sense of security and accomplishment. If the assets in the group together are greater than the liability of all individuals, the members contribute; however, in case of lack of cash and liquidity, the members are unable to pay, and the group disintegrates. This chapter explores how homogeneity in profession, neighborhood, and culture fosters solidarity and strengthens the bonds among group members.

Keywords: Conflicts; group lending; trust; loan allocation; repayment issues

Introduction

All the members selected in a community lending program under Ajeevika are homogeneous, said one of the group leaders. They have a correlational hierarchy, and when they start, all their traits in terms of domicile and geography are similar. Yet during lending, variation happens and the risk profiles of the members change. This transition leads to divergence and conflicts in the group. Generally, a

Development and Conflict in Community Lending Programs, 47–68

Published under exclusive licence by Emerald Publishing Limited
doi:10.1108/978-1-83708-290-220251009

community lending group goes through various stages such as Forming, Storming, Norming, Performing, and Adjourning. During the forming stage, the members choose the other members and members of the same risk profile come together. In the storming and forming stage, the rules of the group are formalized and accepted with the consensus of all the members. After formation, the groups perform, and this is during this stage that further variation takes place and group members diverge as good and bad members in terms of their financial behavior. Various causes lead to this divergence, and only in certain cases do the group members again converge and work harmoniously toward the achievement of the group objective of financial sustainability. The groups function as a bank and the extractive members or members with bad repayment history defaulting jeopardize the financial access to formal loans for all the members of the group. Keeping in mind that in a homogenous group all the members of the same risk profile, it is important to discover what leads to the divergence in behavior of some of the member. And what are the different mechanisms adopted by the groups to improve the payment behavior of the risky and bad members? Most of the studies highlight that the physical conditions of a group, such as the working environment and access to infrastructure, are generally not the cause for the conflicts and breaking up of the group. However, this study still needs to explore the impact of the physical and facilitating conditions, such as working space, access to basic amenities, stationery, and grievance mechanisms, on the financial health of the group. To help the members co-adapt and co-evolve, the defaulting members are provided the financial training in the form of intermediation. This study also aims to explore the role of financial literacy in keeping the groups together. Generally, in a group, the change in the profession and a lack of adoption of livelihood opportunities can lead to conflict. The reasons for the change in the risk profiles of the members are more affective, such as low trust, bad leadership, or disputes with the leader; ethnic or religious bias; discrimination based on income or caste basis; and mutual conflicts. This study establishes that divergence in the behavior of the members in a group is an outcome of affective factors such as biases, lack of trust, and discrimination that crop up during the operation of the group. This study uses the qualitative research methodology using the hermeneutical approach to assess the impact of affective factors on the behavior of group members leading to conflicts in the group.

Literature Review

Community Groups

Community refers to a specific geographic area with defined boundaries and comprises people with homogenous interests and activities. These organizations refer to the entity that comes together to serve the common good. Murray G Ross refers to the mechanism through which the community recognizes the objectives and resources of the organization (Internal/External) and leverages these resources to achieve the goal. These community organizations aim to achieve their objectives through the effective utilization of resources and shared norms and values. Microfinance is a challenge for the people at the bottom of the pyramid due to the lack of collateral. Collective organizations provide a substitute for physical capital in the form of social capital and enable financial inclusion for micro borrowers. The key to financialization is learning with the people, creating a new knowledge database, and creating institutional capacity. Community organizations enable collaboration and empowerment. Community organizations refer to the process through which the community's resources are diverted toward the welfare of society. Mohd. Shakil and Mizrahi define community organizations through a framework of 14 principles. These include maintaining organizational balance, viewing planning as a complex and value-driven process, establishing a basic decision-making structure, addressing resistance to change, fostering change from within, ensuring proper record-keeping and documentation, recognizing the unpredictability of media, and balancing both products and processes effectively. Sarma and Mehta (2014), in their study of the microfinance-based (Self-Help Group [SHG] Bank linkage) model, emphasize that both the bank and MFI model derive their advantage from the population's competition and homogeneity.

Thus, besides the planning, maintaining organizational balance, adherence to group norms, the opposition to change are the major factors that impede the successful working of the groups as a financial institution. Desai and Joshi, in their study, highlighted that exposure to the SHG Bank linkage program increased the women's participation in group savings. Micro borrowers at the bottom of the pyramid do not have access to collateral, and hence formal financial institutions are not ready to lend them. Community development initiatives or place-based activities focused on generating assets to improve the quality of life in low- and moderate-income areas ensure access to financial services to the people at the bottom of the pyramid. Cooperative ownership models, which give communities a voice, rely on community-based social capital to succeed.

Social Capital

Social capital is defined as the aggregate of resources obtained by a person or a group by possession of an enduring network of more or less formalized ties of mutual acquaintance and recognition, writes Bourdieu (1986). The social organization aims to achieve its objective using its resources. Social capital refers to comradeship, collective efficacy, connectivity in network and structural equivalence, or uniformity of nodes across structures. Through the theoretical lens of Resource-Based View (RBV), social capital in a community setup provides members of the network with benefit from collectively owned capital. A hierarchal network resource comprises positions, authority, rules, and agents connected to the source. Social capital refers to the investment in external relations by the members, by which they gain access to valuable contacts and information. And by investing in internal linkages, the members can exercise effective governance. As per Olives and Kawachi (2015), social capital includes structural and cognitive components. Coleman refers to the network-based interpretation of social capital. As per the author, the social capital is located in the network structure. And situated in a network facilitated by closure and multiplex ties, it leads to the emergence of cognitive capital as norms, attitudes, trusts, and sanctions. Norms, values, attitudes, and beliefs that produce and perpetuate positive interdependence of utility functions are called cognitive, social capital. Rules, processes, precedents, and networks are examples of structural social capital that help people work together for mutual benefit. Social capital comprises norms, exchange reciprocity, group membership, and social engagement. There is no consensus on the definition of social capital, and different authors have given different definitions of social capital. As per the extant literature, the colonial capital has been designed as (1) the relations an actor maintains with other actors, (2) the structure of relations among actors within a collectively, or (3) both types of linkages. As per the relations that an actor maintains, social capital is defined as a resource that allows a focused actor to take action on behalf of another actor. And thus, membership in a social network facilitates actor action through direct and indirect ties. As an outcome of relations, an actor maintains with other actors; the social capital is defined as the ability of the people to work together by informal values or shared norms. Social capital has further been described as a culture of trust in which networks emerge. Inglehart (1997) and Putnam defined social capital as organizational features such as norms, networks, and social trust that led to cooperation and coordination. Emphasizing the web of cooperative relationships, Brehm and Rahn (1997) define social capital as a means to resolve the collective action problem. From the perspective of social structure, social capital has been described as a social structure that facilitates specific actions of individuals within the structure. It has been defined as a resource that actors derive from specific social structures and pursue interests. From the dual perspective of relations between the actor and structure of relations, the colonial capital has been referred to as the sum of actual and potential resources embedded within and derived through a Network of relationships possessed by an individual or social structure. Hence, to summarize, the set of resources made accessible to a group through group members' social relationships within the group's social structure, as well as in the broader formal and informal structure of the organization, is referred to as social capital.

Model of Group Social Capital Based on the Source of Social Capital

Extant literature defines social capital through the conceptual framework of (1) Networks, (2) Norms, (3) Beliefs, (4) Rules, and (5) Trust. Adler and Kwon and Nahapiet and Ghoshal (1998) have defined three different dimensions of social capital: (1) Structural, which is based on network ties; (2) Relational, based on trusts, norms, and obligations; and (3) Cognitive based on shared code of language. The study motivates the structuralist ontology of social groups based on social structures. The structure is often referred to as a lattice of relations dependent on social structure. Social structure, as a general category of social phenomena, comprises social practices, conventions, roles, and hierarchies. The extant literature refers to this as the Goldilocks constraint, where social networks are dependent on social factors and are created intentionally. Ritchie and Adler and Kwon have highlighted three different sources of social capital, namely, (1) Network, (2) Norms, and (3) Shared beliefs. However, few researchers highlight the origin of social capital as social networks. Structural analysis of this kind bifurcates the social capital into indirect and direct ties (Adler & Kwon, 2009). Within the social structure, i.e., broader formal and informal structure, the social capital resides within the configuration of the social structure conduit. Regarding the structure of the social capital and strategy formulation, the literature discusses two types of social structure: (1) internal structures that give rise to cognitive social capital and reside in the broader network structure. The structure in this context comprises closure or bonding relationships that include strong ties, exchange reciprocity, and valence. This form refers to the horizontal structure of linkages between the members of a homogenous nature in terms of domicile, education, and employment. The conclusion of a relationship often fosters increased cooperation, stronger adherence to agreed-upon norms, and more open sharing of information. Contrary to this, sparse networks with redundant ties lead to more collaboration and structural holes. Another state of network relations between the members through internal structures is bridging relationships. Bridging refers to the relationship among members of unlike groups. This is also a form of internal relations in the form of vertical and horizontal relationships. Bridging refers to the connections formed among members of different groups. It represents a type of internal relationship that can take both vertical and horizontal forms. These connections are often characterized as weak ties, linking individuals and groups from diverse social and ethnic backgrounds. (2) External structures give rise to the Linking relationship, which refers to the hierarchal relationship due to the difference in power. This kind of relationship exists between the community members or social organizations and the Government.

Fig. 13 provides details of the model of social capital in the context of group lending.

Krishna and Uphoff provide a disintegrated approach to define social capital, which comprises the cognitive and structural components. (Nahapiet and Ghoshal's (1998) model of social capital is used for analysis. According to the authors, social capital comprises three dimensions structural, relational, and cognitive. The structural dimension includes network ties, network configurations, and appropriable organization. According to network theorists, the social network impacts the social network both through direct ties and indirect links. The cognitive dimension comprises shared codes, rules, and narratives, and the relational size includes trust, obligations, and norms. The structural

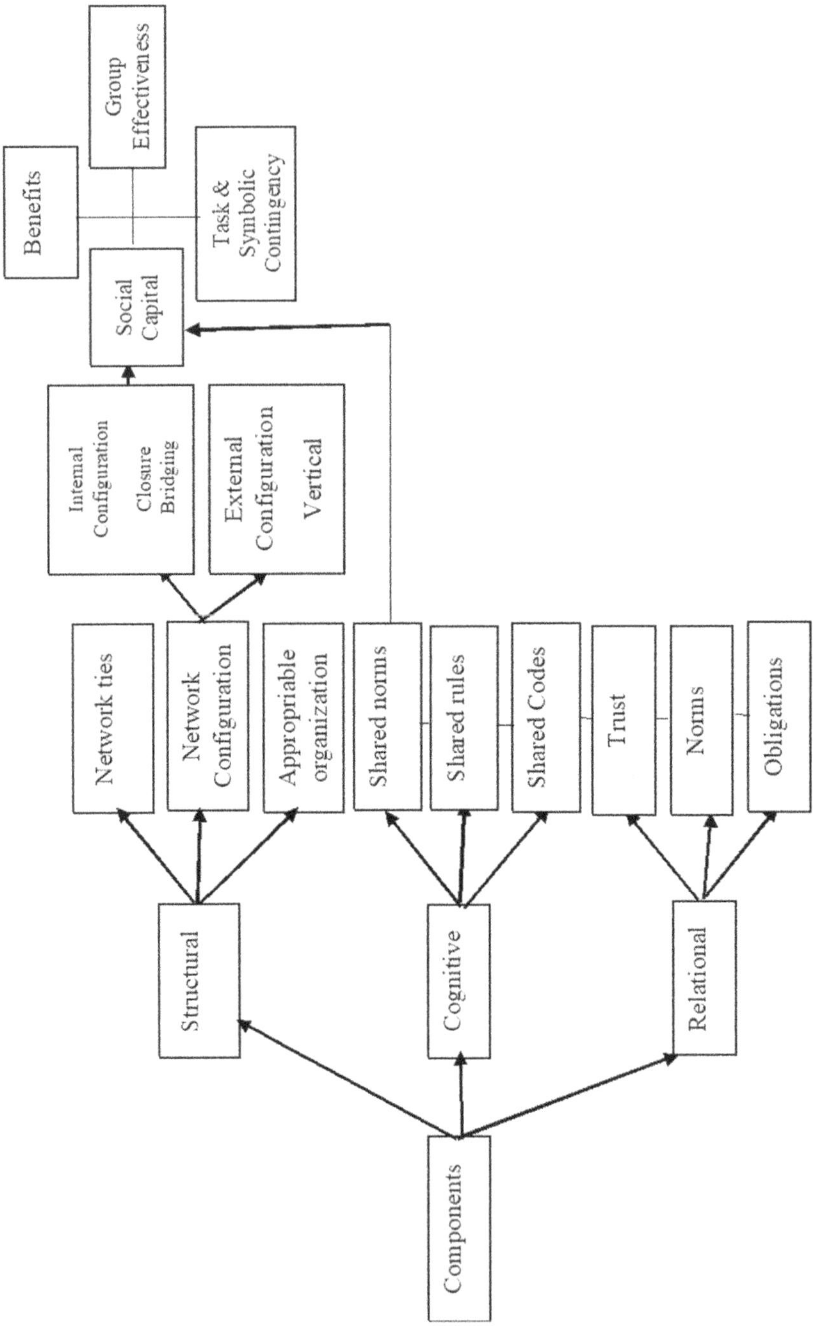

Fig. 13. Model of Social Capital in Context of Group Lending.

component refers to the networks in an organization, and the cognitive component refers to the shared codes. This structural cognitive and relational component leads to social capital. Network refers to the critical source of wealth within a given social organization. Depending on the nature of the network configuration, which could be external or internal, the social capital differs. Seibert et al. and Edwards and Foley have highlighted the role of shared norms and beliefs, which, according to the author, determine the social capital's sociocultural component. This sociocultural component provides the context for the sociocultural. Portes (1998) refers to the norm as generalized reciprocity among members. Nahapiet and Ghoshal (1998) refer to the importance of shared belief, and forms of strategic management lead to social capital. Nohria and Berkley refer to the formal institutions and rules that impact social capital. External network configuration refers to vertical relationships between the borrower or the social organization and the external agencies. This is referred to as a linking organization and involves dealings with state and government agencies. And the horizontal relationships refer to the relationships within the network. It could be an intrafirm or closure, or bonding organization. Otherwise, it could be an intrafirm or bridging organization, which involves a relationship with the distinct groups. This form of social capital leads to task contingency and symbolic contingency. The benefits generated from the social organization lead to group effectiveness. As suggested by Coleman, the closure form of an organization leads to better coordination. In contrast, the sparse network that comprises the gaps in the network is called the structural hole. Walker et al. provide an incentive for the gatekeepers and other catalysts to provide access to resources. In the case of the open organization, any violation of norms goes unnoticed. Thus, the structural holes in a community network can be analyzed from the RBV.

Role of Relationships Between the Members in Promoting Social Capital

As per our study, human capital can augment the role of social capital in promoting the group's effectiveness. We have included this component in the form of a relational element, which comprises the norms, trust, and obligation to promote social capital and the group's effectiveness. Coleman argues that human capital without social capital is not sufficient to augment the group's effectiveness. In this regard, our study corroborates the affective component's role, which comprises the emotions, attitudes, feelings, and culture in augmenting the social capital. These are also referred to as attitude-based factors, also referred to as community psychology. Hughey et al. refer to this as informal, community-based attitudes comprising social support, community satisfaction, and pride. Putnam highlights the importance of the affective components and attitudes such as motivation on a group's effectiveness. We have included these constructs as part of the relational model. Ideological schism refers to the separation and conflict among the people due to ideological differences. This difference can be due to external and internal factors, where external factors include competition and homogeneity of population. Internal factors include factors such as leadership, culture, and strength (Sarma & Mehta, 2014). In a capitalist economy, social relations and symbolic interactions are transferred in money as a means of maintaining relations. New trade relations are set in the context of financial mutuals in the maintenance of networks and identity. Knowles and Luke (2018) in their study highlight that harmony within community lending is identified as bonding, bridging, and vertical relations between the group. Sarma and Mehta (2014) state that in the case of microfinance, various conflict management mechanisms are used by community lending groups, which include group cohesion and cooperation. Hence, collaboration is an important strategy for conflict management. Another dimension of conflict is task conflict. Task conflict can lead to better group effectiveness, and various studies highlight that task conflicts lead to better group outcomes (DeChurch & Marks, 2001). Conflict cannot be avoided, and it is inevitable between people and groups. Various methods exist to manage conflicts, which include self-awareness, conflict communication, and establishing an institutional structure. Park and Burgess (1921) highlight that conflict is inevitable among the members of society. Conflict is neither good nor bad but can be utilized as a primary force for social change. Thakore (2013), in his research, highlights the origin of species that conflict concerning resources, and conflicts help the *homosapiens* to further evolve. The studies highlight that integrative conflict management is more effective in the resolution of conflicts than confrontation and avoidance styles. Inequity leads to discrimination due to affective factors such as gender, culture, leadership, and ethics. The cognitive factors that lead to conflict include various factors such as tasks and access to financial resources to name a few. There are various modus operandi to resolve the conflict, including establishing an integrative conflict management system, which is more efficient than conflict resolution. According to various strands, of literature, there are two very important reasons for conflict among the members, which include emotionally laden reasons, such as gender, demographics, ethnicity, caste, and race, which can lead to inequity and inferiority and hence conflicts. Besides, this idea and task can also lead to conflict, which comes under the purview of cognitive factors. Access to money or capital is a cognitive factor that in a capitalist economy leads to myriad conflicts. There are various approaches to tackle conflict, including collaborative and competitive approaches. In case of emotionally laden conflicts that originate on the basis of religion or marital status, they can be resolved only with the intervention of legitimate authorities like state agencies and police. In other cases, which include tasks and ideas, their collaborative and competitive approach is a good approach for the resolution of the conflict (Tjosvold et al., 2006). Various studies highlight that avoidance and collaborative strategies are not strategies to tackle emotionally laden conflicts. About the groups, competitive victimhood has an important role to play in propagating the conflict among the members of the group. Ideally, in a group, the members are impacted by various affective factors such as inequity due to discrimination, gender bias, racial discrimination, and ethnicity. These affective factors lead to competitive victimhood ness among the marginalized sections of society. Thus, the members are impacted by the in-group identity, and in these circumstances in group forgiveness has an important role to play in promoting empathy and trust among the members of the group (Noor et al., 2008). The literature highlights that conflict is inherent in the case of teams working independently. There are various circumstances in which team performance improves due to the inherent conflict (Bradley et al., 2015). According to various literature, scarcity, competition, equilibrium, and specialization play an important role in conflict resolution among the members of the group. To cope with the changes, various strategies are adopted, which include innovation/exchange and evolution. According to the literature, reciprocation brings us to interactions that imply helping the helper. There are various kinds of reciprocations, which include unconditional help; in return, he allocates reactive income for helping. And then there is reciprocation from the unconditional helper, there is potential gain from mutual aid (Hirshleifer, 1978). In contemporary literature, status conflict is often defined as a dispute over people's relative status in a group hierarchy. As per the literature, the status conflict impacts the group's performance.

Discussion and Analysis

In an archipelago of the group, the members diverge after forming the group due to myriad affective reasons that include gender, religion, ethnicity, trust, and leadership, to name a few. The issue at the heart of all conflicts is the divergence from the main purpose or objective of financial solidarity. Various reasons lead to this distrust among the members of the group. Moreover, besides the affective factors, the changes in the facilitating conditions are also cited as one of the factors responsible for the conflict among the group. The groups for lending are generally formed among the members from the same geography and the same profession. If the members face a loss of social capital in geography due to affective factors such as caste, ethnicity, and cultural norms, they tend to diverge, and it also leads to migration to the other regions. This sort of divergence also leads to conflicts and breaking up of the groups or moral hazard among certain risky members. In addition to this, lack of a good working place for conducting meetings, lack of institutional sustainability of groups, lack of social norms and basic amenities, and lack of banking facilities also lead to divergence and conflict among the members of the group. Thus, the facilitating conditions within the group and in the diverse geographies also lead to conflict among the members of the group. Besides the facilitating condition, the lack of good leadership and direction also leads to divergence and splitting up of the groups. Various kinds of coping strategies adopted by the members of the group, such as social intermediation, financial literacy campaigns, counselling, state intervention, and support, motivate the members to adapt and acculturate them to ensure the institutional sustainability of the group. However, many times these coping strategies are not adequate to ensure the institutional and financial sustainability of the groups. Various strategies are adopted to ensure financial discipline, which include the maintenance of the group financial records, attendance registers, and meeting chronicles. Despite all efforts, the lack of intermediation and adherence to group norms leads to the breaking up of the group due to the lack of financial and institutional sustainability of groups. Thus, to ensure solidarity in the groups, the convergence of diverse members through incentivization and better opportunities becomes indispensable. The state in India has undertaken various initiatives such as providing financial aid to the members in the form of subsidies, grants, marketing support to advertise and sell their products on different national and international platforms, livelihood training, awards, and recognition to enable the members to achieve financial and institutional sustainability. Moreover, within the theoretical framework of agency, the moral hazard exists in the form of deliberate designs, which give rise to bias and discrimination. Initially, in a homogenous group, the members start from a common point, and then they diverge and vary due to differences in living conditions. The designs include the use of power hierarchies, agency, and self-interest to jeopardize the process of achieving group institutional balance or equilibrium. Along with the use of power hierarchies, the group members also exercise noncooperative enforcement, such as isolation of the members who do not punish the particular identified member. This second order of noncooperative behavior becomes a norm in the group and leads to the disintegration of the group or to conflicts in the group. The coping strategies to ensure the sustainability of the groups are to ensure convergence to the common point through circularity in the form of incentivization for the good members, intermediation, and financial literacy.

"Ever since our arrival from Pakistan, our group has been engaged in the occupation of manufacturing handicrafts. These women have been manufacturing handicrafts since the country's independence. Karigars pursue handicraft as an ancient artform in several of the Karkhanas and markets. We make leather products, Kurtis etc. If some woman member is not able to pay the loan, all the members get together and visit the home of the said member. Repayment is obtained from failing members through collaboration and peer pressure. Members of the Ajeevika block play a critical role in ensuring the organisations' self-sustainability. These Ajeevika block officers visit once a month, and bank officers come once every 2 to 3 months to persuade the delinquent members to make the payment. They persuade the members to stick to a strict budget."

Case Against Second-Order Noncooperative Equilibrium as a Coping Strategy in Social Selection to Achieve Convergence

Divergence leads to unhappiness, and that leads to conflicts. Divergence of an individual should not be a flimsy allegation considering it leads to exploration or moral hazard with minimal chance of convergence with the mainstream. For a group member, divergence could be saving less and not repaying debt or overspending the money for nonproductive purposes. One coping strategy is the use of negative reinforcement or second-order equilibrium for anyone who has diverged is a bad strategy. In certain groups and social contexts, there are instances of provocation of members by regular doses of exercising social pressures (depending on the level of divergence), leading to more divergence, exploration of the lost social capital, and radicalization with little chance for peace without retaliation or hope of convergence in tradition. Peaceful retaliation takes the form of stressful lives and migration and its evolution, a response to complex conditions. If the members could develop an additional trait like literacy, it would lead to higher adaptation and acculturation in the group. Thus, the state intervention in the support of such individuals is a great coping strategy to set right the imbalance in the polity of a group.

Conflict as a Strategy for Management

Conflict is an inevitable part of any organization, and it can be used as a strategy to get work done. Moreover, conflict plays an important role in getting things done through others. An integrative conflict management system is important for improvising task management and improving the achievement of task goals.

Excerpt From Interview

The respondent mentioned that they come from a family of bankers, with the profession tracing back to their grandfathers. Our group has taken the loan under the SHG linkage from the bank. Earlier, it was the Swarn Jayanti Rozgar Yojana, and now it is Deendayal Antodaya Yojana (DAY). As per the respondent, since all the members of the group are from the same profession, this helps in reducing the rate of loan default. This group, according to the members, is extremely old, and members came together since the implementation of the SHG bank linkage program. The members are selected as per the type of profession. Though members do not generally default, if the members default, then the entire group that stays nearby counsels the member. Even in monthly meetings, the member is counseled. He drew an analogy that all the fingers in a hand are not the same, and some 10% of people always default, and as a result, some members default. The members are all in the same profession, and through monitoring, it is ensured that they do not misuse the funds. If they do, they are warned, and mostly they can repay their bank loan. The interview highlights that the members of the group are generally homogenous, and this creates a common goal and objective. However, in case of default, the member is counseled by the other members of the group.

Excerpt From the Second Interview

"There are 10 people and they work regularly. They start at 11 a.m. and till 5 p.m. Terracotta pottery is our ancestral job. Our membership is not restricted to the Kumhar community and anybody can join. But they are from this village. Ajeevika's department has helped us to form this group. Since joining the group the self-efficacy of the group has improved. Since joining the group, the big officials have started coming and our group is near Khajuraho and foreigners have also been coming to Khajuraho. Since the members are in the same group, they help each other. If some member is making the Ganesh ji chair or Ganesh ji statue then the woman who is making the craft is guided and helped by other members. We have taken the training and then we have taken the bank loan. Our bank loan has increased from Rs. 30,000 to Rs. 100,000. If the members need a loan, we all pool together and permit loan sanction to the needy person. Our group meeting is conducted per week. In each meeting, members maintain accounts and records. Banks visit the site and the Ajeevika officials to inspect the work and find out if the work is as per the standard. Members are confident of each other, that if the loan is taken it will be paid off. Once, a member of the group was unable to pay the loan as they mis-utilized the loan and spent it for non-productive purposes and then we expelled them from the group. In our group, the members of the group understand that if the loan is taken then it has to be paid back. Due to bank sanctions, that bank will not give the loan even if one of the members does not work, the members pressurize the other members. In our group, we have Adhyaksh, Kosha Adhyaksh, and Sachdev. We also show our accounts to the Ajeevika and show our books to the other members of the group. We make small, big diyas, lamps made of mud and when it is baked in the fire it becomes terracotta. And if talk about utensils like hands, and plates, we do not color them. Our family, grandfather started this business when he was 22 years and now after 40 years, my father and myself started pursuing this art. Ajeevika gives us fellowship to exhibit the items at fairs and we have been to the international trade fair, Saras Mela. Women who are not educated take help from the educated member. My mother is Adhyaksh and other members are from other families to maintain a democratic and fair system. We are not joined to cluster, we get letters from Patan vihbaag, NRLM exhibition, and NRLM vihbaag and if we do not get funds, we get loans from these agencies. Even the honorable Chief Minister has visited our facility to see our work."

As indicated in the interview above, the divergence in group members' behavior is evident in the form of differing attitudes, responses, and patterns of interaction.

Factors Impacting Conflicts in a Community Lending Group

In the case of a SHG, the conflict could arise due to cognitive factors such as nonrepayment of loans or due to affective factors such as gender, caste, and race. This can lead to conflicts of interest and rifts among the members of groups. In the case of affective factors, the likelihood of strategic default and misappropriation of scarce resources increases manifold. This is called a divergence in behavior, and this kind of divergence leads to conflict. This includes misutilization of funds for nonproductive purposes. Divergence in behavior leads to exploration and a high level of risk of nonpayment of loans. This could be psychological divergence, which might be due to environmental factors, life cycle, or lack of resources, which can further lead to bad financial behavior. Oversight and monitoring of financial behavior lead to better repayments of loans. However, there is a role for neutral intermediation, as in the case of peer monitoring, there is a risk of moral hazard and bias. *The case in point is an interview with members of leather product-making self-help groups that migrated from Pakistan during the partition.* For Karigars, handicraft is a traditional art form. We make Kurtis and other leather products. If one of the women members is unable to repay the loan, the other members unite and visit the home of the specified member. Collaboration and peer pressure are used to extort money from disgruntled members. Members of the Ajeevika block (state intervention) are crucial to the organization's long-term survival. Hence, though social capital is a source of improving the mental and social wellness of the members of the group, in many cases psychological factors that are individual-specific lead to conflict among the group members due to divergence. This could be due to race, gender, ethnicity, or demographics. Thus, state intervention and monitoring or hand-holding play an important role in improving the financial wellness of the group. Besides that, social capital also helps in reducing the conflicts among the group members by providing access to more resources. Despite divergence in behavior, if social capital and access to resources increase, it leads to better cohesion and solidarity among group members. However, in a few cases, group members cite discriminatory practices as the main reason for conflict among the group members. In these cases, lack of good leadership is the main reason for conflict among the members of the group. Only good leadership and intermediation can enable the convergence of the diverged members into the group.

Fig. 14 shows the various factors that lead to conflict in the group.

As per our study, human capital can augment the role of social capital in promoting the group's effectiveness. Coleman argues that human capital without social capital is not sufficient to augment the group's effectiveness. Lack of trust and social capital leads to divergence in the financial behavior of the members of the group. In this regard, our study corroborates the affective component's role, which comprises the emotions, attitudes, feelings, and culture in augmenting the

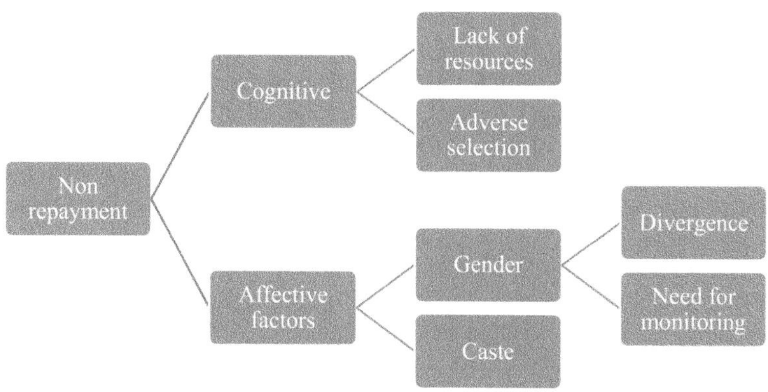

Fig. 14. Factors Leading to Conflict in Group.

social capital (Nebus, 1998). These are also referred to as attitude-based factors, also referred to as community psychology. Hughey et al. (2002) refer this as informal, community-based attitudes comprising social support, community satisfaction, and pride. Putnam highlights the importance of the affective components and attitudes such as motivation on a group's effectiveness.

Excerpt From Interview

Self Help Groups (SHG) works on innovation principles. SHG, when it links to a government agency, gets the required training and guidance. Self-help promoting institution (SHPI) helps in mobilization and also helps in the selection of the members, and it is dependent on the women who are getting selected. If initially the members are wrongly chosen, it will remain like this only. The main target of SHG is entrepreneurship, and SHPI helps in linking of the members. There are many things, as initially, members do not know about how to conduct meetings, how to organize each other, how to maintain a register, and how to organize a business. For the future, what is going to be the business plan? And the Government is giving the money for a business plan. When a few months are left, it is to see the mutual differences between the members. Banks also want to see what businesses should be given to businesses so that they generate business. In one area, if the work is done on a large scale, for example, in Saharanpur, the artisans do Pittal work, and in Hathras, it is metal Zari work, glass work, stone work, then in those places, if people work in closure, they automatically get buyers. After production, market planning is extremely important. The Government of India has established spillers in Mathura, and there is another agency. The Government has given them spillers, but the dilemma is that bad-quality items are selling. If all 10 members work on different items, the group cannot be successful. SHPI has been hand-holding for 4 years. The plan is to maximize the amount of bank loan, agencies can take from the banks. Regarding leadership, when women go to 100 places, they get confident, and through market exposure, they learn how they will handle things, and they learn to talk. As I told you, the women whom we sent to meet Anandipatel—100 of them—out of them, 4 were such who had leadership. They were working together, and there were big units. In the Fareb unit toward Agra, there are many women's units being developed who are into goat rearing. Credit planning is learned in 5 months of incubation. Starting is done at a small level so that they learn to utilize money, and they get the idea that a bank loan is to be paid, and they also learn so that they become trained to handle large sums of money. The sponsored agency also decides that the work that is given to him is proficient in that. When we form groups of 500 members, we select 3 to 4 members to attend training so that they develop an understanding of doing the work. This is an opportunity to learn, and also there are meetings where they get to develop leadership. NPAs are increasing and banks are looking at them as defaulters, and due to this, legitimate groups are unable to get the loan. Neighbors look into the matter and monitor them. If a person has taken a loan of Rs. 30,000, then it is not a criminal offense that the member will be punished, except that the other members can use the social pressure. If the defaulting member is not socially harassed, then there is no way to get back that money. Each of us who is getting money from the Government already has some expenses. In every member's mind, the only thing that remains is that he should get the money so that he can pay back his previous loans. The position is such that the members to whom we have given the money will work for 2 months, but those to whom we have given technology will work forever. This technology will work for him and will work forever. Social change is brought about by these groups. In 2017, we started work in Mathura on a particular craft, and at that time, people came from IIT. And you understand that the visiting of the head of IIT to any place is a big thing. Because the members do not understand the importance of IIT. Women who would not have been out of home go to IIT for giving training. They go to seminars, and there are more than 50 members who are going out and working. This gives them social status. This gives them confidence, and if technology is innovated, this increases their social status. There are members whose children are studying at NIT. Money is not a big thing, but if they get the things or aid, then this improves their income. In the traditional machine the members had various problems, such as spinal problems 90%. They used to sit in Dhanush posture, and now, they are sitting on the table and doing work. If he earns Rs. 100, he invests a significant portion in health; however, with the machine, he can now save time and increase production. Things have developed, and individual members do not get financial support, but when the Government agency gets affiliated with the group, it becomes an opportunity and technology. Any agency in the form of the group should leave an impression that they not only work but also believe in expansion. In 2017, when the group started, there were as few as 500 women, and now, 1,000 women are affiliated to the scheme. There was a time when we as an SHPI used to go to the doorstep of the SHG, but now they come to us. This is an achievement that they are communicating with us. At starting, when we explain to them, it is up to them if they want to understand or not, but once things start working, they understand things are good and going well. Secondly, the Government is also giving them interventions. Some are skilled; some are not skilled. For those who need technology, we are giving them technology training. Some people need innovative designs, and for them, we are conducting an innovative design workshop. In Delhi, there is the INA market; we have given them training and a stipend. The work is going through channel. There is planning for taking the product from production till the point of sale. Bankers are not at fault, as NPAs are very high and banks cannot identify every defaulter. Under the bank scheme, a loan has to be given. Bankers probably default in delaying the money allocation; as if it is given in time, things come out well. Individually, if a member goes to the bank, the bank really harasses him, and if he has to put up the unit today, then the banker gives him a loan in 6 months, so money is invested in the wrong purpose. NABARD does meeting of SLBC Quarterly and monitors banks and the loan applications of SHGs. NABARD is the best agency that is regulating the working of SHGs. This interview highlights the reasons for conflicts among groups, such as the nonhomogeneity of members, lack of financial literacy, and bad attitudes of the bankers. These are some of the cognitive factors that lead to conflict in groups and lead to the breaking up of the group. Proper social intermediation and financial literacy lead to conflict resolution.

Role of Social Capital

Social capital is defined as the sum of norms, networks, and social ties among the members of a community. It refers to a collection of social networks that improve a community's social well-being. Moreover, literature bifurcates literature on social capital based on direct and indirect ties. Baker (1990) has defined social capital as a resource that actors derive from the specific structures and then use to pursue interests; changes in a relationship create it. Bourdieu has defined social capital as the aggregate of the actual possession of potential resources that are linked to the possession of a durable network of more or less institutionalized relationships of mutual acquaintance or recognition. From external ties, one definition describes social capital as a resource derived from structures. The other defines it as resources linked to relations. As per Coleman,

> social capital is not a single entity but a variety of different entities having two characteristics in typical. They all consist of a specific aspect of social structure and facilitate the actions of individuals within that structure. Social capital has been defined as ability due to membership in a group. (Portes, 1998; Brehm & Rahn, 1997)

This definition highlights the internal ties of the members. Fukuyama (1997) defined "social capital as the existence of a specific set of informal values or norms shared among members of a group that permits cooperation among them." More researchers define social capital as a "culture of trust, voluntary means, and processes, expectations for action within a collectivity". The size of a social organization's network also affects its social capital. In community development, social capital has been defined as the norms, Network, and trust among the community members to facilitate cooperation among members of the community and to facilitate the achievement of community objectives. Complementary to both views, Nahapiet and Ghoshal (1998) defined social capital as the sum of both the network and the assets mobilized through the network. Existing literature in social capital tends to focus either on the internal linkages of the community members or the external linkages between the members and the institutions. One of the significant phases in the strategic management of an organization is the organizational appraisal and environmental appraisal. It comprises the strategic direction of the resources and capabilities. These resources include the availability of financial, human, and administrative resources. Effective utilization of these resources is essential to achieve a competitive advantage. Resource availability and resource capabilities can be defined at the individual, firm, and interfirm levels. At the individual level, the resources refer to the norms and values of decision-makers; at the institutional level or firm level, the resource-based refers to organizational culture and politics. The entrepreneurship view comprises three phases: opportunity refinement, leveraging, and championing. Opportunity refinement includes creating awareness of opportunities, leveraging, sourcing, acquiring resources, mobilizing combined resources, and advocating. In the case of microfinancing, the formal financial institutions are not willing to lend to the micro borrowers due to a lack of collateral. SHGs under the SHG linkage program by NABARD aim to provide access to finance for the people at the bottom of the pyramid. These organizations can access finance through loans by a formal financial institution under the SHG linkage program through social capital. Social capital is a unique phenomenon that helps to replace physical collateral with social collateral in a group scenario and facilitates access to finance. Members of a SHG bank linkage program can borrow money from the bank. The State Government machinery, which includes the State Level Banking Committee, the Block Level Banking Committee, and the District Mission Management Unit, is responsible for overseeing the bank loans. Suppose members of the SHG take out loans. In that case, District Mission Managers Block level officials, and counsellors known as CRPs play a critical role in monitoring and motivating them to repay the loan. This is one of the unique aspects of the bank connection program for SHGs. In their study, Srivastava and Samanta use six aspects to define social capital: "Group and networks," "Trust & Solidarity," "Collective action & collaboration," "Social cohesion," and "Information and Communication." In this context, "Trust and Solidarity" refers to interpersonal behavior that fosters better cohesion, "Collective action" refers to the ability of people to work together, "Social cohesion" refers to conflict mitigation, and "Information and Communication" refer to how social capital helps to improve access to information.

Fig. 15 provides details of vertical and horizontal relationships.

The vertical and horizontal linkages are depicted in the diagram above. The borrower has horizontal relationships among its members while standing relationships pertain to the lender's relationship with the borrower. In the case of a

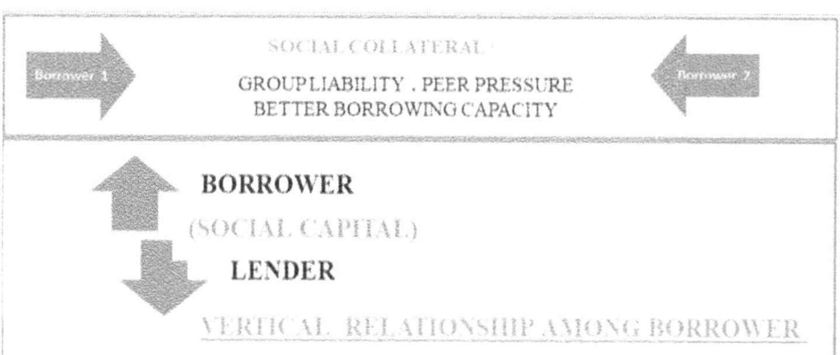

Fig. 15. Depicts the Vertical and Horizontal Relationships.

vertical connection, members are frequently dissatisfied with the relationship with the bank. Borrowers repeatedly mentioned the bank's prejudice.

Monitoring and Its Role in Conflict Resolution

In the interview, the response emphasizes the importance of monitoring by the member. Furthermore, in the case of SHGs, the members are chosen from similar socioeconomic backgrounds, which helps to reduce and mitigate the problem of adverse selection and hence potential conflict of interest among the group members.

Lending to the Women Members

Stiglitz and Halder point out that members of the Ajeevika SHGs are more likely to lend to women. Women are more adept at saving by nature, and lending takes place in a more communal setting where everyone knows everyone, which helps mitigate the adverse selection problem.

Transcripts From the Member

Interview With District Mission Manager. Aside from that, group members share the same background in the same location and village. Therefore, they are familiar with one another. Peer monitoring is possible among the members. Members share money concerns because they are from the same society and village. A loan is granted to the needy person from the savings of all the members. Members' peers watch each other due to their social network and relationships. We call a meeting and suggest that the leader penalize the member who takes the loan and uses it for nonproductive purposes. The locals are all familiar with one another. They talk about money whenever they get together in the village. The entire society keeps an eye on things and builds up pressure. Family members and SHG members inquire about and supervise the loan amount used. For example, if a person has taken a loan of Rs 100,000, the members will enquire about the loan repayment. Our group is like a family because it consists of four diverse houses. There have been occasions of counseling and disagreements, but it has helped us ensure better loan payback. Varian emphasizes the impact of the selection criteria, i.e., assortative and random matching, on the respondents' financial outcomes. Wei Zhang highlights the relevance of banks' progressive lending in enhancing a SHG's economic outcomes.

Moral Hazard and Peer Monitoring Are Reasons for Conflict Among Members of the Group

Joint Liability Group, according to, helps to mitigate the problem of moral hazard through the use of social links, information flow, and dynamic incentives such as progressive loans to borrowers with lower interest rates, longer terms, higher loan amount, and lower transaction costs. Assortative matching permits group members to be matched. Our tribe has been working in the handicraft industry since we arrived from Pakistan. Since the country's independence, these women have been producing handicrafts. In various Karkhanas and fairs, Karigars practice handicrafts as an ancient art form. We make Kurtis and other leather products. If one of the women members is unable to repay the loan, the other members unite and visit the home of the specified member. *Collaboration and peer pressure are used to extort money from disgruntled members. Members of the Ajeevika block are crucial to the organization's long-term survival. The formation of SHGs is not uniform and is not based on activity. Guidelines allow for houses on the same lane coverage, with some households making pottery and weaving, and the next family running a minor business.*

These are nonhomogeneous take-out loans through the SHGBLP, with one member using the money for ceramics and the other for weaving. As a result, loans are not repaid. Members of a homogeneous SHG can keep an eye on each other. Thus, the interview highlights that there are nonhomogeneous members, which leads to conflict. However, conflict can also be used as a source of development by channelizing the group dynamics for welfare. This can only be achieved through specialization and delegation of work. Hence, in a nonhomogeneous group, to reap the fruits of diversity, specialization, and delegation of tasks through transformational leadership can lead to the achievement of group goals. Though transformational leadership can make a difference, lack of good leadership and oversight can lead to misuse of financial resources and wealth. Thus, the lack of good leadership in any group is a major reason for conflicts and the breaking of the group. In case of external conflict, the marginalized group, when it interacts with society at large, such as visiting a commercial bank, it leads to a conflict of interest. In case of external conflicts, state intervention through intermediation, use of literacy campaigns, creating champions for the cause in the external environment, and glorifying the skillset of the members through livelihood training and recognitions can play an important role in reducing or mitigating external conflicts. In an interview, the leader highlighted that one of the members of his group got an opportunity to visit America along with the chief minister. These kinds of recognition give a lot of recognition to the members of the group.

Fig. 16 provides reasons for conflicts among members.

A case in point is the interview with the bank officials, where the official highlighted that the group will not give loans to the members if they come alone. However, when they come with other members, generally we provide them the loans based on social capital or state intervention. In a homogenous group, internal conflicts can arise due to cognitive reasons such as nonrepayment of loans, and this can be resolved through the use of peer monitoring.

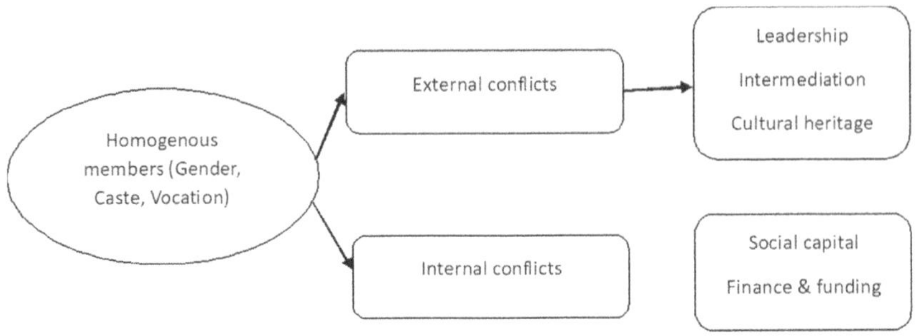

Fig. 16. Reason for Conflict Among Members. *Source:* By Authors.

Process of Peer Monitoring

Fig. 17 provides the source of conflict and challenges in SHGs.

Peer monitoring, delegated monitoring by banks, and Ajeevika block-level officers or employees are examples of different types of monitoring (National Rural Livelihood Mission). Due to a lack of financial incentives, banks are not interested in monitoring their customers. In the case of indigenous loans, peer monitoring produces excellent results at a low cost. The block officials monitor the performance of the borrowers and enforce increased repayments in the case of external loans or bank loans under Self Help Group bank linkage. In terms of information asymmetry, which includes moral hazard and adverse selection, Fig. 15 emphasizes the obstacles faced by the lender in extending credit to micro borrowers. The peer mechanism helps prevent moral hazard by reducing the probability of adverse selection through peer selection and peer monitoring. Along with better credit development, this leads to better payback and thrift. SHG is a social structure made up of people who belong to the same social group and have similar employment responsibilities, social relationships, and

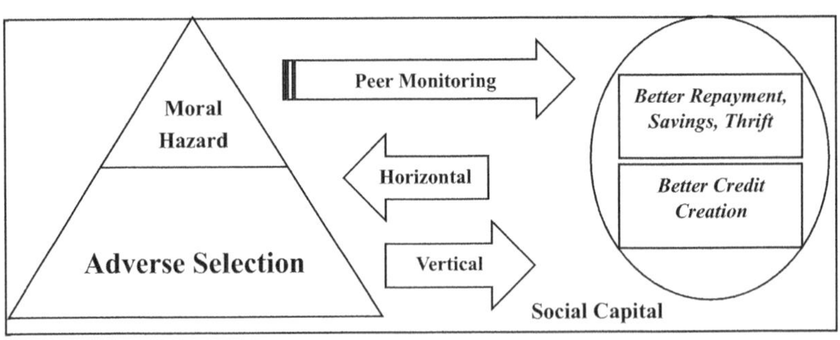

Fig. 17. Source of Conflict and Challenges in Self-Help Groups. *Source:* By Authors.

commercial connections. These social organizations function according to a set of standard norms and institutions. These activities result in more excellent financial results in terms of repayment.

Theoretical Coding—Process of Peer Monitoring

Theoretical coding for peer monitoring reveals that there are three stages to the monitoring process: (1) peer selection or group formation, (2) peer monitoring, and (3) peer enforcement. We can see from the codes that the size of the group, composition of the group, and shared norms are crucial criteria at the stage of group formation. Tuckman's theory of group formation refers to this stage as group formation and storming. The institutional structures and processes define the process in the second stage, norming and performing. Institutional arrangements, such as bookkeeping, recordkeeping, and meetings, are implemented at this stage. This ensures the group's proper management. Following this stage, the group's performance begins in savings/thrift, inter- and intra-loans and is referred to as the performing stage. At this point, it's critical to keep an eye on things. The group exercises sanction and enforcement due to shared liability and restricted individual liability. The final level is known as peer sanction and enforcement.

Fig. 18 provides theoretical coding for stages in group information.

After analyzing the data, it becomes clear that there are two alternative management models for the groups. One of the models used by banks is the Power and Control model, in which the bank bears the monitoring and screening costs and the high transaction costs. The formal structure of this model distinguishes it. The banks do not know the borrowers in this arrangement, and the risk is passed from the lender to the borrower. The second form is the cooperative model, in which the members decide the Panchsutras. The members of the group are in charge of peer monitoring, penalties, and enforcement. The members of the group choose the leaders.

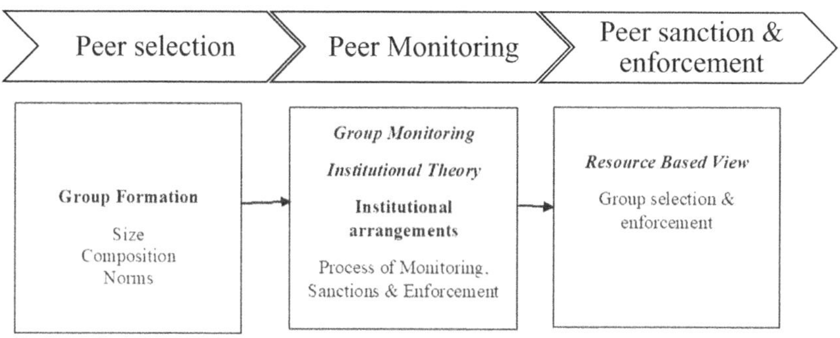

Fig. 18. Theoretical Coding 7—Stages in Group Formation.

Peer Monitoring as a Cause of Conflict

Peer Monitoring often serves as a source of Conflict.

Conclusion

Social finance, as per the study, plays an increasingly important role in promoting the welfare of the people at the bottom of the pyramid. In the case of a group formed by the members who belong to the homogeneous group, the social capital provides the financial support to ensure access to finance for the people at the bottom of the pyramid. Within a group, the peer mechanism plays an important role in ensuring the financial discipline within the group to ensure the financial sustainability of the group.

References

Bradley, B. H., Anderson, H. J., Baur, J. E., & Klotz, A. C. (2015). When conflict helps: Integrating evidence for beneficial conflict in groups and teams under three perspectives. *Group Dynamics: Theory, Research, and Practice*, *19*(4), 243–272.

Brehm, J., & Rahn, W. (1997). Individual-level evidence for the causes and consequences of social capital. *American Journal of Political Science*, *41*(3), 999–1023. https://doi.org/10.2307/2111684

DeChurch, L. A., & Marks, M. A. (2001). Maximizing the benefits of task conflict: The role of conflict management. *International Journal of Conflict Management*, *12* (1), 4–22.

Hirshleifer, J. (1978). Competition, cooperation, and conflict in economics and biology. *The American Economic Review*, *68*(2), 238–243.

Knowles, G., & Luke, B. (2018). Creating conflict or harmony? The impact of microfinance programs and self-help groups on social order in poor communities. *Third Sector Review*, *24*(2), 35–56.

Noor, M., Brown, R., Gonzalez, R., Manzi, J., & Lewis, C. A. (2008). On positive psychological outcomes: What helps groups with a history of conflict to forgive and reconcile with each other? *Personality and Social Psychology Bulletin*, *34*(6), 819–832.

Park, R. E., & Burgess, E. W. (1921). *Introduction to the science of society*. s.n.

Portes, A. (1998). Social capital: Its origins and applications in modern sociology. *Annual Review of Sociology*, *24*, 1–24.

Sarma, S. K., & Mehta, M. H. (2014). The best model for micro-lending: Self-help group or joint liability group? *Journal of Rural Development*, *33*(3), 247–260.

Dr. Thakore, D. (2013). Conflict and conflict management. *Journal of Business and Management*, *8*(6), 07–16.

Tjosvold, D., Law, K. S., & Sun, H. (2006). Effectiveness of Chinese teams: The role of conflict types and conflict management approaches. 罗胜强, 孙海法, trans. *Management and Organization Review*, *2*(2), 231–252.

Chapter 4

Leadership a Panacea to Cause of Poverty Reduction and Financial Inclusion Through Self-Help Groups

Abstract

Community lending programs suffer from various inherent conflicts due to diversity and conflict of interest among the group members. Transformational leadership plays a vital role in providing conflict resolution through hand-holding. This chapter will use the transformational leadership theory to explore the impact of a transformational leader in ensuring consensus and a sense of ownership among the members of the group. This chapter will use the single case study method to study the role of group leaders in the success of the group. Through negative case analysis, this chapter will provide a comparative analysis of the groups without strong leaders vis a vis the groups without leaders. The primary data will be collected by using the semi-structured interview. The secondary data will be collected using the existing published literature. For data collection, the samples will be selected using purposive random sampling. The scope of the study will be community lending initiatives in Asia. In addition to transformational leadership, this chapter will also look at the role of the financial leaders in achieving sustainability and financial goals within the groups. The abuse of power within a group can lead to the exploitation of the marginalized and can further lead to social evils like homicides through the use of peer pressure. It will also explore the role of leaders in ensuring adherence to group norms and increasing organizational commitment among the members of the group. This chapter will include case studies from Europe, Germany, the United Kingdom, and the Asia Pacific, including India, Bangladesh, and China.

Keywords: Microfinance; community lending; financial access; usage; transformational leadership

Development and Conflict in Community Lending Programs, 69–99

Published under exclusive licence by Emerald Publishing Limited
doi:10.1108/978-1-83708-290-220251012

Introduction

Community lending refers to a social phenomenon that brings together people from marginalized sections of society for the achievement of group goals like poverty reduction and sustainable development. A good leader has a great role to play in the success of the group. Without good leaders, the groups are like skeletons without life and lack control and coordination. Leadership helps to bring about circularity and convergence to the behavior and lives of the members of the group. Without group leaders, the members suffer from divergence and find it difficult to create a consensus or solidarity among themselves. The conflicts among the group members take the form of cognitive expression such as nonrepayment of loans and money taken. Through motivational skills and power dreaming, they can give rise to action in the group. In a community lending group, the members choose their leaders through the consensus, and the leader is responsible for laying down the group norms, preparing the books of accounts, and motivating the members to work toward the mission of financial sustainability of the group. Not only the leader has the power of a dream, but he is also able to appeal to the emotions of the people at large and motivate them to achieve the group goals. Leaders in a group are thus born out of necessity and are not Minerva that sprung up from the mind of Jove. This chapter aims to study the impact of transformational leadership in mitigating the conflicts among the members of the group. This chapter uses the qualitative case study method to discuss the impact of leadership on the sustainability of the group, and for this study, the data have been collected using the semi-structured interview method.

Literature Review

The self-help group (SHG) has been defined as providing help and support to the members of the group in dealing with their problems and improving their psychological function and effectiveness (Levy, 1976). SHGs or community lending groups have existed across the world for ages, and in India, the SHG linkage program was introduced in the year 1992. These institutes were aimed at providing livelihood and promoting self-reliance, among rural women. Beyond Financial Access and Usage, without the use of Financial Collateral & Monitoring through Peer Pressure, SHGs ensured sustainable livelihood for millions of marginalized women in India. In the year 1990, NABARD introduced the SHG Linkage Program, which is the key strategy for delivering financial services to the poor in a sustainable manner. According to the latest NABARD Annual report, 45% of the SHGs have been able to get access to Credit Linkage once. There are various studies on the importance of SHGs. However, there is a lack of literature in the domain of low average loan size and dismal credit creation under the bank linkage program. There is of yet no study to explore the causes of Low Credit Off taken under the SHG Linkage Program, and there is no study on the impact of digitization on the sustainability of the SHGs in India. From the Scientific Evidence analyzed from the analysis of the relevant literature, it is established that the main cause of low credit offtake is the set of lack of good leadership and hand-holding for these groups. Bankers lack motivation to lend to the SHG members due to lack of documentation, lack of adherence to the Panchsutras, and lack of protocols and adherence. Most of the current research is limited to the physical outreach and Social Role of SHGs. There is not much research in the field of models for monitoring, problems of moral hazard and adverse selection, and digitization of processes of the SHG Bank Linkage program. This chapter aims at understanding the impact of Financial Literacy and monitoring through various models. This model will be of importance to academicians and policymakers. Lasting peace cannot be achieved unless large population groups find ways in which to break out of poverty, and that "across cultures and civilizations, Yunus and Grameen Bank have shown that even the poorest of the poor can work to bring about their development," The Noble Committee. SHGs, next to more broadly defined savings groups (SGs), are a form of community-based approach to microfinance. The SHGs have emerged as the medium of financial intermediaries and the major channels of disbursement of finance. The Self-Help Bank Linkage Program introduced by the NABARD in the year 1992 has been touted as an Alternative Capital Funding Model for meeting the needs of the Microfinance Industry in Rural India and as a cost-effective model of Microfinance program and as the channel of disbursement of Microfinance. There is extant literature available on limitations and various challenges faced by this program, and most of the studies highlight the issue of lack of good leadership as the cause of financial exclusion. Various nations have adopted financial Inclusion as the Sustainable Development Goals (SDGs) by the World Bank. And SHGs are considered to be the major driver of the Financial Inclusion program through the famous Bank Sakhi Model. This review also aims to study the various challenges faced by the members of the SHGs.

SHGs are extremely important to achieve the objective of women empowerment.

- Women's Empowerment: The extant literature makes a mention of the dominant role of SHGs in achieving Women's Empowerment. The analysis of the extant literature shows that the SHG leads to the Empowerment of the Women. This empowerment can be in the form of Social Empowerment, Women Empowerment, and Political Empowerment.

Table 1 provides details of the literature review.

Typologies

Tankha (2012) suggests that Self-Help Groups (SHGs) can take diverse forms. Globally, in rural parts of South East Asia, Latin America, and Caribbean, there existed informal groups called as Rotating Savings and Credit Associations (ROSCAs). Kenya has majority of women who participate in community saving through ROSCAs. Vlack et al. (2014) elaborate that ROSCAs arrived from West

Table 1. Literature Review.

Author	Description
Brody (2017) High Confidence	Women's SHGs have a positive effect on women empowerment, political empowerment, women's mobility and women's control over family planning.
Dr. Gopalaswamy et al. (2016)	Microfinance has positive but small effects on income, women's empowerment, employment, asset creation, and consumption expenditure. The poorest of the poor are likely to experience large positive effects on household consumption.
Maren Duvendack & Philip Mader (2020)	There is no reliable evidence for impacts of microcredit on women's control over household resources, making it unlikely that microcredit has a substantial impact on women empowerment in a broader sense.
Stewart et al. (2010)	Micro savings has no significant effect on engagement in economic opportunities, and there is relatively weak and inconsistent evidence that microcredit has a positive influence on incomes.
Duvendack et al. (2011)	A study on microfinance report on positive effects but offers no convincing evidence of impacts on overall well-being due to the evidence base being too weak to draw robust conclusions.
Steinart (2011)	Savings promotion has a small but positive impact on intermediate outcome (Savings income and propensity) and poverty measures (Household expenditure, food and safety).

Africa and became a part and foundation of African ancestry community in Caribbean. ROSCAs are part of the ancestral culture in Bahamas, where people contribute a sum periodically to the common pool (H. M. Srinivasan, n.d.). SHGs are supported by the nongovernment organizations (NGOs) and by the Government agencies. The report highlights role of the Self-Help Promotion Agencies (SHPAs) in promoting the SHGs. The report highlights that there are three kinds of SHPAs: (1) NGOs, (2) government agencies, and (3) banks. The NGO Model of SHG is promoting the formation of SHG. The basic function of these groups is loans for consumption, clearing outside debt, social, medical, education, business, agriculture, etc. A typical household starts with own savings and then is promoted by the NGO (Shiyani & Namboodiri, n.d.).

Microlending Schools and Technologies

Microlending schools can be classified into four major schools: (1) Solidarity Group, (2) Grameen, (3) SHG, (4) Village Banking, and (5) Individual Lending.

Solidarity Groups: Solidarity Groups use the peer pressures to control the credit risk. Generally, the lenders deploy the stepped approach to lending. This approach helps to generate the data regarding the Credit History while reducing the exposure to the Formal lender and risk is controlled easily. Only one account is opened in the bank for the Group.

Grameen Model: In this model, a self-selected group of 4–5 other groups from the village form a center, and this structure enhances the financial viability of the project. Compulsory training of 4–5 months is given before the loan. Moreover, the loans are provided to the members in a staggered manner. After one or two months of payment, the Group becomes eligible for the second loan. The savings kept serve as collateral for the members. Also in some cases, the depositors are not allowed to access their savings.

Self-help group: Under the SHG approach, i.e. the SHG Bank Linkage model, the members have only one account with the SHG and not with the banks, and the banks do not have direct dealings with the banks. If the SHG member decides to make regular savings contributions and members can borrow from each other, the SHG opens a group savings account and deposits funds that are not loaned, and the SHG maintains a meticulous record of group attendance, savings, and internal lending activities (Cheryl & Craiz, n.d.).

Various perspectives exist on the origins of SHGs.

Perspectives on SHGs (Self-Help Groups) Include

(1) Financial System Approach.
(2) Poverty Lending Approach.

The financial systems approach emphasizes large-scale outreach to the economically active poor—both to borrowers who can repay microloans from household and enterprise income streams and to savers. It focuses on institutional Self Sufficiency (Robinson, 2001). While the poverty lending approach concentrates on reducing poverty through credit, often provided together with Credit are complementary services such as skills training and the teaching of literacy and numeracy, health, and nutrition. Through these institutes, Donor and Government-funded credit is provided to poor borrowers below the market rate of interest. Costs serve as another important perspective in the domain of SHGs. One of the fundamental poverty/sustainability questions is whether services can be delivered at a cost that is affordable to clients and can these groups be self-sustainable. Most of the studies highlight the lack of good leadership as the reason for the failure of community lending.

Based on Financing and Promoting Agency

Model 1 encourages banks to form and finance SHGs and government agencies promote the group, and hence, the issue of lack of leadership does not impact the borrowers. Model 2 encourages NGOs to form groups giving small cash grants and training as an incentive and then link them to the local bank where NGOs or government agencies promote the group. In Model 3, NGOs MFI and group clusters are banks financed by intermediate loans to SHGs, and banks promote the group (Christen & Ivatury, 2007).

Participation From the NGOs

NGOs have also started participating in disbursing cash and credit to the people at the Bottom of the Pyramid, and NGOs know what they do not have in terms of good staff, trained in managing cash, in conforming to regulations, forecasting reserves, and minimizing frauds. The poor have a high rate of aversion to risk-taking. Thus, the groups have higher power to bring the news about the lower rates of interest and affordable insurance and other financial services to the members of the SHGs. Sustainability is one of the major benefits of the SHGs. This involves the quantification of the Perceived Value of the Utility, and it is linked to the Source of Consumption Loan, Source of Production Loan, Link to get the Banks, and ability to solve the social and community problem, elevate the social status, and link to other agencies in the Government. Unsubsidized Group Self-Management and Benefit stream to each member leads to the sustainability.

The practice of Thrift: Women members talk to each other, and they plan how to save the Thrift, and Thrift differs from Savings. *Internal Credit:* Internal credit is the other reason for the existence of the SHGs. Simple Task Forces for the SHGs include the Panchayat Leadership, Health Development, Education and Literacy, and Economic.

Successful Case Studies Regarding SHGs

Case Study: This is the case study about the Natural Village defined by Watershed and disasters. In this Natural Setting, the SHGs can help to mobilize the natural village and lessen the impact of Natural hazards. There are numerous examples of SHGs managing the disasters in the State of Orissa.

Loan Elasticity: Case Study of Banswara Village

Microfinance for villagers considers the natural cycles of rural life. Rather than following a strict monthly schedule, many villagers prefer to meet for loan repayments in the evenings, with the timing linked to lunar cycles. Some banks, such as those in Banswara, have adapted their repayment schedules to align with the rhythms of nature. They ask villagers to repay loans when a specific tree, known as the "Flame of the Forest," blooms. SHGs acknowledge the importance of the harvest and sowing seasons and provide for repayment as per the seasons and natural events. Internal Loans from the SHG vary widely. SHGs offer various benefits to the members, who are mainly illiterate and landless. SHGs have helped to increase the income and assets of the members in the SHGs. SHGs help reduce the interest rates charged by the Money Lenders, and they extend credit to the poorest and help to form groups for the poorest of the women, with NGOs' support SHGs' help to promote social development.

(1) Do SHGs help in promoting schemes like Swarnjayanti Grameen Swar Rozgar Yojana? There is a lack of differentiation between the Swarn Jayanti Rozgara Yojana and SHG Bank Linkage program. (2) The poorest of the people in the community are still overlooked by the SHGs. Exclusion is one of the major problem areas, e.g. NGOs in North East India. (3) SHGs are basically suffering from the issue that can SHGs really do everything? Distractions from the core financial activities can undermine the quality of the Financial Benefits. There are very few studies on whether group is better off with the Social Performance. The case in point is the Darjeeling CRS, and the confusion is how much can the SHG take before it imploded.

Savings Help Groups were started in India by the Women members of SEWA International under the leadership of Ela Bhatt. In 1985, the Mysore Resettlement and Development Agency (MYRADA), a non-governmental organization (NGO) based in Southern India, began promoting the concept of Self-Help Affinity Groups (SHAGs), which were later named Self-Help Groups (SHGs). This marked a significant point in the history of the SHG movement in India. In 1987 NGO PRADAN introduced *Savings Groups* for Poverty alleviation in Rajasthan. In 1989 IFAD promoted Informal Borrowing and Lending program. During this period from 1987 to 1990, the Government was busy in promoting and supporting the NGOs. Nationalization of banks was done in 1969–1971, Mandatory system of Priority Lending in 1972, Establishment of Rural Banks in 1982, and piloting and mainstreaming of the SHG movement in 1992–1996. Most of the SHGs were formed based on concept of Saving First and Credit Later (Reddy, 2005).

In 1992, the Government recognized the SGH as an alternative credit model. This model was based on the principle of Graduation, which refers to how SHGs move up the ladder in terms of income and the factors that can promote it. SHG Bank Linkage involves partnership between the SHG, NGOs and banks (Badatya & Puhazhendi, 2002).

Gaps in Self-Help Group Bank Linkage Program

According to Aggarwal (1996), enforcement of stringent prudential norms, capital adequacy stipulations, setting up of the Board for Financial Supervision (BFS) and pressure to reduce NPAs have made banks so risk-averse that they have reduced their exposure to private loans with even a modest risk of non-recovery. The SHG suffers from the following challenges lack of transport facilities, long distance market, lack of training on economic activities, members not attending meetings, and no economic activity other than microlending were major problems faced by the women SHG members. The lack of transport facilities, lack of training on economic activities, long distance of the market, and dominance of group leader were the major problems faced by the nonmembers. The lack of training on economic activities, the dominance of the group leader, members not giving monthly savings, members not attending regular meetings, no economic activity other than microlending, and less profit from products prepared were major reasons for SHG dropouts. Thus, lack of good leadership is often touted as the reason for the failure of group.

Bank Sakhi Channel

In 2006, RBI (Reserve Bank of India) announced the Business Correspondents and Bank Sakhi channel for Rural Banking channel. Customer service points and Business Correspondents facilitate last-mile connectivity. The Bank Sakhi model has facilitated the access to financial services. According to the report, the **Bank Sakhi Model**—where a Self-Help Group (SHG) member is trained as a **Business Correspondent**—is a key driver of financial inclusion. Banks allowed appointing third-party correspondents. State level rural livelihood mission (SLRM) deploys SHG members as Business Correspondents. The State Mission provides grants and incentives. Bank Sakhi is paid as per the transaction until SLRM has made the progress as Business Correspondents. In 2020, completed SLRM also provided the training support in the form of Capacity Building. For the implementation of Bank Sakhi Model, SRLMs have been deployed by the Regional Rural Banks and Business Correspondents. Digitization of the Community-Based organization facilitated biometric identities through signatories through real-time ATMs. The model support migration from Bank to Bank Sakhi model. Individual accounts were linked to the SHG Bank Account in the CBS. Through this system, there is more transparency. A credit transaction history can be gradually built. This Dual technology can be used to transfer funds from SHGs to the individual account. National Rural Livelihood Mission (NRLM) has developed a model to promote Business Correspondent agents to ensure the usage of Bank Accounts. The SHG Member-based SHG Model is a far sustainable model (Nair, n.d.).

Bankers Model of Financial Development of a Group

There are three major phases of Financial Development:

Phase 1: Savings: In this phase, the group chooses common amount to save each month. Hence, the group opens a savings account at nearby bank. It leads to the discipline of thrift and creation of assets.

Phase 2: Interlending: This phase deals with the savings, and the group lends savings members (Charges interest) and basic book keeping begins. This way groups learn to lend and borrow with small amounts of cash at stake and dependence on money lender reduced.

Phase 3: Bank Linkage: This refers to the within group saving and lending, and the group approaches the bank credit up to four times the amount saved. This leads to the development of the relationship with the mainstream financial institutions and group can borrow up to four times savings.

Phase 4: Sustainability: The group manages savings, internal lending, bank credit and book keeping without subsidized support. The group continues indefinitely (as long as members enjoy benefits).

Group Linkages bring unexpected benefits to the Group members, and the members can motivate the members to lend the money. And Bankers can lend money to the SHGs at rate much lower than the Microfinance Institutions (Wilson, 2002).

Driver of Sustainable Banking Growth

The critical review of the chapter reveals that the SHGs lead to the sustainable growth of the Banks in the company. SHGs following "Panchsutras," namely conduct of regular group meetings, regular savings within the group, internal lending, timely repayment of loan, and maintenance of proper books of accounts, are considered to be of good quality and over years have proved themselves to be good customers of Banks, *NABARD*. Further, the review of the chapter reveals that the SHG leads to the number of innovations in the disbursement of the credit. Recognition by the formal credit structure of self-management capabilities of the poor through SHGs and a linkup between the two is expected to result in specific advantages to both systems. Under the linkage project, the main advantage to banks would be externalization of a part of the work items of the credit cycle – assessment of credit needs, appraisal, disbursal, supervision and repayment, reduction in the formal paperwork involved, and a consequent reduction in transaction costs. Improvement in recoveries and also in the margins leads to a wider coverage of the target group. A larger mobilization of small savings is equally advantageous. For the groups, advantages lie in the access to a larger quantum of resources as compared to their corpus generated through thrift, access to better technology and skill up gradation through different schemes of banking sector, and a general improvement in the nature and scale of operations that would accelerate economic development, *NABARD*.

The Self-Help Group Bank Linkage Program helps in the reduction of operating expenses as well reducing the delinquency rates (Srinivasan & Sriram, 2006).

E Shakti Digitization

The objective of this initiative was to digitize all the social and financial data of the SHGs and the members. It aims at providing easy access to all the information about the SHGs to the stakeholders at their doorsteps. In Phase I, this project was rolled out in two districts: Dhule (Maharashtra) and Ramgarh (Jharkhand).

The e-Shakti project has been implemented all over India. A major challenge for Self-Help Groups (SHGs) was a lack of proper record-keeping. To address this issue, the **e-Shakti** initiative was launched to digitize their books of accounts. In the first stage, the Master data were created, and when all the data were uploaded on the server, the SHG was called unboarded. Hence, e-Shakti was made operational through Mobile App and the Go live. This project creates various kinds of data including member wise information on SHG saving, credit history of the members, microcredit plan of SHGs, Bank linkage details, and other periodical MIS. This initiative facilitates banks to take application of SHG loans online, provide access to all the information online, and generation of reports (Kagwar, n.d.).

Types of Cost in SHG and Bank Linkage Program

There are various kinds of costs involved in SHG including Cost of Money, Cost of prudent financial services, and Transaction costs. Transaction cost comprises of Direct Costs and Indirect Costs. Direct Cost comprises of the cost of formation of group, training of the group, administrative cost, branch supervision, cost of appraisal of group, and the Monitoring costs.

Impact of SHG Linkage Program on Credit Creation and Savings

The SHG Linkage Program has led to increase in SHG Savings to 23,324 Crore, and Loan Outstanding has increased from 58,320 Crore. Also, SHGs form the highest proportion of the Loan Outstanding.

All the form of banks such as Commercial Bank, Regional Rural Bank, and Private Banks has been given targets to disburse the amount of loan. Commercial Banks contribute the maximum to the loan amount or credit, and Cooperative Banks contribute the least.

Credit Rationing

One of the major challenges facing the SHGs is the low Credit Creation and Credit Rationing by the Bankers. Interaction with the SHG Members indicate that they seldom have access to the Credit Amount.

Extant literature cites various reasons of Credit Rationing:

(1) *Supply Side Factors*—These factors include parameters such as individual household characteristics, household production skills, household previous day credit history, and ability of the household collateral. The various factors that impact credit rationing include Viability of Production, Ability to loan, and Operation of Production

(2) *Demand Side Factors*—Factors that impact the Demand side factors include inability to provide collateral, lack of network with the formal financial institutions, and transactions costs.
(3) Repeat Loan and Credit Linkages as the form of Financial Sustainability SHG BLP is aimed at magnifying the rate of Savings and Credit level within the group. The extant literature lays emphasis on sustainability through the repeat loans from the client. For the sustainable growth of the microcredit through the SHGs, the extant literature emphasizes the need for the reduction of the Transaction cost (Rhyne, 1998).

SHG–Bank Linkage Program (SBLP), *the channel to reduce the transaction costs*: The Self-Help Group Bank Linkage Program has emerged as a Cost-effective channel to reduce the Operating Expenses and the Delinquency Costs. Within this organizational format, SBLP have the high recovery rates, reduced transaction costs & provide an opportunity for business in future (Srinivasan, 2008)

SHG Sustainability

Factors such as recovery of loans, per capita *savings and linkage,* with an SHG federation, lead to higher sustainability (Parida & Sinha, 2010).

SHG federations are crucial for improving the sustainability of Self-Help Groups (SHGs) (Nair, 2005; Shylendra, 2018; and Chakrabarti, 2004).

Sustainability of SHGs was well established in terms of:

- increase value of assets and saving rate;
- better access to institutional loans;
- higher rate of repayment;
- elimination of informal sources and impressive social empowerment, Badatya & Puhazhendi, (2002).

Saver Graduation and built in tendency toward membership expansion leads to sustainability (Ahlin and Townsend, 2007). These days various measures of Sustainability have been developed. With evolution of Panchsutras as the foundation of a successful Self Help Group Linkage program, Sustainability index as metrics of Panchsutras compliance has become the benchmark to screen and evaluate the workings of SHGs (Guha & Das, 2019). The Panchsutras framework comprises scores for several dimensions of sustainability: managerial, organizational (measured by dropout rates), and multidimensional. The multi-dimensional score, in particular, assesses the frequency of group meetings, member attendance, the maintenance of group records, the decision-making process, the rotation of group leadership, and the group's capacity for conflict resolution. Sustainability is defined as a Self-Help Group's (**SHG's**) non-reliance on any external sources. Despite all the efforts, sustainability of SHGs is slightly doubtful due to non-adherence to the Panchsutras. As per the extant literature,

SHGs work on the Principle of Social Relations and Proximity, Inclusion, Social and Peer Monitoring, and Discipline and Refrain (Morduch, 2005). Extant literature is of view that SHG members must have self-regulation to make SHG a success. And in order to ensure peer monitoring and self-regulation, there is a need for effective leadership and hand-holding in the form of intermediation.

A theoretical lens for the Sustainability is the set of Principles to ensure Financial and Operational viability of the SHGs. It includes *discipline, refrain, inclusion and peer monitoring, and social relations and proximity* (Morduch & de Aghion, 2010).

Challenges to SHG comprise higher costs of monitoring and transaction costs. Lenders and financial institutions like Banks are vary of lending to the SHGs due to the problem of Moral Hazard and Adverse Selection. As per (1) Adverse Selection, banks cannot easily identify the customers who are likely to default and (2) Moral Hazard, banks cannot ensure their customers to put in the required level of efforts to make the financed projects successful (Morduch & de Aghion, 2010).

Adverse Selection: Adverse selection refers to the information problem that includes subsidizing the bad members that do not have collateral and about whom credit worthiness information is not available by the good members. The bank deals with such problems by having information networks. Thus, safe borrowers would like to have safe partners and risky partners to have risky borrowers. Lenders can also discover the type of borrower by looking at the profile of the partner.

Non-availability of the collateral: In such case, safe borrowers would have to subsidize the bad borrowers that push up the rate of interests extremely high. The bank can offer two types of contracts: One with high level of Joint Liability and lower level of interest costs and other with the lower level of Joint Liability and higher level of interest costs. Safe borrowers will select the high joint liability and lower level of interest costs, and risky borrowers will select the lower joint liability and higher level of interest rates.

Moral Hazard: In case of the Joint Liability Projects or Community initiatives like SHGs, the project payoff depends on the actions of the borrowers. Ordinarily borrowers choose action where Marginal Benefit is equal to the Marginal cost. But in case of Asymmetric information, the borrowers who will not be able to offer the collateral will have a different objective (Ghatak & Guinnane, 1999).

Theories of peer monitoring deciphers that the incentives for Peer Monitoring and Peer selection are responsible for the higher repayment rates. Despite all the arguments, the rate of default among the Community groups and SHGs defies the Principle of Peer Pressure as a motivating factor to repay (A, Diagne, 1998). This is due to *internal selection bias* and *social costs.* Biased member selection in groups can remove the incentive to monitor or be monitored. The reason for none functioning of Peer Monitoring is also fraught with Free Rider problem (Diamond, 1984), and the reason of not paying is not the inability to pay but the unwillingness to pay (Alliou, 2000). Thus, there is relevance for the third-party monitoring (Stiglitz, 1990). Good borrower will have to bear the burden for bad borrowers, and banks will extend the benefits in form of lesser interest rates.

Group lending hence improves the welfare and repayment. There are two options for the borrowers under Joint Liability or Community initiatives either to work cooperatively or noncooperatively (J, Tirole, 1993). If the members are working cooperatively, the author suggests a Nash Equilibrium where there is a cost for disutility built into the model, and also the cost of the project failure is built into the model (Conning, 2005). The borrower incurs cost to monitor the actions of the partner. Under the Joint Liability, the social sanctions are effective, and monitoring cost are low enough. Joint Liability leads to improvement in the repayment through peer monitoring. The Joint Liability Group facilitates the screening, monitoring and repayment of loans facilitating financial viability of SHGs. The author mentions that the reason for low cost is social capital, intensive monitoring, which are the outcomes of effective leadership and trust. This chapter has enumerated the problems of *SHG* as (1) Adverse selection, (2) moral hazard, (3) enforcement, and (4) auditing costs due to lack of good leadership. The author highlights that the reason for the failure of the SHGs is the inability to recover the loans from the poor people and self-selection into the problem. The author has propagates that JLLG promotes rural credit through impacting the borrowing and lending behavior of the poor or the Transaction costs. By auditing the individual member, the Joint Liability Group reduces the cost of auditing and monitoring.

NPAs in SHG Bank Linkage in India Microfinance

Total NPAs out of loan outstanding has balanced to 6.12% in 2017–2018 but again fail to 5.9%. "Poor economic conditions, non-cooperation among members, expenses incurred on marriages, social ceremonies and medical emergencies are some of the factors that have turned the loans extended to the Self-Help Groups (SHGs) non-performing assets (NPAs)." (Source: the Hans India website). Main causes for increasing NPAs are (1) Poor economic conditions, noncooperation/nonrepayment by other members of the SHG expenses toward marriage/ceremony, medical emergency, etc., and expectation of loan waiver from the government in that order, as the main factors behind the unhealthy growth of NPAs.

In wake of the literature, the factors' demand can be divided as the Supply Side factors such as Access, Price strategies & wards and Cooperate Governance with *Supply side* factors such as:

(1) Access to Financial services:
- access exclusion;
- condition exclusion;
- price exclusion;
- marketing exclusion;
- self-exclusion.

(2) Usage.
(3) Outreach.

(4) Ease of Use.
(5) Size of Bank.
(6) Type—Commercial and Rural.
(7) Transaction Cost.
(8) Credit Books and *Demand side* factor comprise of:

- financial literacy;
- cost for transactions;
- livelihood profiles;
- gender and age profiles.

Women Empowerment

From the analysis of the reviews conducted under the meta analysis, it becomes clear that there are few studies that establish a Positive impact of SHG Programmes on the Empowerment of the Women. In terms of *Economic Empowerment,* the *Members* of SEWA Experience Positive Impact on Income, and Econometric Evaluation of SHGs. Income generation for members of the SHG is influenced by factors like loan amount, amount of saving, years of existence of SHG, education level of the group leader, and availability of the training facility. However, SHG-wise efficiency scores varied across the geographies due to different sociocultural dimensions. Women Empowerment as a phenomenon is the most studied concept and one of the most celebrated social objectives in India (Swain & Varghese, 2014).The authors assert that there is consensus on what does the Women Empowerment means. Kabeer (2002) has defined the women empowerment as the process through which those who have been denied the ability to make strategic life choices acquire such ability. This ability has been defined as resources which include the access to resources both the material and social resources, agency which includes the process of decision-making, negotiation, deception, nepotism and manipulation, and achievements that are well-being outcomes. Further, SHGs provide the members the required training and workshops to cater greater awareness. Similarly, supports from the various group members also empower the women. Also, the group meetings bring the members closer toward the Government officials, bank officers and workers in NGOs. SHGs cover all the microenterprises and aim to create self-employment and livelihood for the marginalized section of society (Sarkar & Baishya, 2012).

Social Empowerment

The aim of the review is to critically analyze the impact of SHG on Social Empowerment. Members of SHGs experience positive impact on decision-making and Women's Empowerment on Rural Community.

Determinants of Social Empowerment through decision-making.

- Decision-making can be classified as Participatory decision-making (*decision-making related to purchase of expensive items, children, child ill, child's wedding*) and Work Participation (engaged more than 240 hours in salaried work, business activity, or nonagriculture wage work during a calendar year) (Desai & Choudhuri, 2018).
- The SHG movement in India began in the early 1980s as a social mobilization tool, truly scaled-up when a NABARD-led initiative in 1992 linked a small number of SHGs with banks under the SBLP, and 25 years since its existence, the SHG movement has evolved by acting as a platform for not just financial access but also as a means of social justice and mobilization (Korada & Shruti, 2018).

Social Outcomes

This review aims at analyzing the impact of the SHGs on the achievement of the social objectives such as the Alleviation of Poverty, promoting good habits such as Thrift/saving among the Poor people, Promoting Livelihood and Nutrition and Health, Economic Growth and Development and the factors that drive the Economic Growth of Banking Sector.

Social Outcome/Thrifts

- The extant literature has yet to reach a definitive conclusion regarding the impact of the SHG microfinance program on the financial habits of the poor.
- SHGs are small informal group of 10–20 individuals who are homogeneous with respect to the social and economic background and come together voluntarily to promote saving habit among members and for a common cause to raise and manage resources for the benefit of group members (NABARD, 2018).
- The major form of microfinance in India is that based on women's SHGs, which are small groups of 10–20 members. These groups collect savings from their members and provide loans to them. However, unlike most Accumulating Savings and Credit Associations (ASCAs) found in several countries, these groups also obtain loans from banks and on-lend them to their members (Nair, 2005).
- SHGs promote participatory Credit Management and fill the void created by the lack of Formal Finance. In India, SHGs facilitate Economic Empowerment of women and weaker section.
- Microcredit does not have a Transformative effect, and the effect is conditional on the individual's characteristic. The effect of micro savings seems more promising while microinsurance suffers from limited take up (Beck et al., 2018).
- No meaningfully positive, policy relevant, income effect arising from the micro lending.

Promoting Livelihood

SHGs play an extremely important role in promoting the Livelihood of the people at large. "Across rural India, poor women are changing their lives and their children's lives. In the aptly-named 'Self Help Groups', millions of women are coming together to fight long-held prejudices" (Bhatt, 1997a, 1997b).

Nutrition and Health

- Its primary purpose is to provide a help and support for members in dealing with the problems and improving their psychological function and effectiveness (Levy, 1976).
- An SHG is a voluntary group of people formed to attain common goal, most of its members have social identity, heritage, cost or traditional occupations and come together for common cause and manage resources for the benefit of the group of people by NABARD (NABARD, 2018).
- SHGs are all about creating a safe space for these women, helping them socially and financially first by helping each other. The first and foremost necessity of forming an SHG is understanding that your peers act as your collateral and putting in trust, forming a bond before anything else (Bhagalakshmi, 1993).

Drivers of Economic Growth

The critical review of the chapter reveals that there is a positive relationship between the SHGs and the Economic Growth and Development of the nation. For the development of the country, SHG are the major vehicle (Hindu, 1998). In India, the SHGs constitute a widely accepted development strategy for poverty reduction as they are perceived as powerful vehicle for the promotion of microcredit and microfinance, especially for women (Chen et al., 2007).

Moreover, the author argues that there is a positive relationship between the SHGs and Economic Growth and Development of the nation. Credit access and terms have discriminated against the poor due to various reasons such as inability to provide collateral, small-sized loans, and high transaction costs for bank formalities. Microfinance through rural SHGs is a significant medium of poverty alleviation and empowerment. It aims at financial inclusion through the delivery of financial services at an affordable cost to the vast sections of the disadvantaged and low-income groups (Pereira, n.d.).

SHG and Financial Inclusion

From the critical review of the chapter, the SHGs help in achieving the goal of Financial Inclusion. According to the literature, Financial Inclusion is "The process of ensuring access to financial services and timely and adequate credit for vulnerable groups such as weaker sections and low-income groups at an affordable cost." The SHG can help achieve the SDGs of Gender Equality and Poverty Eradication. Self-Help Groups (SHGs) play a vital role in advancing the

Sustainable Development Goals (SDGs), particularly those related to gender equality and poverty eradication, as highlighted in PwC's analysis of data from the UN's SDG report. Financial inclusion refers to the process of providing vulnerable and low-income groups, including weaker sections of society, with access to affordable financial services and timely, adequate credit (Rangarajan, n.d.). Financial inclusion will act as a catalyst for not just economic growth but also eradication of poverty. It will also help in achieving the SDGs set by the United Nations (UN).

According to the policy document, NRLM, and State Rural Livelihood Mission, the chapter discusses the National Rural Livelihood Mission, which was named as Deendayal Antodaya Yojana (DAY) NRLM. The mission also aims at the introduction of Financial Inclusion model, loan from banks, association and coordination with banking and financial institutions and coverage from loss of life and health.

Transaction Costs in Group Credit

In the context of group microcredit in India, transaction costs can be categorized into three types: (i) the cost of money, (ii) the cost of prudent financial practices such as provisioning for loan defaults, and (iii) the cost of operations, which includes activities like screening candidates, documentation, and follow-up. Transaction cost is not proportionate to amount lent. Cost is higher due to the smaller size of the loan. The moot question in this regard is to ensure sustainability the group should charge interest rates. In this regard with interest rates growing at exorbitant rates, the policymakers have suggested for a cap on these loans. But these caps have not been the solution and the cost has been rising consistently. Besides, transaction costs there is cost of supervision. The author cites that the involvement of NGOs can lead to reduction in the transaction costs. In case of NGOs as promoting institutions, more the number of years of experience, lower is the transaction cost. Transaction costs comprise the direct cost and indirect cost. Direct cost comprises the cost of formation of the group, training of the group, administrative cost that include cost of documentation, disbursement and other administrative expenses, branch supervision, cost of appraisal of the group, cost of documentation, cost of disbursement and monitoring costs and the indirect costs. The author has selected 3 case studies, in group lending domain to study the transaction costs. In each of the MFI, the field workers are selected and appointed for monitoring and supervising and group formation. The Manager of the MFI surveys the villages and decides the groups for lending. After the first group formation meeting, in second meeting, the loans are disbursed for period of 55 weeks. The field worker is responsible for the monitoring the activities of the group.

Informal Savings

The research paper written by Lori Beaman, Dean Karlan, and Bram Thuysbaert discusses that the high cost of credit and contracting cost often leads to cost and market failures in the developing economies. The paper mentions that the use of the Informal Savings through the use of technology such as Oral Accounting helps in increasing the success of the SHGs. This approach does not introduce any kind of formal contract but leads to financial inclusion through an informal group

Discussion and Conclusion

Are the leaders born or born out of necessity? In short, great leaders are born and are also products of occasion and are the fruits of the spiritual influence and guidance of their gurus, mentors, and Government's efforts, which invest in training the influencers to become leaders. The analysis of the literature highlights various factors such as social networks, business culture, funding sources, composition of the board, staff structure, loan intake, and collection tools that lead to loan delinquency among the members of the group. In the tapestry of leadership, the center or the community group is the main leader or the consensually chosen head of the community or the clan that defines the success of the group. Alongside the group's center or its democratically chosen leaders, it is often the margins—the underprivileged sections of society—that also shape the group's future. Hence, the leadership in a community is the clan that defines the success of the group. Within the community, the anxiety flows from the tapestry or margins, which are the margins of leadership to the center. In a marginalized group suffering from a lack of access to resources, the anxiety flows from the periphery to the center in case of misutilization of resources. This free-floating anxiety is called peer pressure, which is channeled depending on the center which is the origin of all kinds of leadership. Leadership toxicity often leads to unrest and chaos, which amplifies the conflict within an organization. Various factors such as predominantly economic and social deprivations lead to inequities at the margins, which further leads to anxiety at the center, with the peer pressure taking the form of conflicts and strife leading to the disappearance of the civic sense. In an SHG, the primary question is institutional survival and not corporate mission. Thus, the structure of the group requires the members of the group to follow the group rules and channelize the group dynamics in the form of peer pressure through an able leadership to create social capital and commitment to leadership. The declining social capital is yet another reason for the breaking up of the groups and conflicts in the group.

Ethical dilemmas in leadership: Leadership is fraught with various ethical challenges which include conflict of interest, resource allocation, whistle-blowing, transparency, loyalty, and short-term versus long-term goals. The leaders in a group have access to resources, and their policies define the modus operandi for the allocation of the financial and material resources among the members of society. Many times, there is a conflict of interest among the members of the society, which leads to ethical dilemmas. Moral hazard could be due to a change in the behavior of the members of society, after taking the loan. As a panacea to the evils of moral hazard and conflict of interest, the members of the community must adhere to the norms laid down by the leader of the group and must ensure that there is a whistleblowing policy in place with adequate disclosure to ensure transparency and fairness.

Leadership and conflict: Nature of rivalry among the members: Community and leadership are intertwined, and life in the group depends on leaders. Leadership is the center and origin of the community in the case of a group lending vehicle. Conflicts in groups and rivalry might arise due to leaders and access to resources. A great community leader takes the members into their stride. Rivalry might arise due to large group size, and community leaders ensure optimal group size. Rivalry might arise due to the savings already deposited as sunk cost by good members. Rivalry might arise due to the barriers to exist and slow growth of the group finances or resources. Community leadership plays a great role in the sustenance of the group. Thus, the conflicts as mentioned earlier are caused due to cognitive factors such as nonaccess to the financial resources and capital and affective factors such as nonaccess to social capital and personal relationships.

Transcript From Interview

Conflict among members due to nonadherence to group norms and the role of leadership in ensuring financial discipline: One of the major issues faced by Rural India is the lack of access to financial services. One of the major perquisites to facilitate poverty reduction and sustainable development is to facilitate access to financial services. Financial access or access to Financial services facilitates leveraging the economic opportunities for growth. Rural poor lack financial access and cannot make use of the economic opportunities that come their way. Thus, Financial Access can help the rural poor overcome poverty. Access to finance for the poor is a challenge despite the various schemes adopted by the Government of India, including the Nationalization of Banks, Lead Bank Schemes, Regional Rural Banks, and Service area approaches to financing. One of the major reasons for this lack of access and outreach is the lack of effective delivery mechanisms for the poor. If there is sufficient delivery of financial services to the poor, it could lead to sustainable growth and poverty reduction. The NRLM has taken the task of promoting Financial Inclusion among the poor. The NRLM includes various financial services such as Credit, Savings, Insurance, and Payment and Remittance facilities. This program includes various financial services such as opening up the bank accounts for the SHG, facilitating the access to Bank Credit to meet Production and Consumption needs, provision insurance, services, and pension products.

National Rural Livelihood Mission

National Rural Livelihood Mission, which was Swarn Jayanti Gram Rojgar Yojana (SGRY), has been named as DAY NRLM. This scheme is implementable at the Block and the District level. The Department of Rural Development, under the Ministry of Rural Development, Government of India, is responsible for policy formulation, monitoring, and evaluation of the program. Under these schemes, one member from each member household will be brought under the

SHG. This will be federated at the village level, and the mission will comprise of various components such as social mobilization, community institution and capacity building, financial inclusion, livelihood promotion and congruence, training and capacity building, and this mission also aims at training the rural youth, placement, training, self-employment, innovations, infrastructure support and market support. Community Investment Fund (CIF) is provided to the SHGs in intensive blocks to the SHG through the Federations to advance loan. The mission also aims at introduction of the Financial Inclusion model, loan from banks, association and coordination with banking and financial institutions and coverage from loss of life and health. The NRLM will introduce the suitable linkages at the District level with District Rural Development Agencies (DRDAs) and Panchayat Raj Institutes (PRIs). The beneficiaries for this scheme will be the rural poor. This mission is implemented through an Advisory committee which comprises the representatives from the Civil Society Organizations (CSO), Financial Institutions, Industry Associations, Academicians and Poverty and Development Experts. This committee will comprise of the experts from various fields to manage the mission. The SMMU assist the CEO in the implementation of the mission. This committee comprises the experts from various areas like Social Mobilization, Capacity Building, Bank Linkages, etc., and this committee is responsible for the designing policies and implementation guidelines at the state and districts levels, monitoring the progress and providing implementation support, ensuring quality implementation, and managing partnerships. District levels will interface with the district administration and other line departments with the District Rural Development Agencies and Panchayati Raj Institutions. SHGs are set up and federated at the district level.

Interviews: Leadership and Its Importance in Enhancing Group Solidarity Through Financial Training

Financial literacy plays an extremely important role in ensuring the success of the group. If the members of the group get together and strategically default in that case other members exercise peer pressure as they have the dynamic incentive to do so. The leader in the group helps the members in the group to maintain regular books of accounts and also conduct formal meetings to get an oversight of the workings of the group. However, in most of the groups, the members are not financially literate, and they lack financial skills. In such cases, the person who is chosen the leader of the group helps the other members to prepare the books of accounts. Below given are some real-life examples of conflicts among the group members.

Interview 1: Absolutely, members of a group are trusted by the bank, and if an individual member approaches the bank from the group, the bank remains skeptical that they might not pay. Banks are further motivated by the regular monthly meetings. Our group conducts weekly meeting in which we decide the amount of loan to be taken, and the savings amount to be collected. One member in the meeting is selected as the leader of the group. In our group, there are no instances of loan default. If the member does not pay, he is expelled from the group. Peer monitoring and social sanction help in reinforcement and better repayment of loans. Since all members take loans for productive activities and are aware of the joint liability, they engage in peer monitoring. Each member understands that they may need a loan in the future, and that defaulting could result in expulsion from the group. So, they work sincerely for the success of the group.

Interview 2: The leader of the group selects member with the skill set and gives him livelihood and attaches him to the group. All the members in the group are acquaintances. In the group, members get the livelihood, and we feel that the Government is not cooperative in providing the loan. The bank loan is cheap in terms of the interest rate. The process of providing loan is tedious, and bank officials are wary of lending to the members. They are very arrogant and do not know their work. We do not apply for loans; instead, we generate surplus income from handicrafts, and our products are ISO-certified and carry barcodes. Thus, the difference in the skill set also leads to the conflict among the members of the group.

Interview 3: Conflict due to strategic default: In our village, we have service area, and we discuss with the artists, and out of those who have basic idea of the artform, we select the people and then we give them SHG form. We individually visit the village and collect the data, and after that, we conduct 2 group meetings and explain the benefits from the Government and us and then we form the groups. In the rural area, most of the people work banyan bait, they make the mats and weaving, and it has great demand. They also make coral mats and some other items such as handicrafts, and hand embroidery is also made. We also develop them, and this art is family art. In the beginning, we provided them the loan, and after their development, they take loan from the banks. Nowadays, groups are undertaking group meetings, and they are discussing the matters in the group. They are maintaining the attendance registers, financial registers, and pass books. Only after the first period of performance, they get the loan. Initially, they get a loan of Rs. 10,000. Sometimes, if a member is not able to pay, the group members pay back the loan, and after two to three days, they collect the loan. One or two groups this kind of problem is coming of strategic default, but these days, we are closely interacting with the groups and taking drastic steps. CRP (Community resource person) is doing social audit, and banks are grading the SHG performance. Bank officers do not visit generally. It is only in case of loan default that the bank officer visits the SHG and we help them. We are NGO Committee, select the officers for field visit and train them, we do the audit and then give them training, and we also give them training. The NGO is not giving individual loan, and the loan is given to the SHG. Insurance is also provided, and we weekly visit the SHG. And in case of any problem, we visit them and solve the problem. These days SHG members are given the digital literacy, especially to the leader. They are proficient at using the WhatsApp and mobile. We conducted the digital and financial literacy training for the members. They become independent in some time then we leave them. Their families have been reaping the benefits of these initiatives. The Government is providing them support to visit and attend the marketing events. They provide funds to these people, and NABARD is also supporting them. We are providing them the training regarding the color and designs. At the time of joining, they are brainwashed and trained. Only when we tell them and influenced by 2 and 3, they come to the bank. Through this program, women members have received training and have become both technologically and financially sustainable. NABARD is supporting our organization, and we are creating lot of awareness for financial literacy program. Hence, lot of members receive the financial literacy.

Interview 4: Conflict due to lack of infrastructure and facilitating conditions and network relations.

Theory of Networked Governance

Development and sustainability of the SHGs is a bottom-up approach toward sustainable development of the poor regions. SHGs are informal groups, but the moment they come within the ambit of the NRLM, there is an increasing need for Networked Governance. Under the NRLM, the funding is provided to the SHGs under the Bank Self Help Group linkage program. In order to make transition from self-sufficient SHG model to SHG Linkage model, there is a need for collaboration between the banks and SHGs in an integrated fashion.

Self-Help Groups

SHGs are unorganized and work without collateral on the basis of the social collateral and work through the peer pressure to ensure proper utilization of resources. Though SHGs can borrow credit from the various sources including the informal sources, under the Financial Inclusion the Government has major thrust on including the SHGs within the ambit of Formal finance.

Theoretical Perspectives on NRLM and SHG Bank Linkage Program

Under NRLM, a separate scheme, namely DAY NRLM has been introduced. This scheme is implementable at the Block level. This scheme is Government-led and is aimed at creating the Community groups and are federated at the village level. The mission of this program is Mobilization, Community Institution, Capacity Building, Financial Inclusion, Livelihood promotion, Training, and Capacity Building. Under the Financial Inclusion Model, loan and credit will be made available to the SHGs from the banks. In order to ensure effective monitoring of the activities of the agents, the monitoring agency has been set up at village level in the form of Bank Linkage sub committees. These committees are called as Block Mission Management Units (BMMU). This committee document and monitor the level of the performance of SHGs. Besides that, at the Community level there are Business Correspondents called as Bank Sakhis that assist in Monitoring SHG repayment to the banks. These Bank Sakhis are selected by an informal committee with representatives from the different SHGs. The officers at the DMMU (District Mission Management Units) conduct various workshops, trainings, and Capacity Building initiatives to sensitize the members of SHGs about the importance of the Financial Inclusion.

Fig. 19 depicts the networked Governance for SHG Bank Linkage.

Networked Governance SHG Bank Linkage

Development and sustainability of the SHGs is a bottom approach toward sustainable development of poor regions. SHGs are informal groups, but the moment they come within the ambit of NRLM, there is an increasing need for Networked Governance. Under NRLM, the funding is provided to the SHGs under the SHG Bank Linkage program. In order to make the transition from Self-Sufficient SHG Model to SHG Bank Linkage model, there is a need for collaboration between the banks and SHGs in an integrated fashion. The four-tier structure of SMMU, DMMU, BMMU, and VO is a network that aims to mobilize and engage the citizens and the Government bodies, banks, and regulatory authorities, such as RBI, NABARD, in development, implementation and Monitoring of the SHGs. Though in most of the Network structures, technology is the key driver and in case of SHG Bank Linkages. Most important level in SHG Bank Linkage is the Block Level. Generally, the District level Officers visit the Blocks and call a quarterly meeting of the Bankers. Most important thing in management is the visit to the SHGs as these units do not understand the importance of Credit and Cash Credit Limit. District Managers are responsible for sensitizing the SHGs to use the Cash Credit Limit and understand the importance of availing bank credit for sustainability. District Managers are responsible for strengthening this financial transition to formal credit and monitoring the units continuously so that the SHGs do not break up. Many a times in lack of follow up, the SHGs stop following the Panchsutras. Any livelihood activity, they have to be guided and supported. For Financial Inclusion, it is important to monitor them and collaborate to create a Micro-credit Plan. There is lack of integrated interface between the lender and the borrowers and monitoring agencies. In remote areas, the SHGs do not have infrastructure, and they are not literate in using the digital mode.

Excerpts from interview: An open-ended interview was undertaken with the DMMU, District Mission Manager, Nainital, Uttarakhand, India—Mrs. Sangeeta. According to the District Mission Manager, the key challenge in SHG–Bank Linkages lies at the block level, which is considered the most critical stage. Generally, the District level Officers visit the Blocks and call a quarterly meeting of the Bankers. Most important thing in management is the visit to the SHGs as these units do not understand the importance of Credit and Cash Credit Limit. District Managers are responsible for sensitizing the SHGs to use the Cash Credit Limit and understand the importance of availing bank credit for sustainability. District Managers are responsible for strengthening this financial transition to formal credit and monitoring the units continuously so that the SHGs do not break up. Many a times in lack of follow up, the SHGs stop following the Panchsutras. Any livelihood activity, they have to be guided and

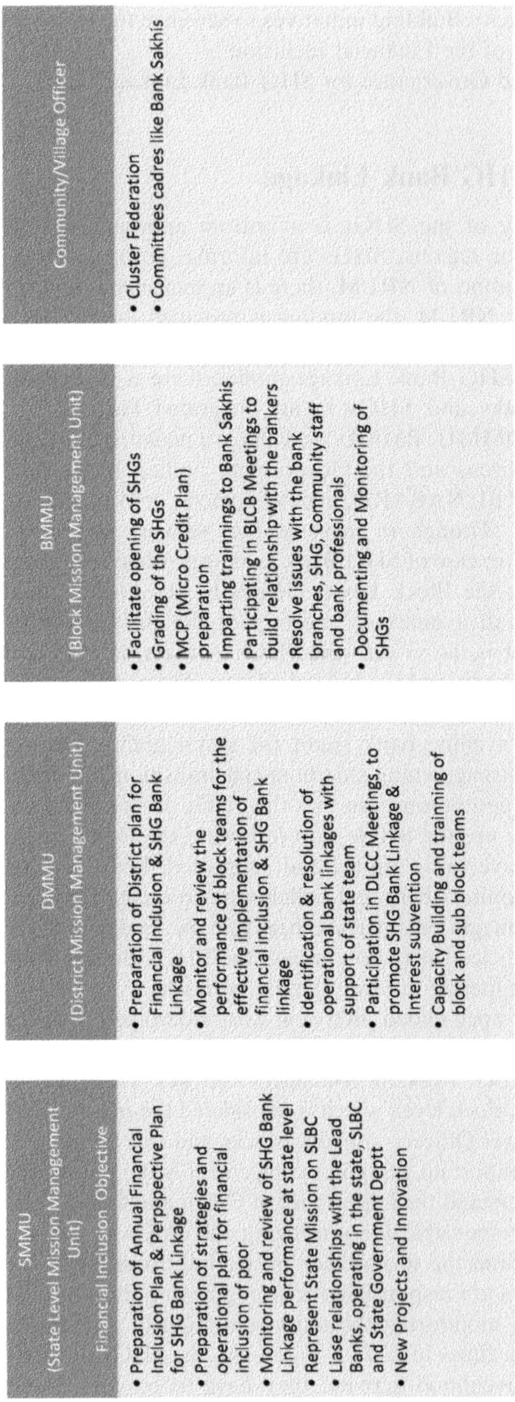

Fig. 19. Networked Governance for SHG Bank Linkage.

supported. For Financial Inclusion, it is important to monitor them and collaborate to create a Microcredit Plan. There is lack of integrated interface between the lender and the borrowers and monitoring agencies. In remote areas, the SHGs do not have infrastructure, and they are not literate in using the digital mode. From the interview, it becomes apparent that the lack of facilitating conditions and access to resources is the reason for conflict among the members of the group. And leaders are deem to be the central force that is responsible for providing access to community resources to the marginalized sections of society. The margins at the society look toward the center or the leadership for providing them the access to resources. Inequities in the margins lead to the anxiety within the group, which leads to conflicts and all the while the forces within this panorama of group keep on moving toward center leading to acute peer pressure due to the social contract among the community to support each other and provide emotional and financial support to the defaulting member. However, excessive defaults and lack of financial attitude among some members lead to the disappearance of the mutual faith among the members of the groups leading to the expulsion of the defaulting members from the group.

Future course of action: In first phase, there should be pilot and digital mode which will be beneficial. Financial Literacy regarding the Financial products is most important. Also, the bankers need to be trained on handling SHG clients. Many a time, the lender or the bankers demotivate these SHGs; hence, SHGs transition to informal sources. For women, there should be awareness programs on financial behavior, including expenditures and savings habits. DMMU conduct lot of programs with Banks and Health officials for the overall development of the SHGs as part of Capacity Building and Institutional Development. For the SHGs, the physical access to the branches at distance is a major problem. Under Financial Inclusion, the Bank Sakhi Model is indeed very successful. In Nainital, the block has 500 SHGs, and the Bank Sakhis are doing a wonderful job and act as the bridge between the Bank and SHGs. In case of Women SHGs, the issue of reliance on male members, and diversion of funds is a major problem so the Block Level Members, CRPs, and Area Coordinators continuously monitor and visit the SHGs.

Case *study from China:* China is the largest economy in the world in terms of Purchasing Power Parity, and it ranks second in term of nominal GDP. Termed as Asian Tiger, China is one of the world's fastest economies in the world, with approximately 10% GDP growth rate over last 30 years. The public sector and the State contribute for the lion's share in the economic growth, with Private Sector growing at a rapid pace. Known as the world's factory, China has one of the major manufacturing bases in the world and is also one of the biggest exporters of manufactured goods across the world. It is one of the fastest growing Consumer market and is the second largest importer of developmental good and services. It is trading partner of the major trading nations and plays a significant role in the world trade. It has also developed potent trade relations and treaties with the rest of the world. Some of the significant treaties are China–Australia Free Trade Agreement, China–South Korea Free Trade Agreement, ASEAN–China Free Trade Area, Switzerland and Pakistan. China was ranked 77th on basis of Per Capita income that was computed using the Nominal GDP and 89TH as per the PPP GDP in real terms, the IMF report. This nation also suffers from the Rural and Urban divide, with the coastal region more developed and industrialized as compared to the hinterlands. As China's economic importance in the world has grown, so has been the attention to the structure and health of its economy. In China, the importance of health care has increased manifold with the increase in the economic growth. China is a Communist country and one of the most powerful of all the developed of all the Asian countries. Often, it is referred to as the Asian tiger. Manufacturing contributed to the maximum percentage of the GDP. Banking is the main source of credit creation in China. China being a Communist regime, never promoted the entry of the foreign and international banks till 2002. The first time foreign banks were allowed in China in the year 2002. Chinese banking comprises of the State-owned Commercial Banks, City Banks, Policy Banks, and Tier-2 Commercial Banks. The Central bank of China, the People Bank of China, is responsible for monetary policy formulation and all kinds of quantitative and qualitative restriction for credit creation. China is the most populous of the nations in the world. Despite high levels of GDP growth, there is a group chunk of population that is dependent on Agriculture and hence not economically independent. Other major issue is the with regard to the Communist regime. China is a Communist nation, and it has not provided the entry to any of the foreign banks till 2002. Moreover, the Central Bank of China regulates most of the credit creation and policy framework in the nation. There is a need for the opening of the economy. After joining WTO (World Trade Organization), still China has not adhered to the obligations as a WTO member and has tried to take monetary measures that can impact the economic interest of the neighbors and economic partners in the world.

Case *of Chinese Township and Village Enterprises and role of township leadership in ensuring success of microfinance:* China's township and village enterprises have been one of the most successful institutional formats for providing access to the people at the margins of the society. Marginalized sections of society do not have any kind of collateral due which the banks are unwilling to provide access to finance for the people at the bottom of the pyramid. However, in China the township and village enterprises lead to the increase in the financial inclusion and access to finance during the period 1985–1987. The introduction of the joint liability lending as part of township and village lending enterprises further leads to the success of the microfinance in the hinterlands. The township leaders appointed by the state are made responsible for monitoring and oversight, which makes these township and village enterprises the most success institutional format for facilitating access to finance for the people at the bottom of the pyramid. Besides the township leadership, the literature highlights the importance of the favorable conditions such as greater firm profitability, large group size to name a few. In a survey, Park & Burgess (1921) found that two third of the local government and state agencies acted as the guarantors for the loans taken by town and village enterprises and for the 42% of the borrowings in general. In all the loans where the government is the guarantor during

1994–1997, the undertaking and guarantee is either by township government or township enterprises. Data highlight that during 1994–1997, the township leaders solicited the loan applications, by bringing the borrowers and lenders together. During this period, the township leaders also played an extremely important role in conducting the group meetings, which increased to 37.4 during the period. Also the survey highlights that in most of the cases of loan defaults, the groups prefer taking the help from the township leaders in ensuring the repayment of the loans. Thus, the increased involvement of the township leaders in bank lending in China during 1994–1997 led to the better repayment of the loans in China, until individual leadership replaced the group lending and borrowing.

Case *study from Nepal:* Until the mid of the 20th century, Nepal used to be an isolated, agrarian society, and it entered the modern era in the decade of 50s without education, healthcare, provision for roads, telecommunications, power, civil service or industry. The country, however, is committed to economic liberalization. Nepal marched on to the path of planned economic development with a series of five-year plans. In the year 2002, Nepal completed its Ninth Plan when its currency has been made convertible. Foreign aid constitutes more than a half of the overall economic budget. Since 1975, rural development efforts and improved administration have been the emphasis of Government policies. Agriculture constitutes principal economic activity, giving employment to 70% of the population and generating 37% of GDP. The staple food crops are Rice and Wheat. Agriculture surplus emerges from the lowland Terai region produces, which is the supplier the food-deficient hill areas. There is heavy economic dependence on remittances from foreign workers. Social services and infrastructure development have not made much of a progress in Nepal. Primary education system is under-development across the country, and Tribhuvan University boasts of several campuses. Road provides a robust link between Kathmandu and India and nearby hill regions. Nepal is the Himalayan neighbor. Its economy is mainly an agricultural economy. Nepal banking comprises of the Commercial Banks, Development Banks, Finance companies and Microcredit development banks. Nepal Central bank is the central bank of Nepalese economy. Nepal being an agricultural economy is facing various problems at the supply side of the credit creation. Credit creation is deficient, given the higher demand for credit. Indian banks have a major presence in Nepal. State Bank of India has a major presence in Nepal along with the other domestic banks.

Community lending in Nepal: Nepal has a vast chunk of population which is below the poverty line, and many financial services such as deposits, loans, payment services, and money transfers are provided by the microfinance channel. Microfinance provides an important tool to offset poverty by providing access to financial services and loans. Microfinance in Nepal is facilitated through the informal finance sector and community lending and microfinance institutions in the formal sector. By 1992, two regional rural-level microfinance and development banks had been established in the Eastern and Western regions. Many state-level players such as Grameen Bikas Bank, and Nirdhan Utthan Bank Limited. Three private commercial banks jointly own NUBL, Grameen Trust Bank of Bangladesh, and clients of banks. Core microfinance services are delivered using the group center concept. The members of the group are homogenous but not close relatives. The group is monitored through uniform norms, adherence to which ensures the financial discipline. The bank is based on the subsidy model from the Government, which ensures the financial sustainability of the group. The contribution to the savings of the groups is done by the members together.

Case *study of community lending groups—Bhutan:* Bhutan is a small kingdom located in the mountain of Himalayas. Bhutan is mainly a cash less economy that is dependent on informal financial services for trade and commerce. Formal financial services form a very small percentage of the total financial system. The citizens of the nation find it worthy to store the cash in the vaults and in the wardrobes. The rural areas of the nation are not at well served by the banks and financial system, and there are no ATM (automated teller machines) in the vicinity; hence, the citizens must rely on the parallel economy, cooperatives and shopkeepers. There is a large financial disparity between the rural and the urban community. The rural community saves infrequently and saves depending upon the seasonality of harvest and agricultural production. Similarly, there is a vast gender disparity as the males in urban areas use formal finance much more frequently as compared to the rural youth. The biggest challenge faced by the rural people in accessing microfinance was the lack of access to financial services and the need for flexible terms of loans. Saving clubs in the form of *kidu tshogpas* are the main vehicles for generating wealth and creating income. The lack of financial literacy is one of the major challenges faced by the people in Bhutan. Most of the Bhutanese citizens rely on the informal sector that includes the shopkeepers, moneylenders, and relatives for accessing the finance. In this scenario, the groups play an important role in promoting legitimacy in banking and promoting good financial habits among the villagers in Bhutan. Still the use of technology in the form of internet and mobile banking is in the seminal stages, and there is no use of this technology for banking by the people of Bhutan.

Conclusion

Leadership is an important factor that impacts the existence of the community lending groups. The SHGs through their social capital play an important role in providing access to finance at the door steps of the citizen India. Without good leadership, the margins of society that are part of the community lending groups face acute financial anxiety leading to peer pressure within the group. This peer pressure further leads to the conflicts and flights within the group. Transformational leadership further provides solidarity and cohesiveness within the group, leading to self-sufficiency within the group. It provides resilience and financial sustainability to the group, by ensuring financial discipline and adherence to the group goals and objectives.

References

Aggarwal, S. (1996). *Rural Development, Banking and Sustainability of Self-Help Groups*. New Delhi, Discovery Publishing House.

Ahlin, C., & Townsend, R. M. (2007). Using repayment data to test across models of joint liability lending. *The Economic Journal*, *117*(517), F11–F51.

Alliou, D. (2000). *Design and sustainability issues of rural credit and savings.*

Badatya, V. & Puhazhendi, K. C. (2002). *SHG-Bank linkage programme for rural poor.*

Beck, T., Behr, P., & Guettler, A. (2018). Gender and banking: Are women better loan officers? *Journal of Banking & Finance*, 1279–1321.

Bhagalakshmi. (1993). Environment of women through thrift and credit groups. *Gramvikas Newsletter*, 18.

Bhatt, E. (1997a). *Self employed women's.*

Bhatt, E. (1997b). *Women and development alternatives micro and small scale enterprise in India.* West View Press.

Brody, T. A. (2017). *Economic self-help group programs for improving women's empowerment: A systematic review.*

Chakrabarti, R. (2004). 'The Indian microfinance experience: Accomplishments and challenges'. In: B. Debroy & A. U. Khan (eds.), *Integrating the Rural Poor into Markets*, Academic Foundation, New Delhi. pp. 137–151.

Chen, M., Jhabvala, R., Kanbur, R., & Richards, C. (2007). *Membership based organizations of the poor: Concepts, experience and policy.* Routledge.

Cheryl, F., & Craiz, C. (n.d.). *Making microfinance work: Managing product diversification.*

Christen, P. B., & Ivatury, G. (2007). *Sustainability of self-help groups in India: Two analyses'.*

Conning, J. (2005). *Monitoring by delegates or by the peers ? Joint liability loans under moral hazard.*

Diagne, A. (1998). *Default incentives, peer pressure, and equilibrium outcomes in group-based lending programs.*

Diamond, D. (1984). *Financial intermediation and delegated monitoring.*

Duvendack, M., Palmer-Jones, R., Copestake, J. G., Hooper, L., Loke, Y., & Rao, N. (2011). *What is the evidence of the impact of microfinance on the well-being of poor people?*

Ghatak, M., & Guinnane, T. W. (1999). *The economics of lending with joint liabilit Theory and Liability.*

Gopalaswamy, A. K., Babu, M. S., & Dash, U. (2016). *Systematic review of quantitative evidence on the impact of microfinance on the poor in South Asia*, London: EPPI-Centre, Social Science Research Unit, Institute of Education, University College London.

Guha, P., & Das, T. (2019). *Measuring women's SHG sustainability: A study of rural Assam.* Sage.

Kabeer, N. (2002). *Resources, agency, achievements: Reflections on the measurement of Women's empowerment.* https://doi.org/10.1111/1467-7660.00125

Kagwar, S. (n.d.). *International journal of advanced research in management sciences.*

Korada, I. B., & Shruti. (2018). Uptake of digital financial services: Behavior change a challenge. *IFMR Lead.*

Levy, H. (1976). Stochastic dominance and expected Utility: Survey and analysis. *Management Science*, *22*(12), 1116–1124.

Maren Duvendack & Philip Mader. (2020). *Impact of financial inclusion in low- and middle-income countries: A systematic review of reviews.*

Morduch, A. A. a. (2005). *The economics microfinance.*

Morduch, J., & de Aghion, B. A. (2010). *The economics of microfinance.* MIT Press.

NABARD. (2018). *Status of Microfinance in India 2017–18*. Mumbai: National Bank for Agriculture and Rural Development.

Nair, A. (2005). *Sustainability of microfinance self help groups in India: Would federating help?* World Bank Policy Papers.

Nair, A. (n.d.). *Sustainability of microfinance self help groups in India: Would federating help?*

Park, R. E., & Burgess, E. W. (1921). *Introduction to the science of society*.

Parida, P. C., & Sinha, A. (2010). "Performance and sustainability of Self-Help Groups in India: A gender perspective." *Asian Development Review*, *27*(1), 80–103.

Pereira, M. (n.d.). [Online]. https://www.mkgandhi.org/articles/gwomen.htm

Dr. Rangarajan, C. (n.d.). *Committee financial inclusion, Reserve Bank of India*.

Reddy, C. (2005, October). *A keystone of microfinance*.

Rhyne, E. (1998). The yin and yang of microfinance: Reaching the poor and sustainability. *Micro Banking Bulletin*, 6–8.

Robinson, M. (2001). *The microfinance revolution*.

Stewart, R., Van Rooyen, C., Dickson, K., & Majoro, M. (2010). *What is impact of microfinance on poor people?* A Systematic Review of Evidence from sub-Saharan Africa', Technicial Report, EPPI-Centre, Social Science Research Unit, University of London.

Sarkar, S., & Baishya, S. (2012). Impact of micro finance in women empowerment of Assam: An impact study of SHGs in Assam. *BARNOLIPI: An Interdisciplinary Journal*.

Schueffel, P. (2016). Taming the beast: A scientific. *Journal of Innovation Management*, *4*(4), 32–54.

Shylendra, H. S. (2018). Federating the Self-Help Groups (SHGs) in India: Emerging conceptual and policy challenges. *International Journal of Rural Management*, *14* (2). Article first published online: October 9, 2018; Issue published: October 2018.

Shiyani, R. L., & Namboodiri, N. V. (n.d.). *Potential role of self-help groups in rural financial deepening*.

Srinivasan. (2008). *Microfinance India: State of the Sector Report 2008*. New Delhi: Sage Publications.

Srinivasan, H. M. a. G. (n.d.). *Self help groups in india A study of lights and shades*.

Srinivasan, R., & Sriram, M. S. (2006). *Micro finance in India: Discussion*.

Steinart (2011). *Microfinance*.

Stiglitz, J. (1990). *Peer monitoring and credit markets*. World Bank Economic Review.

Syna Desivilya, H., & Eizen, D. (2005). Conflict management in work teams: The role of social self-efficacy and group identification. *International Journal of Conflict Management*, *16*(2), 183–208.

Swain, R. B., & Varghese, A. (2014). Evaluating the impact of training in self-help groups in India. *The European Journal of Development Research*, *26*(5), 870–885.

Tankha, A. (2012). *Banking on Self-Help Groups: Twenty Years On*. New Delhi: SAGE Publications India Pvt. Ltd.

Teinemaa, T. (2013). *The impact of group lending on participants' entrepreneurial resources*.

Dr. Thakore, D. (2013). Conflict and conflict management. *Journal of Business and Management*, *8*(6), 07–16.

The Fintech revolution. (2015). A wave of startups is changing finance—For the better. *The Economist*, *13*, 8937.

Thompson, V. A. (1961). Hierarchy, specialization, and organizational conflict. *Administrative Science Quarterly*, *5*(4), 485–521.

Tirole, J. (1993). *Collusion and the theory of organization*.

Tjosvold, D., Law, K. S., & Sun, H. (2006). Effectiveness of Chinese teams: The role of conflict types and conflict management approaches. 罗胜强, 孙海法, trans. *Management and Organization Review*, *2*(2), 231–252.

Triandis, H. C. (1977). *Interpersonal behaviour*. Brooks/Cole Pub. Co.

Venittelli, T. (2022). Is group lending a collateral for informal credit? *Progress in Development Studies*, *22*(4), 392–407.

Vlack, K. V., Stoffle, B W., Stoffle, R. W., & Minnis, J. (2014, January–June). *Women empowerment and community resilence rotating savings and credit association*. Caribbean Studies.

Volk, M. (2012). Estimating probability of default & comparing it to credit rating classification by banks. *Economic and Business Review*

Wilson, K. (2002). The new microfinance: An essay on the self-help group movement in India. *Journal of Microfinance/ESR Review*, *4*(2). Article 11. https://scholarsarchive.byu.edu/esr/vol4/iss2/11

Chapter 5

Transformational Financial Leadership: A Key to Conflict Resolution in a Community Lending Program

Abstract

This chapter will explore the impact of state intervention in ensuring the resolution of conflicts within the group. A group is generally fraught with various power imbalances that lead to conflicts among group. Without any state intervention, the scarce resources within a group cannot be allocated equitably. The state intervention enables the members of the group to achieve an equitable allocation of resources. If left to the dynamics of the group, the community lending initiatives suffer from the risk of exploitation and deprivation. With the thrust on financial sustainability and the discontinuation of a charity-based approach, the groups are required to be self-reliant. In this context, state intervention and hand-holding by the Government have come to play an important role in the success of the groups. The secondary data will be collected using the existing published literature. For data collection, the samples will be selected using purposive random sampling. A case study method will be used to explore the role that the state is playing in implementing various community lending programs in countries across the world. The data will be collected through semi-structured interviews and hermeneutics. This chapter will also provide a discussion on various policy initiatives by the state and their role in ensuring the success of groups.

Keywords: Self-help groups; financial sustainability; charity-based approach; microfinance and economic inclusion; financial literacy

---

Development and Conflict in Community Lending Programs, 101–118

Published under exclusive licence by Emerald Publishing Limited
doi:10.1108/978-1-83708-290-220251015

Introduction

Globally, 1.7 billion people live below the poverty line, and they do not have access to finance due to the lack of collateral and creditworthiness among the poor. The large banks and credit institutions, which are part of the formal financial system, are wary of lending to the poor and marginalized due to the information asymmetry about their creditworthiness. The social innovation of group lending provides a panacea to the problem of financial exclusion and poverty by providing access to finance to the poor based on the social capital. Group lending as a source of finance has existed for centuries in various parts of the world. In India, this scheme exists in the form of the self-help group (SHG) bank linkage program. While in other parts of the world such as Germany, this scheme has existed in the form of cooperatives and Ireland in the form of Rotating Savings and Credit Associations (ROSCAs). Group lending is a vehicle for the democratization of developmental finance for all through access to social capital. Social capital refers to the social relationships and cultural bonds that exist among the various members of society. These relationships and networks enable the members to access finance through the formal sector. When the social realities of marginalization of these poor members interact with the social membership, a cohesive force in the form of social capital facilitates access to microfinance. The success of these groups in ensuring 90% repayment rates is primarily because of the structural dynamics in the form of sociocultural factors. At the time of the formation of the groups, the selection of the members is done based on some form of homogeneity. The members in the group are homogenous in terms of profession, trade, or neighborhood. This proximity helps in reducing the adverse selection and ensuring that the members who form the group are from the same sociocultural background. Leadership in the group also plays an important role in the success of the group. The adverse selection of the members in the group can lead to the risk of nonrepayment of loans. Good leaders help create homogenous groups of members who have the same risk profile. A priori information about the other members of the group due to the same neighborhood and the same locality increases the likelihood of repayment increasing the financial sustainability of these groups. This chapter delves into how groups through social capital help to mitigate the problem of financial exclusion of the poor and what is the complex process of interaction of social membership of the poor members in a group with the social realities such as the perception of the bankers about the repayment of the loans, which leads to access to finance for the people at the bottom of the pyramid? Even then, for many reasons, the proposition of earning a livelihood in the group is fraught with various challenges. *Economic viability* of the group is determined by financial sustainability, which implies the ability of groups to earn sufficient profits. The use of technology in the form of collaborative digital platforms and computers to ensure access to finance for the people at the bottom through the Drone Didi determines the financial viability of these women at the bottom of the pyramid. Technological interventions help to achieve the objective of financial inclusion through access to finance for the people at the bottom of the pyramid. At the same time, the *institutional sustainability* of the groups is determined by the proficiency of the workforce and the skill set they acquire. The social efficacy of the groups and sustainability depends on the existing social norms, cultural norms, and social capital within the group. Better network relations with the group lead to better access to finance for the people at the bottom of the pyramid by promoting a better *entrepreneurial ecosystem (EE)* through human resource development and *capacity building*. The absorptive capacity (AC) of the ecosystem further impacts the financial and institutional viability of the members of the group.

Research Problem

Financial inclusion of the poor and marginalized sections of society has been defined as a **Sustainable Developmental Goal (SDG)**. For people, without physical collateral and creditworthiness, access to finance is a great obstacle in the achievement of the sustainable development goal. This chapter seeks to study how the *social capital or the existing relationship* among the members of the groups in the form of sociocultural norms helps them to access finance to the people at the bottom of the pyramid. The lack of adequate leadership, social intermediation, and an assimilative and supportive *EE* leads to decimation of the small enterprises and SHGs. The AC of the ecosystem determines the success of SHGs and community lending programs. In an EE, the actors who are part of the economic businesses receive information from external sources which include the Central Bank of Small Business NABARD and various nongovernment organizations (NGOs) and the AC of the system ensures the institutional sustainability and viability of the SHGs or small businesses. The AC of the ecosystem is determined by various strategic drivers, which include the strong network relations and availability of skilled individuals. SHG clusters often play an extremely important role in promoting product innovation within a business enterprise. Moreover, support in the form of ancillary services plays an important role in promoting the collective knowledge base of the ecosystem. The AC is often referred to as capability, which includes various organizational routines and processes that ensure convergence with the higher goals of an organization. The AC of a financial system thus plays an extremely important role in determining the success of the small enterprises within a financial cluster. AC plays an extremely important role in promoting institutional sustainability and the financial viability of SHGs and enterprises. This research study aims to analyze the impact of the AC on organizational growth and learning while reducing the conflicts among the members of the group. Further, the organizational agility of the community group or the small enterprises in terms of financial sustainability is determined by the various dynamic capabilities that provide a competitive advantage to the groups or small and medium enterprises.

Theoretical Lens

In this study, systems thinking and dynamic punctuated equilibrium theory have been adopted to capture the dynamics of leadership in a group. Transformational leadership has become a key factor in determining the success of social innovation such as SHG linkage programs and in promoting the cause of financial inclusion in achieving the sustainable development goal of poverty reduction among the poor. Besides that, the social intermediation by the self-help promoting institutions and NGOs play an extremely important role in ensuring the financial viability and sustainability of the groups and small enterprises.

Discussion and Analysis

The United Nations emphasizes poverty reduction through financial inclusion, highlighting the challenges faced by women in the unorganized sector who lack access to credit due to the absence of physical collateral. SHG bank linkages facilitate credit access, but proactive strategies are needed to manage collective efforts effectively. The context of the discussion in this volume is how socio-cultural factors and local leaders who are sensitive to social realities and marginalization are more successful in driving the programs to achieve social goals like poverty reduction and financial inclusion. This chapter will further highlight the impact of complex interactions of social realities like inequities and gender differences with group mechanisms on achieving broader goals. The chapter will further contest the resource-based view (RBV) and emphasize that scarcity of resources is not the main cause of underdevelopment and nonachievement of SDGs. Rather, it is the organizational context in the form of the EE that determines the success of the SHG and community groups. Within the EE, it is the existence of the supportive sociocultural context in the form of cultural norms and social capital that determines the success of the SHGs. In case of lack of transformational leadership or bad leadership, it can lead to various conflicts among the members of the group or community lending programs. As within an ecosystem, the number of competitors increases the conflicts among the members of the group increase manifold. The difference in dynamic capabilities such as resource endowment and skill set further accentuates the conflicts among the members of the group or the community. The study highlights the way the resources are allocated and the role that the interaction of subjective biases originating through sociocultural practices and milieus plays in creating rifts and cleavages responsible for increasing inequities and marginalization. The chapter discusses how cultural factors, analyzed through the Hofstede cultural prism, influence the financial sustainability of groups. Varied geographies exhibit different cultural norms, impacting the financial orientation of communities, such as the matriarchal societies in South India and patriarchal societies in North India. Additionally, rural societies vary in collectivism and individualism, affecting group financial behavior. This exploration aims to understand how cultural factors impact financial behavior and member orientation within SHGs. The interaction of cultural factors and social realities poses various challenges that lead to conflict in the groups, such as increased rates of abuse. This chapter explores the impact of financial leadership and sociocultural practices, such as SHG bank linkage programs, on the financial inclusion of the poor.

Besides that, it is important to increase the absorptive and assimilative capacity of the members of the community through continuous social intermediation and hand-holding. Moreover, transformational leadership and high entry barriers and lower exit barriers can help to resolve the conflict among the member's group.

Digital Transformation

Financial exclusion of the poor is a major problem and challenge to the achievement of developmental goals. Due to the exclusion from mainstream finance, because of a lack of creditworthiness history and social capital, the poor suffer from social exclusion and are caught in the death trap of poverty. Over, the centuries the cause of financial inclusion of the poor has caught the attention of policymakers and social researchers alike. When the poor and marginalized try to access formal finance, they are rejected by the banks and formal financial institutions due to the lack of access to physical collateral and information asymmetry. Group lending provides access to social capital and leadership, which enables the marginalized section of society to access microfinance. Leadership in a world fraught with inequalities is no longer an individual concept but is a characteristic of the dynamics of a system that emerges in diverse ways according to various traits and attributes. In a group lending scenario, the process of financial process starts with the selection of a leader, who is not only a controller but is a messiah and has complete knowledge about the other members of the group. He is an individual who selects the people with the same risk profile and is responsible for maintaining the relationships and motivating the other members of the group. Through discourse and his existing knowledge, he selects members who are all homogenous in terms of risk profile and he is sensitive to issues such as ethics and integrity. Till the 1980s, the groups were charity-based organizations, and the role of the leader in the group was that of an authoritarian. He was responsible for the allocation of the resources, and efficiency and productivity were not major concerns. After the 1990s, the role of the leader transformed into that of a controller, who was responsible for the efficient allocation of resources and productivity. However, with the advent of technology and the adoption of SDGs, the role of the leader changed to that of a nurturer, focused on motivating and encouraging the members to adhere to the group's shared norms. In today's scenario, the leader in a group is a coach, who is more literate than other members of the group, and he helps the other members of the group to maintain their books of accounts and adhere to the social norms. Thus, the role of a leader is empowerment and leadership is more distributed leadership. In contrast to the RBV which propagates that the lack of financial resources and physical collateral is the reason for the exclusion of the poor, the systems thinking propagates that leadership beyond the radical and participatory governance process is a social influencing process. With the emergence of social media and influencers, the role of leaders as social change agents has emerged. Today, leadership in a system is a distributed process driven by discourses and interactions rather than the policy and changes made by an individual leader. Thus, in a group, the operational dynamics that lead to the emergence of leadership is the web of influences, through which the leader mobilizes the members of society, neighborhood, or profession to join the group. In this study, discourse analysis will be used to analyze the impact of transformational leadership on the success of the groups. Below is the discourse from the semi-structured interview with an official working as part of the state banking level committee, which is responsible for implementing the SHG linkage. The discourse highlights that, in the case of the SHG linkage program implemented in India, the influencers play an important role as transformational leaders. In modern times, in developing nations like India, the state has come to play an important role in the selection of local leaders. Known as the "Bank Sakhis" or "DigiPay Sakhis," these women are banking correspondents, who are not appointed individually for a particular group but are selected by the state or NGOs, trained by the banks and the Government to provide support and assistance to members of group in banking with ease at their doorsteps with the use of technology. This type of assistance and systems-level support creates distributed leadership as Didi's who champions the cause of behavior modification and attitude building through financial literacy.

Case Study: Digital Transformation Through DigiPay

Lack of an EE, in the form of a lack of access to finance at the individual level, is the main cause of the divide and conflict among the members of the group. Thus, further collaboration and access to resources through digital collaborative platforms ensure the equitable distribution of the resources among the members of the group. In one of the SHGs, 1 gram panchayat, and 1 Bank Sakhi Mission are being undertaken under the Deendayal Antyodaya Yojana under the aegis of the National Rural Livelihood Mission under the Ministry of Rural Development. This program, according to Sh. Dhananjay Bhatt, facilitates the ease of banking in remote locations. This program aims to provide banking services in every Gram Panchayat in rural India. The initiative is named "One Gram Panchayat, One Business Correspondent Sakhi" program aims to increase digital transactions among self-help groups and their members. Under the aegis of this program is enshrined the concept of DigiPay Sakhis. CSC (Common Services Centre) has emerged as a major channel to facilitate the local delivery of citizen-centric services. Till the implementation of the Digital Sakhi program, the members had a lot of difficulty in using technology due to their lack of proficiency or digital literacy. Under the Deendayal Antyodaya Yojana-National Rural Livelihoods Mission, has signed a Memorandum of Understanding with CSC (Common Services Centre) e-Governance India limited to engage women members as "DigiPay Sakhis." These DigiPay Sakhis empower the members' lives of the SHGs by providing them access to local citizen-centric services, including senior citizen pension services. DigiPay Sakhis also enables village women to get access to bank loans. This channel also allows the delivery of pensions to senior citizens and subsidy dissemination to the disabled and the disadvantaged at the doorsteps. It also enables the member working under the aegis of MNREGA to access monetary compensation at their doorsteps. The CSC-enabled AEPS services were initiated in 2016 with the help of National Payment Corporation of India (NPCI). Thus, through capacity building and infrastructure, these programs have played an important role in promoting the growth of small and medium enterprises. This mechanism is channelized through the State and the Central Government agencies to provide services such as Social Security Pension, Vikalang, and Vridhawastha Pension to the beneficiaries directly through the AEPS and biometrics. In July 2018, the Ministry of Rural Development signed a Memorandum of Understanding under the aegis of DAY NRLM and CSC SPV to facilitate banking and delivery of citizen-centric services through the Digi Sakhi, BC Sakhi, and CSC Sakhi to the members of the SHGs. This program aims to empower the members of the SHGs to work as the Village Level Entrepreneur (VLE), Digi Sakhi, and Business Correspondent (BC) Sakhi. These services provide new avenues of earning for the members of the SHGs. The Common Services Center has issued approximately 62,000 Common Services identity numbers to the members. The executive stated that the members of the SHGs use the services of DigiPay Sakhi to deposit their savings and pay for loans. This way, the members need not travel to the remote banks, which are approximately 18–20 km from the villages. The members can download the Digi Application from the Mantra on their mobile phones. This initiative has made depositing, withdrawing, and accessing the mini-statement easy. DigiPay Sakhis are local women proficient in the local language, so they can easily mix up with rural women and promote citizen-centric services. Thus, they can create a market for themselves. In a woman-enabled center, the women feel incredibly convenient and easy to visit. According to the executive, this facility has enabled the delivery of bank services at their doorsteps. The DigiPay Sakhis are provided the training in digital banking; moreover, according to Sh. Dhananjay Bhatt, there is a concept of Champion Didi. Champion Didi uses peer influence to sensitize women regarding net banking. These Didis, who work as VLEs, are provided the commission and transaction charges. These Didis also peer monitor the working of DigiPay. Under the Saksham program, financial literacy training is offered to the members of the SHGs covered under DigiPay. As part of Azadi ka Amrit Mahotsav, several Center for Financial Literacy & Service Delivery (SAKSHAM Centers) are launched under Deendayal Antyodaya Yojana—National Rural Livelihoods Mission (DAY-NRLM) of the Ministry of Rural Development. SAKSHAM Centers are managed by the SHG network, mainly at the Cluster Level Federations (CLFs) level, with the help of trained Community Resource Persons (CRPs). The Ministry of Rural Development and the National Academy of RUDSETI (NAR) organize financial literacy sessions for the members of the SHGs in six domains, personal investment, savings, insurance credit, etc., to name a few. The DigiPay Sakhi enables the availability of banking services to the members of the SHGs 365 days a year. Thus, special drives like SAKSHAM centers and DigiPay Sakhis play an important role in promoting organizational learning and growth among small and medium enterprises.

DigiPay is an Aadhar-based technology, which is also called AEPS (Aadhar-Enabled Payment System).

Fig. 20 highlights that in a group in India, under the SHG linkage program, the group is formed by the Government or the NGO. At the time of formation of the group, the state-level agency or a NGO provides support for the selection of members, who are from the same profession or the same neighborhood and have perfect information about the risk profile of the other members of the group. The leaders selected are responsible for the empowerment of group members and for training the members or institutionalizing the shared norms among the members of the group.

H0. Does social capital have an impact on the success of the SHG?

Since these members are from the same locality or risk profile, they generate social capital in the form of bonding social capital, which refers to closer ties among the members of the group. Another type of social capital is the linkages with external members such as banks and financial institutions. Moreover, the groups also provide access to networks with NGO and self-help promoting institutions. Bonding social capital refers to the close relationship among the members of the group that leads to better social standing and hence access to finance at the doorstep for the people from the bottom of the pyramid. The bonding social capital refers to the close relationship among the members of the group. These relationships originate from the deep relationships among the members of the group. It is also often called the within-group social capital and is good for the group to get by. For getting ahead, there is another kind of social capital, which refers to the bridging social capital. This is the capital between the groups and is important for getting ahead. In a group, the members are selected based on some homogenous criterion, which includes the homogeneity of profession, neighborhood, or the existing social relationship. Thus, the bonding social capital includes the within-group, intra-, and closed-group social capital and the horizontal relationship between people of the same class and category. It refers to the strong social ties among the groups and thick trust and is often

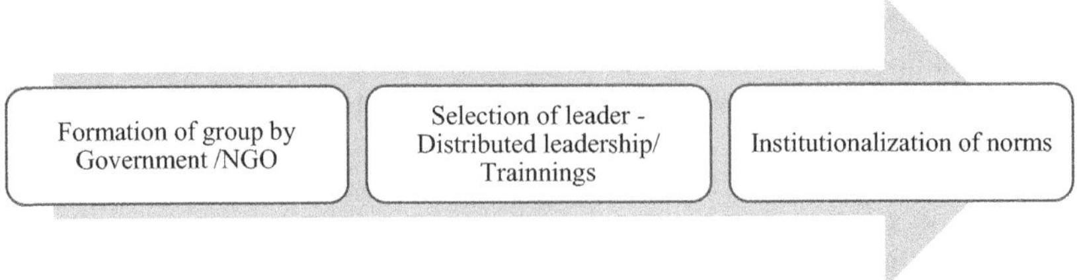

Fig. 20. Process of Group Formation and Enabling Factors. *Source:* Author's creation.

referred to the network closure among the people, which facilitates access to financial services without any physical collateral (Burt, 2002). Friendship refers to the relationship that exists among the people with the same background and between the people with the common characteristics. The members of the group share a common set of information, as they come from similar social and cultural backgrounds. Thus, social and cultural factors have a major impact on the success of the groups. The organizational context or the social imperative in the form of sociocultural norms have an impact upon the stability or viability of the community lending groups.

In excerpt from the interview is given below:

We classify the members who approach joining the group based on their vocation. Some people are interested in block printing, some are interested in Dye painting, and so on. Then we help them open their bank accounts. Then we provide them the passbooks, accounts book, and meeting book. Every month the members have to submit the savings amount and update it to the bank. These members get a loan from the bank without any collateral. The bank manager provides the loan based on application to the members of the group for the discussion around financial transactions.

There is also a subsidy provided to the members of the group. At the stage of formation, the members are grouped based on the like-mindedness of the members. The members of the group make regular payments and maintain the books of accounts. There is a tally application for updating the loan amount. Members of the group monitor each other.

H1. Entrepreneurial Ecosystem has a positive impact on the success and sustainability of group

The analysis of the interview transcript highlights that the like-minded people in a group share a common social–cultural background. The social–cultural background refers to the common vernacular and a priori information about the work proficiency and productivity of the members of the group. In the above interview, the members are from Madhubani in Bihar, and all of them pursue the Sikki art. They have been pursuing the Sikki art for generations, and this provides them proficiency in the work. This provides them with a cultural edge and improves the cohesion within the group. Due to the common culture and social milieu, the members of the group enjoy common bonds. The existence of cohesion within the group further promotes camaraderie and promotes a better quality of art and craft. In another interview, the respondent emphasized that the criteria for selecting group members are their knowledge, skills, and business relevance. This helps to promote the success of the group and mitigate the risk of failure of the groups. Within group factors include the a priori information about the other members of the group. In yet another interview, the executive highlighted that the groups are formed by the members who know each other before the formation of the group. These groups have complete knowledge of each other, which helps the members of the groups to get access to microfinance. Not only this, the within factors in the group include the appointment of the leaders from among the other group members. These leaders are democratically appointed by the members of the group and are responsible for providing direction to the group. Transformational leaders play an important role in changing the attitude and behavior of the members of the group through financial literacy workshops and social intermediation. Generally, the leaders enable the members to prepare the books of accounts. All the members in the group are not financially literate, and they select the most literate member, who is generally responsible for the preparation of the book of accounts. He is also helpful in imparting the necessary knowledge and skills to the people. In a group, the leaders are the people with the highest strategic orientation and are the people with higher financial literacy and financial knowledge. As per one of the SHG banking committees, the members of the group have complete knowledge of each other, and the leader is a member with a better knowledge and better social influence. Thus, in a bonding social group structure, the leadership and homogeneity of members play an important role in the success of the group. Thus, though in an economic world fraught with dichotomies and conflicts, the members try to create a small world, that is inhabitable and defending for. Let's look at an interview from an SHG.

"*Regarding leadership, when women go to 100 places, they get confident and through market exposure and through this they learn how they will handle things and they learn to talk. As I told you the women whom we sent to meet Anandipatel, 100 of them, out of them 4 were such who had leadership. They were working together and there are big units, which they were handling.*" Thus, the analysis of the interview shows that international exposure helps to nurture local leadership among the members of the group. Further, the woman highlighted that "*Women who would not have been out of home, go to IIT for giving training. They go to seminars and there are more than 50 members who are going out and working. This gives them social status. This gives them confidence and if technology is innovated this increases their social status. There are members whose children are studying in NIT.*" Thus, our study establishes that leadership qualities are not innate but can also be learned and nurtured. The example given above highlights that women who visit international seminars and workshops get an opportunity to develop leadership qualities, which leads to better confidence and develops leadership qualities among the members of the group.

H2. Does the social capital impact the resource allocation capacity of group?

In this study, it is hypothesized that social capital improves the capital allocation efficiency of the firms. In a group trying to access formal finance, the agency on the part of the bank leads to financial exclusion. In this regard, the banks often argue that the lack of information about the creditworthiness of the poor and marginalized sections of society is the main reason for the exclusion of the poor. Social capital plays an important role in reducing information asymmetry and ensuring access to finance for the people excluded from the formal financial system. Through social punishments, loss of reputation, and loss of social standing due to bad performance, the members cooperate. Thus, the social capital with the threat perception of the loss of social face motivates the members to work together for a common good. Due to the social capital and joint liability toward the loan for the members of the group, the cost of monitoring the members of the group comes down drastically. Moreover, the source of social capital in a group is relational and cognitive. In the relational or affective form, the social capital for the group remains in the form of the networks, and in the cognitive form, the social capital of the group is enshrined within the norms of the group. The soft information about the members of the group enables the group to access formal finance. The study of Hassan et al. (2017) highlights that the norms or cognitive terms and covenants in the group help to discipline the group. The networks in the group or the relational and affective terms enable the members to achieve an efficient allocation of capital. The capital allocation inefficiency leads to the problem of underinvestment and adverse selection through the rejection of safe borrowers. Thus, besides the availability of resources, the allocation of resources is a bigger impediment to the achievement of the group goals. Most of the conflicts within a group arise due to the unequal distribution of resources or inequities in access to finance for the people at the bottom of the pyramid. Through the group norms and relational networks, the members of a group keep a close vigil on the utilization of resources, and this leads to effective utilization of financial resources. Thus, this study overrides the presumption that the lack of resources leads to inequities; rather, it is the allocation of resources that leads to inequities and inequalities.

H3. Does the leadership in the group impact the social relationships and network relations within the group?

In the 21st century, leadership is not an individual concept rather it is about influencing others. With the advent of social media, leadership has emerged as a transformational concept, which is systems thinking. Leadership is a system of thinking, which is based on the power to influence others. Thus, leadership is no more an individual concept but is rather a social process that is governed by the thinking of other people in the group. In modern times, leadership is about managing the social capital in a social process. This implies that the groups have a certain modus operandi to confirm the behavior of those individuals who conform to the shared norms. Those who adhere to the group norms are generally seen as more upright. Thus, leaders who ensure adherence to group norms are deemed to be more successful than others. This is the new phase of leadership in the 21st century, which is concerned with the use of social influence as a leadership mechanism. Thus, how others perceive the process of resource allocation holds a lot of importance for the efficiency of the process of resource allocation. Through a higher level of shared vision and mutual understanding, the firms can achieve better resource allocation. In the modern-day scenario, the members of a group develop a shared vision through which they undergo a process of socialization. The leaders are the people or individuals who are responsible for providing direction to the other members of the group. The intensity of interaction among the members leads to a higher level of communication and cognitive social capital that refers to the adherence to the social norms. This further leads to a higher level of coordination and hence attainment of financial and institutional sustainability. This adherence to the group norms is often referred to as the structurally embedded social capital, which plays an important role in the sustainability of social groups. Transformational leaders define the terms of group membership in the form of a set of people who adhere to the group norms and become members of the group. In a group, there is a conflict between the marginalized sections of society and the civil society including banks. The use of labels such as "underserving" and "financial failures" becomes a habitus, which means people keep using these labels against the marginalized sections of society.

Given Below Is the Excerpt From the Interview

"The leader of the group selects a member with the skill set gives him a livelihood and attaches him to the group. All the members of the group are acquaintances. In the group members get the livelihood and we feel that the Government is not cooperative in providing thc loan. The bank loan is cheap in terms of the interest rate. The process of providing loans is tedious and bank officials are wary of lending to the members. They are very arrogant and do not know their work. We do not try for loans and from handicrafts we generate surplus and we have ISO certification and barcode. We feel that a loan is feasible for people who do not have their funds. Meetings are conducted regularly, every week. Group formation and sustenance are other things. We make members self-reliant; we give them livelihood. Firstly, we give them livelihood and then we teach them savings habits. All the members are salaried people and then we pool savings from their salary. The members maintain the money dealings, minutes of meetings, savings accounting is done and debit credit voucher is done and then loan appraisal form, loan personal files, and passbooks are maintained. I am a caretaker and there is a woman leader. We are covered under Ajeevika's and we manufacture handicrafts, pickles, chips, curd, etc. We sell our products through the website. During COVID we started manufacturing food products as the sale of food products does not stop even during COVID. We have insurance for each person so that if any person dies, he gets an insurance claim. We open a bank account for each person at the Bank of India. The rate of interest for each person is 1%. We maintain the books of account. Our company is registered under Start Up India. Members discuss the problems with each other. Meetings help to evaluate the amount of savings and loans taken. Leaders are rotated every year; for two years and new members are selected by the women members. The women only know about the rules and regulations; the member's creditworthiness is seen before selecting the members. In the market, we see, what is the reputation of the member. As members jointly responsible and individually responsible for their loan."

Impact of Sociocultural Factors on Sustainability of the Groups

SHGs are generally formed by the people, who are from the same sociocultural background. The homogeneity of members reduces the problem of information asymmetry through the reduction in moral hazard and adverse selection. Since the members in the group have common profession and cultural antecedents, they share a social bonding that promotes social and institutional sustainability among the members of the group. The excerpt from the interview is given here "*He determines the art in which the artist is expert and the Mohalla to which the ladies belong. Then we organize the members into a group on basis of terms and conditions are determined and groups are formed. As the members are from the same profession, they can collect and deposit money. A qualified person from the group monitors the group. After some time SHPI leave them and when the group is sustainable it becomes independent. It is a lineage business and individually the banks cannot provide the loan. Members are joined to each other and have social ties and since they have business correlation, they can pay on time. One of the members who is literate maintains the books of accounts. The members can solicit help from our organization.*" Thus, the sociocultural factors have a vast impact on sustainability of groups.

Transformational Leadership and Leadership as a Social Process

In joint lending groups, the major factors that led to the variance in performance are (1) management by exception, (2) the social process of leadership, and (3) transformational leadership. Management by exception principle highlights that small deviations in group performance or small defaults in performance are not to be pointed, and if only the deviations are considerable, they are to be taken up for sanctions and follow-up. Besides, the small deviations are to be ignored and tackled through counseling.

Management by Exception

Management by exception is the soft approach of banking that highlights that only the most important and significant deviations from the planning are to be taken into consideration and petty deviations should not be considered. A soft approach to leadership implies that extreme measures such as sanctions are to be taken up only in exceptional cases. The following interview highlights the details. The excerpt from the interview is given here "Our SHG is 6 km from the bank and the bank is within the Mandal. If somebody does not make the payment, there is counseling at the Panchayat level. In the monthly meeting, the Sarpanch, bank representative counsels the defaulting member. All groups are linked to the SHG Federations. The interest rate of the group is decided by the group and approved by the leader." In yet another interview, the respondent highlighted that "Though members do not generally default, if the members default, then the entire group which stays nearby counsels the member. Even in monthly meetings, the member is counseled." The interview highlights that in a group lending scenario, the soft approach to the management of the groups includes counseling. This approach highlights the replacement of the negative reinforcement and penalization of the members by positive reinforcement. According to various studies, the soft approach highlights the supportiveness, collaboration, and empathy among the members, which leads to interpersonal relationships among the members of the group. Soft leadership refers to the habit of listening attentively to the other members of the group, empowering decision-making, using the feedback loop, and working to maintain consensus within the group.

The Social Process of Leadership

Today dynamic and complex environments are fraught with vulnerabilities and risks like the COVID-19 pandemic. The modern-day world is fraught with vulnerabilities, which are distributed in a continuous, normally distributed, and increasing fashion. In such a scenario, leadership has emerged as a social process that involves communicating, collaborating through vulnerabilities, or cooperating despite internal and inherent weaknesses. Evolution involves partition and separation through a natural process. However, vulnerabilities in this process of disruption provide the unifying force, but still, it could lead to grave weaknesses. Public leadership offers hope through leaders who can distribute and yet maintain their share of goodness. The continuity of species is the major threat that is troubling humanity, and in this context, SDGs have come to play an important role. Though vulnerabilities, trust, and continuity are at odds, the balance through projections of microfinance and inclusive goals can help to maintain a balance and stability for a brief period. Through the theoretical lens of the punctuated equilibrium model, the brief period of stability is often met with disruptions such as COVID-19 pandemic crises. In such a dynamic environment, organizational agility and alignment depend on technological interventions. If technology drives the mechanics of social finance, then the social process of leadership provides much-needed embeddedness and environment for alignment of social goals to attain sustainability. In the 21st century, leadership is not a stand-alone process rather it is a social process that is exercised by the people using social dynamics such as persuasion, network building, negotiation, and consensus building. Leadership is a process of influencing, communicating, empathizing, empowering, motivating, and coaching the members of the group or the fraternity. In a social process, the members of the group make it difficult for the person to survive as leader, if they do not accept the person as their leader. The members of the SHG are the people, who are drawn from the bottom of the pyramid and marginalized section of society. These members are not literate or proficient and hence they need a lot of hand-holding. Thus, the use of the social process for social intermediation is an act of bonding and building linkages for social change. In the case of the SHGs, the members select their leaders through a consensus-building exercise. There are various ways in which the community leader influences the other members in the organization to follow them for the achievement of the objectives. In the domain of public leadership, another concept that is fast emerging is the concept of heroic leadership. Leadership refers to the kind of personal qualities through which an individual can drive the followers to perform certain functions. Leadership is often cited as a personal trait or the characteristics or personality types that can elicit the required responses from followers. In certain cases, the position that an individual has in an organization also provides authority to the individual to perform various functions and actions that are required for the achievement of the group's goals. Also, in certain cases, leadership is a social process that is driven through the use of social forces. Public leadership is an important trait for the successful functioning of an organization, as it involves developing a good public image and motivating the members to work for the social good and public good. Leadership is a social process that involves providing collaborative direction, alignment, and commitment to the process of management of the group. As per various studies, exogenous shock and vulnerability play an important role in development of the leaders. Any kind of exogenous shock or vulnerability enables the members of the community to come together and work for the betterment of the group. Within Western literature, leadership stands out as a virtue that enables individuals to collaborate and work together for the social good. However, the 21st-century literature highlights that exogenous shocks and vulnerability are not the best approach to exercise leadership. Inclusion and self-imposed leadership are the best forms of leadership. Leadership and collaboration can play an important role in driving people to achieve their objectives and goals. According to the various studies and literature, transformational leadership plays an important role in predicting the outcomes. The existing literature highlights that the social process of leadership leads to better communication, enhances the adaptability and flexibility of the followers and the members of the organization, and helps to reduce the uncertainties in an organization. Transactional and transformational leadership is a term that is often used in the context of the leadership process that aims to create an impact. Transformational leadership is mainly aimed at stimulating the followers to go beyond their self-good to achieve the common good while transactional leadership is mainly aimed at rewarding and punishing the members according to their caliber and individual performance. In the context of the SHG, the style of leadership is mainly transformational and involves motivating the employees to achieve the common good. As a social process, leadership is aimed at reducing the uncertainty in the environment, and it provides various benefits that include enhancing organizational commitment and improving organizational efficacy. Through constant information exchange and participatory approach, the leaders work together to create a consensus and social capital, which increases the trust in a semi-formal organization, such as group, and help the members to raise funds.

Distributed Leadership

The study further highlights that in a group, the leadership is distributed rather than concentrated among one member. In an SHG, the members take the decision through a social process which involves consultation with each other. The process involves deliberation, consensus building, and this creates solidarity among the members of the group. In a group, there is a Chief Accountant, who is proficient in finance and works with the members of the group for the preparation of the books of accounts, and there is a group leader, who guides the members for the attainment of the group goals. The excerpt from the interview with the members of the groups is given as follows: "*In our group, the CM or the Chief (Kosh Adhyaksh) maintains the books of accounts. Members of the group are not literate and they are made aware by the Kosh Adhyaksh. All the members are not literate and illiterate members are apprised of their savings and outstanding loan amount by the chief accountant. Our group members are extremely hard working and they collectively work extremely hard from 11 p.m. till 4 a.m.*" The interview highlights that the Chief Accountant helps the members to maintain their book of accounts. This type of distributed leadership enables the members to work harmoniously toward the attainment of group goals. Also, the leaders in a group work as a role model for the other members of the group. Leaders in the group try to lead by example, where they set a precedence, which is followed by the other members of the society. The state also champions the cause of poverty reduction through cooperation among the members of group. The Government appoint members, who enable the members of the group to adhere to the group norms and attain financial sustainability. "*Ajeevika block members play an extremely important role in maintaining the self-sustainability of the groups. These block officers come from Ajeevika once every month and bank officers also come, once in a period of 2 to 3 months to convince the defaulting members to make the payment. They persuade the members to maintain the financial discipline.*" In a group, the art pursued is a heritage art, which is passed on from generation to generation through the apprenticeship with the master's craftsmen. "*In the cluster 10 to 15 members are operational. Masters' craftsmen are responsible for monitoring the craftsmanship. All the master craftsmen are formed into apex body and the master craftsmen can exercise the pressure in his group and the other group. This craftsman is responsible for covering all the groups and the craftsmen are brought from all over the world including Banaras and West Bengal.*" The interview highlights how the masters enable the members to learn the art form and pass it on from generation to generation. Another excerpt from the interview that highlights the leadership qualities is mentioned as follow: Komal ben is known all over the village. There has never been an issue regarding the non-repayment of loan. "*Even if there is a default due to medical reason or any kind of disease in the family, we support them and counsel them regarding the importance of timely repayment. In our group, members attend meetings regularly. Komalben manages the distribution of the money. This is Komalben's ancestral business and her mother has taught this skill to them. She handles all the tasks like distribution of money. Pach work has been passed on to Komal ben from the generation to generation. Members do cooperate with each other and encourage each other.*" The literature highlights that the leader of the group supports the other members in the timely repayment of loans and promoting financial cooperation.

Hofstede and SHGs in India

According to the literature, as per the Hofstede cultural dimensions, the SHGs are generally formed by the people who know each other extremely well. Thus, the low power distance in a group enables the members of the group to participate equally well in decision-making. In a group, the members work together for the achievement of the group goals. According to the various leaders, the presence of structured rules in a group enables the members to avoid uncertainty. Through disciplined savings and financial habits, group lending promotes restrained behavior among the group members. Thus, an understanding of the culture and cultural affinity helps to develop an appropriate leadership style among the members of the group. Thus, through the Hofstede prism, the sociocultural factors have an important impact on the financial sustainability of the groups. Through the collectivist culture, the SHGs promote savings among the members of the group, provide a mutual support system, and create shared responsibility for success. Generally, the groups are formed to provide, access to long-term finance, which leads to sustainable finance and savings programs that promote financial stability. Further, the social bonding activities among the members of the group lead to better management and utilization of funds.

Exit and Entry Barriers

Entry and exit barriers also play an important role in promoting rivalry among the members of the group. If the entry barriers are high, it can lead to various conflicts among the members of the group, and if exit barriers are low, it makes leaving members from the group far more difficult leading to conflicts among the members of the group. The social capital and network relations within the group further lead to additional entry barriers, which lead to conflicts among the members of the group. Due to the social contract, the members have joint liability, and if one member does not pay all the other members need to pay, this further leads to conflicts among the group members. Fixed costs in the form of regular savings also lead to conflict among the members of the group.

Conclusion

Various studies highlight that leadership enables the members from the margin of the section of society to get the benefit of access to financial resources. Leadership is one of the major factors that lead to conflict among the members of the group. If the leader is effective, he can facilitate the success of the members of the group, and if he is ineffective, he can lead to rivalry and conflicts among the members of the group. Thus, various factors play an important role in promoting harmony and reducing conflicts among the members of the group.

References

Burt, R. S. (2002). The Social Capital of Structural Holes. In M. F. Guillén, R. Collins, P. England, & M. Meyer (Eds.), *The New Economic Sociology: Developments in an Emerging Field* (pp. 148–190). Russell Sage Foundation.

Hassan, Abul, & Saleem, Shamim (2017). An Islamic microfinance business model in Bangladesh: Its role in alleviation of poverty and socio-economic well-being of women. *Humanomics*, *33*, 15–37. https://doi.org/10.1108/H-08-2016-0066

Chapter 6

Communication Strategies and Their Role in the Resolution of Conflicts

Abstract

This chapter will highlight the importance of communication strategies in ensuring the success of the groups through conflict resolution. This chapter will explore the role of communication through mass media and digital channels in conflict resolution using the theoretical lens of the theory of mass communication. The scope of the study will be Asian countries and European countries like France, Germany, and Britain. The case study method will be used to explore the impact of the communication strategies on conflict resolution within the group. In Asian countries particularly, the social factors have an important role in deciding the communication strategy. Generally, the emerging nations use various local communication strategies such as Nukkad Nataks and role plays to ensure the flow of information within the groups. Communication and persuasion strategies play an important role in the success of community lending programs. This chapter will explore the importance of communication strategies to achieve equity and financial inclusion. This chapter will also provide case studies on how the use of mass media and telecommunication has helped ensure knowledge sharing among the group members. The outcome of this chapter will be a conceptual framework of various communication strategies that lead to the success of the group.

Keywords: Communication; storytelling; microfinance; financial inclusion; communication strategies

Introduction

From the well to the WhatsApp group: For generations, village women have connected in the evenings, sharing stories and building community. Now, technology is transforming rural India, bringing new forms of communication and

Development and Conflict in Community Lending Programs, 119–130

Published under exclusive licence by Emerald Publishing Limited
doi:10.1108/978-1-83708-290-220251017

governance to their fingertips. It's a new era of connection and empowerment. Women must lead the charge on issues affecting marginalized women. We need passionate advocates who can champion their needs and ignite their potential. Women are best positioned to understand and address the challenges faced by marginalized women. We need strong, dedicated women to drive change and empower them to soar. Marginalized women deserve advocates who truly understand their experiences. Empowering women to lead these efforts, supported by allies, is essential for creating lasting change. The right communication strategies and policy programs can help to uproot the evil of self-appointed PATIs from the system and also help to resolve conflicts that the members of the group face among each other. In this study, the case study approach has been adopted to study the impact of adoption of mass communication in resolving the conflicts among the members of the group.

Research Problem

The flow of information and opinion building through access to information withheld by the principals or people in authority are the tools to achieve sustainable development and inclusive growth with peace and harmony. In the groups, the members are generally from the marginalized sections of society, and they face moral hazards in terms of misutilization of finances. Inability to pay loans by any member often leads to conflict among the members of the group. The use of mass media is a great tool to ensure the dissemination of information and create information symmetry and harmony. There are many studies on what mass communication is. But there are not many studies that explore how the use of mass communication can help in promoting financial inclusion and reducing the conflicts among the members of the group. The Government of India has implemented various mass communication programs, such as Mann ki Baat and Nukkad nataks, to name a few. This research paper aims to address the question of how the use of mass communication in the form of meetings, nukkad nataks, community radio shows, and programs such as Mann ki Baat is helping the marginalized sections of society to achieve equitable growth and development.

RQ. What is the role of mass communication in conflict resolution among the members of the self-help groups?

Theoretical Framework

For this study, a feedback loop model of communication has been used. The feedback loop model highlights the importance of two-way communication, where the receivers of the messages can respond to the message by interacting with the content creators. Use of media platforms to solicit responses from the members of the group to create content and using mass media to address the grievances or disseminate information are examples of how the Government of

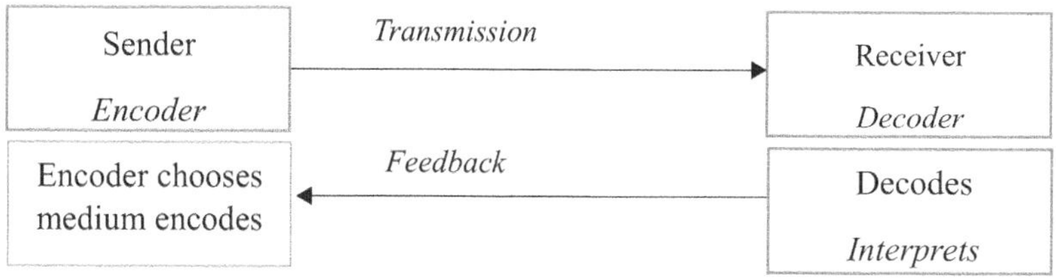

Fig. 21. Two-Way Communication. *Source:* Author's own work.

India is using the mass media to disseminate information and bring about opinion and attitude change among the members of the groups.

Fig. 21 provides the details of two-way communication.

Discussion and Analysis

Problem of Pradhan Pati

The Indian Government has taken some very stringent measures to transform the plight of the women in the Panchayati Raj era by giving them respite from the clutches of the Pradhan Pati. Pradhan Pati refers to the self-appointed leaders called as Sarpanch Pati, Mukhiya Pati in Gram Panchayats. This practice also refers to the proxy leadership that deters male interference in the day-to-day working. In the working of the women's self-help groups, generally the male relatives of women members put undue influence on the working of group. The Government has proposed various initiatives, such as gender inclusive quotas in panchayat committees, level committees, and annual awards for Anti Pradhan Pati championships and the creation of a federation of women panchayat leaders. The Government of India has undertaken various informational campaigns, such as the use of campaign radios, to spread awareness about Pradhan Pati. Under the Panchayati Raj system, the GOI has recommended the use of various modes of information, such as education and communication activities, media engagement, conferences, seminars, training programs, screening of public awareness schemes, and broadcasting of programs through community radio to spread awareness.

Mass Communication and Its Role in Rural Development

Mass media and means of communication are economical ways of providing and imparting information to the poor and illiterate. To impart information to the poor, one needs not be rich or literate. Simply having an economical device, the members of the society can enjoy the benefits of communication being imparted through the radio. Mass media plays an important role in attitude change and improvising behavior through opinion formation. If we look at the other methods of information dissemination, these include conducting meetings, nukkad nataks, the use of fares and melas, word of mouth, religious congregations, and mass gatherings to disseminate information. Mass media has the potential to hold society accountable for the actions of its members and also to ensure discipline. In the villages, the self-help group linkage program has transformed the plight of the members from marginalized society by providing them access to livelihood and means of living. The self-help group linkage program enables the members to get access to bank credit. In villages under the DAY NRLM (National Rural Livelihood Mission) program, the members are required to conduct regular meetings, and these congregations and meetings help them to create awareness regarding their financial position and help the groups to achieve financial sustainability. Thus, mass communication is helping the members of marginalized societies to achieve financial independence and become financially included.

(1) Meetings and their relevance for the group coherence

The members in a self-help group need various group mechanisms such as meetings and bookkeeping to maintain financial discipline and achieve financial sustainability. Every group at the time of formation of the group adheres to conduct regular meetings. These meetings provide the platform for the members to discuss their routine matters, including a collection of savings and distribution of funds as the bank loan and credit. An interview was conducted with the leader of a self-help group to explore the importance of the success of the groups. "*In a month, the members conduct meetings. During these meetings, the members take stock of the financial income generated, and they also distribute the savings among the members of the group. The meetings are a part of shared norms to maintain financial discipline. Generally, the women members of the groups are not that active, and they do not take much interest in the matters relating to community development. The members also disseminate information about the various schemes and Government programmes through meetings. Meetings also provide the platform to resolve conflicts among the members of the group, though now through various initiatives the Government has provided so much work to the groups, that the members have no time to indulge in any sort of politics. Their sole motive is to work for the good of the nation and national development. The members of the group have started using the mass media such as phone and mobile phone to network with the other members of the group. They also use WhatsApp and social media to disseminate information and knowledge about the meetings and financial matters. However, there is one major concern: the social media platforms and mass communication programmes are not broadcasted in the vernacular language. The members of the group highlighted the importance of vernacular language to disseminate information to the group. If the broadcasted messages are in the vernacular language, the members will be able to engage themselves more with the core objectives of the programmes and the ethos of various initiatives.*"

"The groups conduct meetings at least once a month to discuss the financial issues and problems faced by the members of the group. Each member is compulsorily required to attend at least one meeting during the month. The problems in the group and problems faced by the members are discussed in the group. Moreover, the group members also discuss the social problems faced by the members of the group during the group meetings. The Government also organizes various exhibitions and seminars to provide a platform for the members of the group to exhibit their work of art and interact with the external world. Exhibitions are also conducted to resolve the issues and challenges faced by the members of the group. The problems faced by the members are escalated to the social committees formed by the Government of India to resolve social problems faced by the members of the group."

(2) Community Radio and its role in financial awareness:
Program Jan Jan Jankari—Community Radio: Jan Jan tak Jankari is a community radio program that is broadcast through 15 different radio stations in Bihar, Karnataka, and Maharashtra to create an awareness regarding the proxy sarpanch paratha. The Ministry of Panchayati Raj has entrusted the Community Radio with the task of broadcasting these programs. These programs also provide snapshots of various issues, such as women-friendly villages and good governance. The Panchayati Raj also uses the community radios to spread awareness about schemes such as SVAMITA for digital mapping of villages, creating e-Gram Swaraj, Meri Panchayat, Panchayat Nirnay, and Audit online. The use of mass media and communication aids can help to uproot the evil of the marginalization of women from the system. The Government of India has undertaken various initiatives such as Radio programs, Satellite television programs, and the use of local media such as Nukkad Natak to impart knowledge about the community programs to the people at the bottom of the pyramid. Most of the existing knowledge is based on the assumption of free and perfect markets. Whereas most of the community enterprises work in a real environment which do not work on the principle of equity and is fraught with various inequities and imbalances. There is a need to emphasize the importance of bridging the gap between the poor and rich by providing the poor access to rural finance with equity and in all fairness.

(3) Nukkad Nataks and its importance in mass communication:
In the hinterlands, the marginalized sections of society are comprised of members who do not have access to any form of information. Through community lending, the self-help group bank linkage program run by the banks is aimed at providing access to finance and credit to the people at the bottom of the pyramid. Information asymmetry is the major reason that the people in the hinterlands are unable to access loans and credit from the bank. The Government runs various schemes such as Nari Shakti and Ajeevika programs that are aimed at providing information about credit and loans to the members of the marginalized sections of the society. In this regard, mass communication using local traditions and cultural tools such as nukkad nataks play an important role in promoting the welfare of the members through financial inclusion. Nukkad nataks refer to the use of

plays and role plays to promote social causes such as sanitation, water conservation, climate protection, and women's equality. Using the narratives and cultural heritage from the treasure of history, the social groups weave their interactions with the landscape in the form of stories with a message. Various financial institutions, banks, and social organizations have been using traditional folklore as bricolage to portray and communicate the importance of financial inclusion. Through the use of theater, the actors create a natural setting of a village and present various stories and narratives to motivate the members of the group to achieve financial inclusion through compulsive savings and credit. Financial institutions and state agencies often use historical and cultural stories to sensitize the villagers to save money and invest the money for the welfare of the nation and community. In a group, the members are required to follow the shared norms, such as maintenance of books of accounts and conducting meetings for the welfare of the members at the bottom of the pyramid. In this regard, the use of traditional media and folklore, along with vernacular language, helps promote good financial habits and financial discipline among the group members. Nukkad nataks not only provide information but also help in soliciting views from the members of the society regarding the various financial schemes and programs run by the Government of India.

(4) Mann ki baat:
The Government of India has introduced an important community broadcast program, Mann ki Baat, in which the Hon'ble Prime Minister solicits comments and responses from the general community and people regarding their problems, including financial woes such as lack of access to credit. This program is an example of two-way communication, in which the Government of India makes use of the feedback and suggestions from the common public to conduct debate and interactions with the public to address the grievances of the communities. These broadcast series also inform the people of India regarding the newer developments in various fields, including the plans for financial inclusion. This program provides an opportunity to the members for democratic participation and contribute toward the achievement of the goals of sustainable development. Through social intermediation and grievance redressal, mass media initiatives such as broadcast community radios and Mann ki baat play an important role in promoting harmony and conflict resolution through persuasion and counseling. A case in point is the use of cultural heritage such as paintings, various rituals, and sports programs to exhibit team spirit among the members of the society to motivate the members to pursue the objective of community development and excellence. By recognizing the efforts and achievements of the local leaders, the program celebrates excellence and aims to persuade these members to work relentlessly toward the achievement of the group goals. Indeed, the Government of India is also taking various initiatives to develop a sportsman spirit among the members of the group. Mann Ki Baat is an important mass media program that creates content through the feedback that is solicited from the public at large.

Through the dissemination of the information, the Hon'ble Prime Minister not only responds to the grievances of the public but also sensitizes the general public to work toward social and sustainable development. The community programs are an example of the national integration and community participation that absolves to achieve the goal of sustainable development and growth through continuous innovation. The excerpts from the interview highlight the importance of two-way communication and mindfulness in achieving the complete essence of communication. From the design of the program to the speech, communication is an important technique to create awareness and mindfulness. The members in a group are also provided the training to promote mindfulness and create a nontoxic environment. Various initiatives have been taken by the Government of India to reduce the suffering and create happiness among the members of society. The importance of rightful speech cannot be emphasized more than in the business setting. The importance of rightful speech cannot be emphasized more than in a business setting. This includes telling the truth, not exaggerating, being consistent, and using peaceful language.

Conflict Resolution Mechanism in the Workplace

Conflicts in a workplace are bound to occur, and it is in the interest of the members to resolve the conflicts amicably. Those conflicts that cannot be resolved through normal interaction can be resolved through a formal redressal mechanism. A redressal mechanism comprises the representatives from the incubator agency, a representative from District Mission Management Union (DMMU) and State Mission Management Union (SMMU) and representatives in an incubator. These committees can play an extremely important role in reducing the conflicts among the members of the marginalized sections of society. These monitoring committees play an extremely important role in reducing potential conflicts and ensuring open communication among the members of the group. Further, the leaders in these groups also offer the privilege of mediation and intermediation to ensure peace and resolution of the conflicts. In a group, there are often conflicts due to the forked tongue and the double tongue, which implies saying one thing to one person and another thing to another person. The members must communicate the same thing to different people in a group. Communicating different opinions and different rhetoric to different people can lead to fights and mistrust, which can further lead to fights and the misuse of resources. As the famous adage by Buddha suggests, one should speak in a manner that aligns with the listener's mindset and matches their capacity to understand according to the mind of the person who listens and the ability of the person to receive what I say. The members of a community must use the right kind of speech, realizing that the wrong speech leads to conflicts, whereas the right speech leads to the well-being of the members of the group. Often, we come across situations where groups suffer from various altercations and fights, particularly when the members of the group do not pay back their loans at the right time, leading to major strife and fights among the members of the group. In one of the interviews, the respondent, who is the leader of the group, highlighted that the reason for the conflict among the members of the group is the rising non-performing assets, which might be due to the nonrepayment of the loans. The respondent highlighted that often, from the loan provided by the banks under the self-help group linkage program, the funds are misused by the members of the group and their family members for nonreproductive purposes. The non repayment of the loans by the members of the group leads to financial woes for the other members of the group, who are responsible for the payment of loan defaults by the other members of the group. This leads to conflict among the members of the group.

Popular Media of Communication

As per the various studies, the mass communication takes place through the community radios and television, conferences and seminars, nukkad nataks, podcasts and gatherings and congregations. These media of communication enable the members to communicate their concerns and issues with the leader of the group.

Fig. 22(a) provides description of various channels used for communication. And Fig. 22(b) provides description of principles of communication.

In communication for the achievement of the objectives of communication, it is extremely important that the communication must be two-way and there should be a proper feedback loop in place to ensure achievement of objectives of communication. Moreover, the communication should be mindful, i.e., the speaker should keep in mind the sensibilities of the receiver. There should be active listening to ensure that the communication achieves its objectives. The speaker should keep in mind the principle of ethics and integrity to ensure that there is no violation of the basic code of conduct.

Meetings as a Source of Communication

Principles of Communication—A Case Study

How do members in a community ensure that the communication is proper?

Clarity of Purpose

To ensure proper communication among the members of the group, the groups decide and commit to shared norms and byelaws. They also agree to conduct regular meetings. Meetings serve as an important platform to share their views, discuss their problems, influence decision making, and build opinion. The managers generally steer the group, and their performances are also celebrated and audited through the performance review.

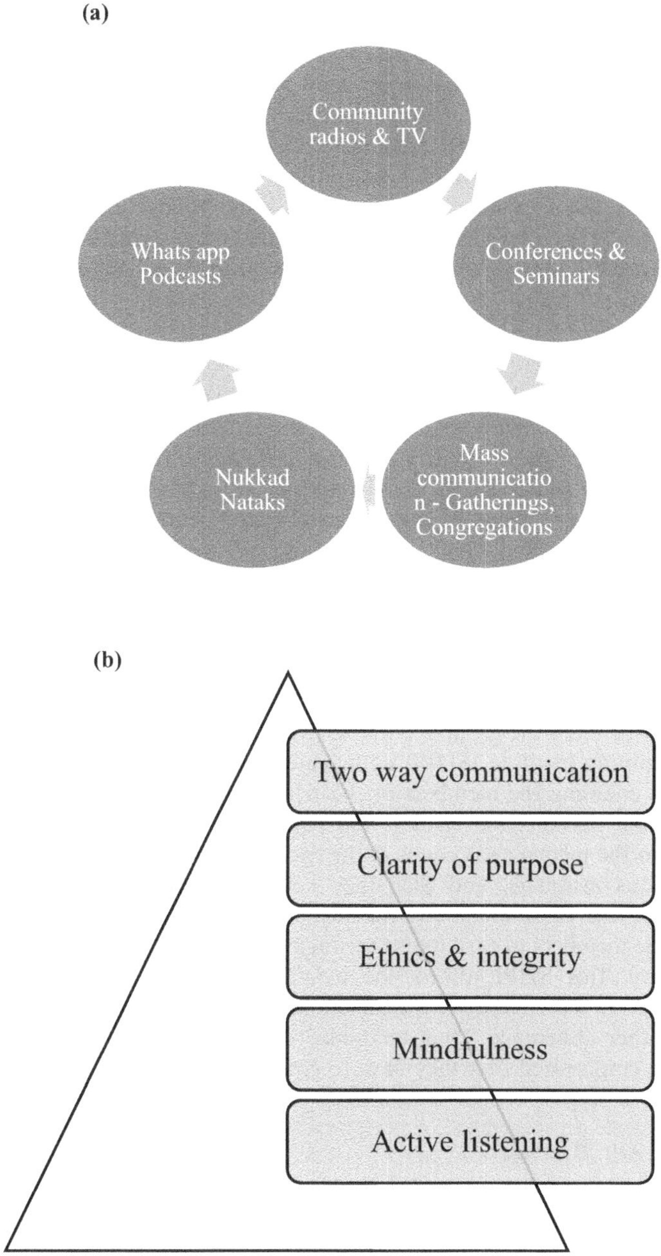

Fig. 22. (a) Refers to Media Used for Communication. (b) Refers to Principles of Communication.

Two-Way Communication

According to the interview, leaders are nominated from among members who demonstrate competence and enjoy wide acceptance. This social capital and relationships among members facilitate seamless communication. The respondent further highlighted that the members of the group in the beginning were not proficient, and then some training was given to them. We also arranged informal get-togethers, such as dance competitions, holy Milan, and flag hoisting on Independence Day, and these all events provided them a platform to speak their mind. Naturally, they started enjoying and wearing good clothes.

Mindfulness

To ensure mindfulness, the members selected are like-minded and of one school of thought. Thus, mindfulness and being empathetic to the feelings and sensibilities of receivers are extremely important to achieve the objective of complete education. This training and social intermediation play an important role in ensuring the completeness of communication and achievement of its objective. The interview above highlights the importance of meetings and formal education and training in promoting meaningful communication among the members of the group. The head of another NGO, a middle-aged gentleman, manages self-help groups comprising about 11 to 15 men. He mainly deals with women's self-help groups in solid waste management. He is extremely passionate about how self-help groups have progressed and how it has led to incremental change in the well-being of the group members. Every month, in the beginning, his Self-help promoting institute (SHPI) contributes to members. He has been instrumental in enabling the members of the self-help groups to sell recycled plastic waste in the markets for Rs 200–300 per day. This amount is then directly credited to the member's account at the end of the month. His SHPI takes only homogenous members, and then they help form a group with institutional governance and rules. He allows the members to form the group, and the bank enables the members to earn interest from money deposited. Similar to the Amul cooperative, this SHPI allows the member to market recycled waste and handicrafts. In his view, all the members live in the same locality and are taken by each other's reference. Thus, he thinks that members can easily monitor each other. He emphasized that they have to conduct meetings at a gap of 15 days.

Importance of Meetings

The SHPI, according to the Head, is where the members can relax and unwind. They are served *tea* and *karah* during the break by the SHPI. Leaders are the lynchpin, and according to the SHPI head, the leader helps the members to maintain the books of accounts. According to him, the primary source of stress for the members of SHPI is the misutilization of loans. The members take the money and misuse it for personal purposes. In a group, the members counsel the defaulting members in case of default, and at times, there is a big fight.

Only the strongest member in the group is made the group leader. This helps in reducing the tension in the group. He calls it a small get-together and party in the slum, where poor people come together. He is happy to see so many poor people enter the prosperous world of higher savings and income. Thus, meetings serve as an important source of communication and a place to discuss their business matters. During the meetings, the members also prepare the minutes of the meetings. These minutes of meetings are an important tool to maintain a record of deliberations and help in decision-making.

"Meetings are conducted regularly, every week. Group formation and sustenance is another thing. We make members self-reliant; we give them livelihood. Firstly, we give them livelihood, and then we teach them savings habits. All the members are salaried people, and then we pool savings from their salaries. The members maintain the money dealings, minutes of meetings, savings accounting, and debit credit voucher is done and then loan appraisal form, loan personal files and passbooks are maintained. I am a caretaker, and there is a woman leader. We are covered under Ajeevika, and we manufacture handicrafts, pickles, chips, curd, etc. We sell our products through the website. During the COVID-19 pandemic, we started manufacturing food products as the sale of food products does not stop even during COVID-19. We have insurance for each person so that if any person dies, he gets an insurance claim. We opened bank accounts for each person at the Bank of India. The rate of interest for each person is 1%. We maintain the books of account. Our company is registered under Start-up India. Members discuss the problems with each other. Meetings help to evaluate the amount of savings and loans taken."

Ethics and Integrity

Leadership positions are rotated annually, with two-year terms, and new leaders are chosen by the women members. The women only know about the rules and regulations, and before selecting the members, the creditworthiness of the member is seen. In the market we see, what is the reputation of the member. As members are jointly responsible and individually responsible for their loan. Our group meeting is conducted per week. In each meeting, members maintain accounts and records. Banks visit the site and the Ajeevika officials to inspect the work and find out if the work is as per the standard. Members are confident in each other that if the loan is taken, it will be paid off. In our group, the members understand that if a loan is taken, it has to be paid back. We also showed our accounts to Ajeevika and books to the other group members. We make small, big diyas, lamps from mud, and it becomes terracotta when baked in the fire. And if we talk about utensils like handi plates, we do not color them.

Active Listening

In a group, the effectiveness of the measures and steps taken depend upon the planning and most importantly how well the strategies are communicated and implemented. Thus, communication plays an extremely important role in the success of the groups. In a group, the communication strategies are suggested by the leaders, and the leaders are responsible for ensuring that the members understand the message intended. In rural parts of the country, the members are not that literate, and the leader makes use of various strategies such as interactive media, vernacular language, and empathy to ensure that the members pursue active listening and understand the message in the intended manner.

Conclusion

Communication plays an important role in ensuring the achievement of group objectives and goals. To ensure attainment of group objectives, the communication should be two way and closed with a feedback loop. Further, the listener in the communication should be active listener and there should be use of local language and vernacular, in the form of nukkad nataks and community radio shows to ensure the attainment of the group objectives.

Chapter 7

Incubation Through NGOs: A Road to Sustainability of Group Initiatives

Abstract

Across the globe, nongovernment organizations (NGOs) and incubators have come to play an important role in promoting social intermediation and conflict resolution among the members of the groups. New groups with no existing network with other banks find it extremely difficult to raise money. The structural factors and rigidities within a group pose various difficulties in the financial inclusion of the members of the group. Self-help promoting institutions (SHPIs) and NGOs play an important role in social intermediation and confidence building among the members of the groups. This chapter will further explore the role of NGOs and incubators in attitude-building and promoting self-reliance among the members of the group. The chapter will provide a conceptual framework on the role of incubators and NGOs in providing financial support and financial intermediation to ensure the achievement of group goals. This chapter will be of immense interest to policymakers and academicians. The primary data will be collected by using the semi-structured interview. The secondary data will be collected using the existing published literature. For data collection, the samples will be selected using purposive random sampling. This chapter will use the case study method semi-structured interviews and hermeneutics to study the impact of NGOs and SHPIs in achieving the success of groups. This chapter will use the theory of collective action to explore the impact of incubation and social intermediation through NGOs and SHPIs on the well-being of small businesses.

Keywords: Incubators; small business groups; self-help groups; self-help promoting institutions and entrepreneur

Development and Conflict in Community Lending Programs, 131–148

Published under exclusive licence by Emerald Publishing Limited
doi:10.1108/978-1-83708-290-220251020

Introduction

Microfinance is aimed at providing access to finance to the poor people at the bottom of the pyramid, who lack physical collateral and record of creditworthiness. Community lending is a mechanism to provide finance to the marginalized sections of society who do not possess any sort of physical collateral. The groups provide the necessary social capital to enable the members at the bottom of the pyramid to access credit and loans. In India, self-help groups (SHGs) were introduced by the Government in the year 1992. These institutes were aimed at *providing livelihood* and promoting self-reliance among rural women. Beyond financial access and usage, without the use of financial collateral and monitoring through peer pressure, SHG ensured sustainable livelihood to millions of marginalized women in India. In 1990, NABARD introduced the SHG Linkage Program, which is the key strategy for delivering financial services to the poor in a sustainable manner. According to the latest NABARD annual report, 45% of the SHGs have been able to get access to Credit Linkage once. From the scientific evidence analyzed from the analysis of the relevant literature, it is established that the main cause of low credit off take is the set of demand and supply factors. Bankers lack the motivation to lend to the SHG members due to lack of documentation, lack of adherence to the Panch sutras, and lack of protocols and adherence. Most of the current research is limited to the physical outreach and Social Role of SHGs. Group formation is a cumbersome process that involves the selection of a homogenous set of people with the same risk profile. As a part of the necessary condition to form groups, only members who already know each other are selected to form the group. The process of selection of members and separation as per risk profile is fraught with various challenges. Various NGOs and self-help promotion institutions play an important role in forming sustainable groups and communities. Many SHGs suffer from the problem of default in loan repayment (Volk et. al., 2012). Financial literacy, adherence to group norms or *Panchsutras, and* Peer monitoring are some of the reasons that impact the success of financial inclusion under the SHG linkage program. Within the social contract of community lending groups, the selection of members gives rise to a precarious problem of agency. The incubators play a key role, as these government-funded agencies provide hand-holding support to the enterprises run by groups through capacity building and change management. Existing literature (Pankaj Baag, 2014), discusses credit risk as risk impacting the total risk of the banks. As per the researchers, this risk refers to a situation of willful default or inability to pay back the loan taken. Most of the literature highlights the role of macroeconomic factors in impacting credit repayment rates (Bruche & Gonzalez Aguado, 2010). However there is a lack of literature in the domain of microfinance through SHG bank linkage programs. Few studies highlight the importance of social capital, weaker informational advantage, and poor financial habits as the main reason for default. This implies that groups with financially illiterate members, with a lack of financial inclusion as account ownership, savings, and credit repayment history tend to default more on their loans. In this regard, the self-help promoting institutes, often called as incubators, are silver lining in the blue sky, and access to credit is like a soft golden glow that offers support to groups and helps them become self-sustainable. How these incubators enable the small community lending groups to become successful is an extremely less-researched area. Nongovernment organizations (NGOs) and self-help promotion institutions (SHPIs) play an extremely important role in laying down the bylaws for the formation of the group and mentoring and counseling the group members to work collaboratively to achieve the group's goals. There are several studies on the importance of community lending, but there are no studies on the importance of incubators in promoting the financial sustainability of groups. This research study aims to conduct a case study to explore the impact of incubators and NGOs in ensuring the sustainability of groups. Incubators help in building an ecosystem for women-led SHGs. This ecosystem will enable these enterprises to access the markets, become financially sustainable, generate employment, and improve the creditworthiness of the women-led SHGs. Many NGOs and academic institutions are working as an incubator for the women-led SHG and enterprises in India. Incubators help corporates to improve their marketing capability and provide access to remote markets.

Research Problem

Incubation is an important medium to provide a foothold to small and medium enterprises that do not have enough physical collateral to access finance from banks and financial institutions. Incubation promotes the adoption of the latest technology by the members at the bottom of the pyramid. The agreement of incubation involves two parties, namely the incubator and incubatee. The incubator provides the right kind of social environment to facilitate the germination of new business ideas and provide the support services such as marketing support and financial support that are required for the flourishing of small and medium enterprises. Through the collateral, the incubator also facilitates access to the necessary physical capital and financial support for the development of local businesses. In the case of the SHG, the NGOs and SHPIs provide the necessary hand-holding and consultation to facilitate the development of the businesses. This study aims to discuss the role of SHPIs and NGOs in promoting the growth of small and medium enterprises. A single case study approach will be adopted to explore the phenomenon of incubation by the NGOs and SHPIs.

> *RQ*. What is the role of an incubator and self-help group promoting institution in promoting financial sustainability of the groups?

Theoretical Framework

In this study, the structural social work theory has been adopted. This theory propagates that society and social work begin with conflict rather than order. Communities are comprised of members from diverse socioeconomic backgrounds with conflicting interests. These members compete for resources and power. Community lending groups are formed by people who are marginalized and living below the poverty line. These members face a lot of discrimination and are often declined loans by commercial banks and formal financial institutions. Thus, the existing conflict of interest leads to the struggle for power among the individuals. SHPIs act as the social intermediaries that help in resolving these conflicts through access to finance for the people at the bottom of the pyramid. These NGOs help to bring together like-minded people to form the groups through a proper selection process.

Literature Review

Several definitions exist for the small businesses. Most of the research papers highlight various firm characteristics, such as the number of employees, performance characteristics such as annual revenue, and industry type, to name a few. Often, small businesses refer to the businesses as a firm that has fewer resources or employees, revenues, or assets (Evans & Lyons, 1999). The state rules define a small business as a privately owned corporation, partnership, or sole proprietorship that has very few employees and very little annual revenue. As per the Ministry of Micro, Small, and Medium Enterprises, a micro enterprise is a business that has investment in plant and machinery of less than 1 crore. And small businesses are the enterprises that have an investment of not more than 10 crore and not more than Rs 50 crore. Cochran (1986) in his research study has drawn an analogy between the weather and the health of the small businesses. The author highlights the lack of data and research on why small businesses fail and the reasons for the same. Various studies have discussed the impact of different factors on the profitability and viability of large firms, but there is hardly any research on the impact of asymmetric information and agency in the form of limited liability of the group members in a community-run enterprise on the financial viability of the small businesses run by the community. Haugh (2021) in his research study has highlighted the importance of incubation in enterprise development and employment generation. Various studies highlight five stages of small business growth: the existence stage, which is concerned with garnering customers and gaining sale; survival, which is concerned with viability of the businesses run by small-size firms; and the success stage. After the success of the small businesses, the next stages are take-off and resource maturity, where the business takes advantage of its network and resource access. Small businesses are well regarded for their potential to create jobs and promote the welfare of the economy (Morrison et al., 2003). However, despite all the assertions, small businesses are fraught with various problems, which include the perceived difference between the current state and the desired state. From the perspective of financial organizations, the problems in small businesses can be defined as about (1) accounting and finance, where accounting defines the book keeping and finance defines the access to the formal finance; (2) internal management; (3) external management; (4) human relations; and (5) Marketing (Walsh &

Ungson, 1988). Incubators and SHPIs help small and business enterprises to gain prominence and become sustainable. Herbane (2010) in his research study has highlighted that the crisis management is absent in the domain of small businesses. Many of the research studies have highlighted that gender, previous government employment, and redundancy had a negative influence on small business. Mukul and Sheeri (2024), in their research study, highlight that the incubation and social capital significantly contribute to rural entrepreneurs' access to resources and knowledge. With ever-evolving, complex entrepreneurial ecosystems, leadership is providing a new direction to these small and medium enterprises.

Structural Theory of Social Work

Fig. 23 provides the structural theory of social work.

The social theory of intermediation, according to our analysis, highlights that market intermediaries help the bottom of the pyramid to get financially included. Intermediaries play an important role in creating an internal force of peer mechanism that involves a social contract to adhere to the group norms and peer monitor each other. Given the trade-off between the welfare of the group and individual welfare, the members with limited liability individually are more likely to shirk responsibility. However, the social intermediaries enable the members of the group to achieve financial sustainability through training, capacity building, leadership development, and attitude change through motivation.

Fig. 24 provides the social theory of intermediation.

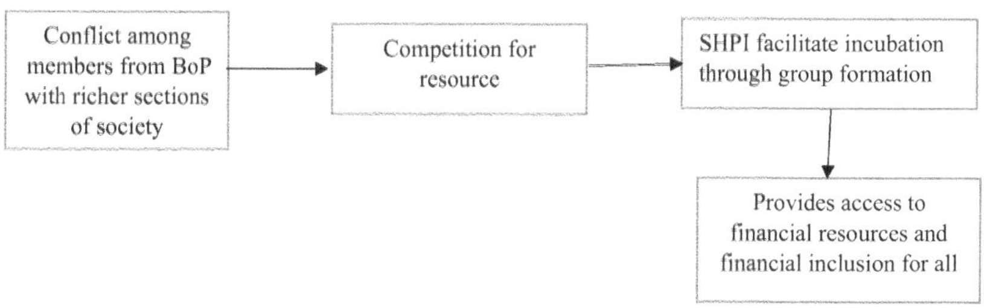

Fig. 23. Structural Theory of Social Work. *Source:* Author's work.

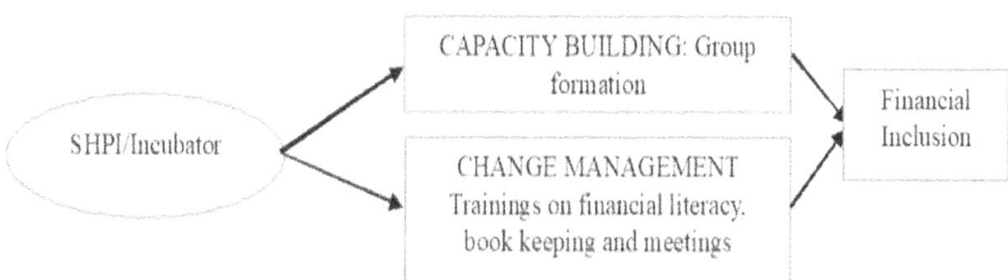

Fig. 24. Social Theory of Intermediation. *Source:* Author's work.

Data Collection and Methodology

The data for this case study was collected using the qualitative methodology and semi-structured interviews. For this study, the data was collected from the heads and directors of the SHPIs and NGOs. In total, six different interviews were conducted with the heads of SHPI and NGOs. Further open and focused coding was done to generate the popular themes in the domain of the role of SHPIs on the wealth of the small and medium enterprises (SME).

Discussion and Analysis

Below is an excerpt from the various interviews taken with the heads of the NGOs and SHPIs. In the functioning of a financial system, intermediation plays an extremely important role. It helps to channel the resources from the savers to the financial institutions. Marginalized sections of society face various challenges, such as a lack of financial literacy and a lack of physical collateral to raise finance and funds. SHPIs and NGOs play an important role in developing financial habits among the poor and channeling the savings from the poor sections of society into the banking system and providing poor the access to loans and credit. Increasingly, SHPIs have gained a place of prominence in providing access to finance for the people at the bottom of the pyramid. In case of the rural poor, despite push to financial inclusion programs, many times they are unable to access bank credit due to lack of financial literacy and efficacy and confidence to bank. Due to this reason, there is a need for hand-holding and intermediation to enable these people from marginalized sections of society to bank with each other.

Intermediation and Role of Intermediaries in the Formation of the Group

Yet another interview was conducted with the head of an SBLP (State help group bank linkage programme) regarding the formation of the SHGs. The respondent explained about the process of group formation. In an SHG, which is homogenous, members can monitor each other. Under SLBC (State-level banking committee), members have different skill sets, some are good at baking, firing etc. In a MAC society as well, people have diversified skillsets. There are two kinds of loans. Loan in the name of society for the purchase of raw materials and another kind of loan is the loan on working capital for the construction of assets. In SHG, members are not able to prepare the books of accounts. SHG is formed by the Government societies, and they have one structure, which is *Sangh Mitra,* under which 10–15 SHGs are formed into the federations or village organizations. At the group or taluk level, a three-tier system is followed in the village system. The SHG is formed by the Government agencies like District Rural Development Agency (DRDA). They have one kind of structure, which is called Sangh Mitra. Ten to fifteen SHGs are formed into a village organization or federation, at the taluk level into Mandal Samkhya and district level one federation. In NRLM, SHGs are responsible for the maintenance of the books of accounts. The member participation in the SHG is extremely less due to the Sangh Mitra, as she is responsible for maintaining the books of accounts.

SHPI and Their Role in Promoting the Sustainability of Groups

SHPIs are the NGOs that are the intermediaries that play an extremely important role in the formation of the group. At the time of formation of the group, the NGOs help to bring people from diverse backgrounds together for the achievement of a common purpose such as financial sustainability. Thus, SHPIs play an extremely important role in reducing adverse selection among the members of the group. SHPIs play an extremely important role in the financial empowerment of the members of the SHGs. SHPIs play an extremely important role in capacity building and providing training to the members of the marginalized sections of society. Thus, NGOs play an extremely important role in promoting the welfare of marginalized sections. SHPIs play an important role in providing training regarding group dynamics, leadership, motivation, bookkeeping, and other income-generation activities.

Fig. 25 provides the role of SHPIs.

Challenges to Group and Role of SHPIs

The main challenge is to have regular meetings and to join some programs with the group to make it sustainable. The groups are formed based on common ground. It is not possible to form a group of the same gender. Men groups are not successful. There are no proper meetings of the group. The members have joint liability, and even if a single member defaults, the entire group is penalized. If the member is not paying the loan, all the members join and go to his door and

Fig. 25. Role of Self-Help Promoting Institutions.
Source: Author's work.

pressurize him to pay the loan. The members in the beginning do not know about the creditworthiness of the members. The group, promoted by the SHPI, promotes the saving habit among the members through intralending for a minimum period of 6 months. This helps them learn lending and saving. Each artisan has art in his hand. Through skill training, the artisan is imparted the training to make their art sellable for the market. These artisans are pursuing the art of Madhubani Sujani paintings. Before corona, the group was provided the marketing support of exhibitions and melas. Through a personal website, we are planning, but not at this moment. In our group, we have Adhyaksh and Kosha Adhyaksh, who provided the training. Thus, the interview highlights that the SHG promoting institutions (SHPI) play an extremely important role in promoting good financial habits among the members of the SHGs and communities.

Structural Rigidities in Group

Structural rigidities in a group refer to the situation where the structural bottlenecks such as lack of communication, lack of consensus on terms of loan such as limited liability of members and unlimited joint liability, lack of financial literacy among the members of the group, lack of required human capital leads to conflict among the members of the group. The community lending groups mainly cater to the members who do not have physical collateral due to which the banks are wary to lend to them. In this regard, various bottlenecks, such as the presence of informal money lenders and merchants, make the financial inclusion of the poor extremely challenging. Various initiatives have been undertaken by the Government of India to facilitate the inclusion of the people from the bottom of the pyramid. This includes the mandatory hand-holding by the NGOs and SHPIs to facilitate the incubation to promote the self-sustainability of these community lending groups. SHPIs are proactively working with the community lending groups in the initial six months to ensure financial discipline among the members of the group, including their ability to pay back their loans and save a fixed amount to facilitate the operational sustainability of the groups. Given below are the following excerpts from the interview which highlight the importance of the SHPIs and NGOs.

Fig. 26 provides the details of structural rigidities in community lending.

Structural rigidities faced by the members of the community lending groups can be defined as follow:

Issues with SHG Linkage Program

(1) Issue of monitoring the performance of SHG bank linkage
The extant literature highlights that in a social contract, there is no incentive for the banks to monitor the borrower due to the high cost of monitoring. The unbanked and underbanked do not have access to formal banking services due to the lack of physical collateral and information asymmetry. Information asymmetry between the borrowers and the lenders further

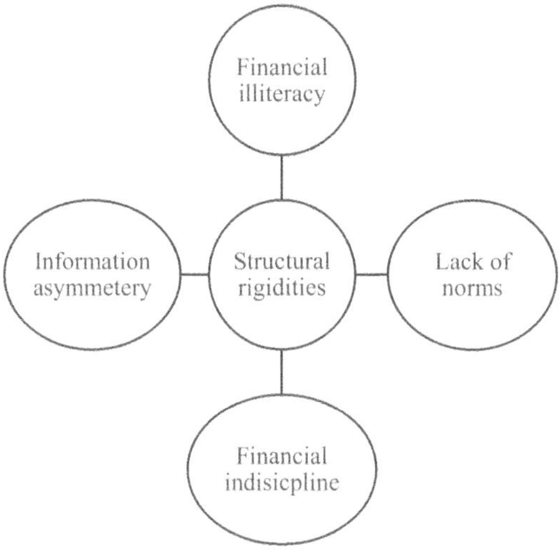

Fig. 26. Structural Rigidities in Community Lending.
Source: Author's own work.

accentuates the problem of moral hazard and adverse selection, leading to higher default rates and credit risk. One of the major problems facing the SHGs is the increasing and vicious circle of credit indebtedness and loan defaults. Many of the banks have proposed to develop community audits for the SHGs, and these could be a game changer for the microfinance industry in India. In a joint liability group with limited liability, many individual members find it beneficial to strategically default or to shirk their responsibility to repay the loan of defaulting members. The strategically defaulting members might find it advantageous to enjoy nonpecuniary benefits and fritter away the loans for nonproductive purposes. The other members, knowing that the repayment of the loan is important to get additional loans from the bank, would invest additional amounts in peer monitoring each other.

(2) Financial literacy

While the extant literature highlights the importance of peer monitoring in achieving financial inclusion through group lending, financial literacy plays an important role in facilitating access to finance for the micro borrowers and reducing the information asymmetry. Various studies highlight the difficulty in mobilizing women members to adopt formal finance in the lack of financial literacy. Though the collective power of the self-help linkage program through personalized channels helps to achieve financial inclusion, still there are many SHGs but very few loan accounts. Existing literature defines financial inclusion as access to financial services at the doorsteps of the people at the bottom of the pyramid. Studies on various supply and demand factors impacting the financial inclusion have identified supply side factors as access exclusion, condition exclusion and self-exclusion. Still in rural India, there is a huge gap in achieving financial inclusion due to lack of credit creation due to various factors. These factors mainly imply that lack of financial knowledge, literacy, and psychological factors hamper financial inclusion. At the outset, there is a need for sensitizing the women and undertaking social intermediation through financial literacy campaigns. Most of the SHGs do not adhere to the group norms or Panchsutras such as maintenance of books of accounts, loan register, savings register. There is a need to train the members to maintain these books. Given fiat and state initiatives like Lakhpati Didi and financial literacy campaigns by NABARD, the plight of rural India is improving, and more and more people are adopting the financial inclusion objective.

Interview 1 (Excerpts)

The Ajeevika scheme under the *Deendayal Antodaya Yojana* plays an extremely important role in promoting small and medium enterprises. During the initial period, the Government officials helped the members to learn the basic skills such as *textile weaving, handloom, people's management, financial planning, and collaboration*. In this regard, in the first three months, the Government officials impart to them the necessary skills, and later on, the members learn self-sufficiency and learn to become financially sustainable.

Interview 2 (Excerpts)

The Government of India has started the Ajeevika program, under which the members initially join the group to earn a livelihood. Then the members from the Ajeevika group, who are self-selected, join the SHG. We have not taken a bank loan, but we have taken a loan under the Cluster-level federation (CLF) Ajeevika program. We do not face any kind of difficulties in making the payments or savings amounts. Our members are aligned to households and are not part of any organization. Our members are extremely versatile in Madhu Bani painting, and this is an ancestral art form. It is a heritage art and is passed on from generation to generation. My mother, grandmother, and great-grandmother used to pursue this art form, and we have become proficient in it. Ajeevika has given a push to this, and our group deposits Rs 10 per member per month, and then we become eligible for a loan. And our women members are very proactive. In our group, the CM or the Chief (Kosh Adhyaksh) maintains the books. Members of the group are not literate, and they are made aware by the Kosh Adhyaksh. All the members are not literate, and illiterate members are apprised of their savings and outstanding loan amount by the chief accountant. Our group members are extremely hard working, and they collectively work extremely hard from 11 p.m. till 4 a.m. None of the members have received any kind of help from any of the other members. Ajeevika National Rural Livelihood Mission (NRLM) block officers do come, and they assist the members in making the loan repayment. Thus, the interview highlights that the Government officials and NRLM enable the members to develop financial proficiency and acumen and also indeed be financially sustainable.

Interview 3 (Excerpts)

Ajeevika block members play an extremely important role in maintaining the self-sustainability of the groups. These block officers come from Ajeevika once every month, and bank officers also come once in a period of 2–3 months to convince the defaulting members to make the payment. They persuade the members to maintain financial discipline. Banks delay the enhancement of loans due to the COVID-19 pandemic. Our bank is 20 km away and there is lot of inconvenience. All the tasks regarding the collection of the money and deposition are undertaken by the chief accountant. These groups play an extremely important role in promoting social welfare objectives such as equity and inclusion. In yet another interview, the respondents highlighted that the Ajeevika members play an extremely important role in promoting the self-sustainability of the SHGs. According to the interview, the members from Ajeevika help to promote financial literacy among the members of the group and also help in the achievement of socially sustainable goals such as equity and financial inclusion.

Interview 4 (Excerpts)

We do Sikki handicraft work. We are from Madhu Bani village, and we train the members on Sikki art. As an apprentice, new members slowly observe the senior members and thus become proficient in this art form. We have not taken any loan from the bank, but we have been supported by the Jio loan. To make our old house into the workshop, we need a loan of Rs 328,000 from the corporate. One lakh rupee was used for the purchase of furniture, one lakh for the purchase of the raw material, and Rs 128,000 for the repair of the house. This house was used as a workshop for making handicrafts. 4 SHGs are joined in the form of an SHG federation. These include Jawala, Bhagwati, Bhairav, and Ganesh. In all the 4 SHGs combined, 35 members are working together. Tula Mohalla comprises of Jawala and Bhagwati. Bhairav and Ganesh are far off, and we find it difficult to reach them. There is no loan repayment problem in the group. If there is a problem in repayment, then the Adhyaksh counsels the defaulters to repay the loan. And sensitize them to the joint liability, in which they are told of the problem of free riding. The defaulting member is told to repay the loans to facilitate the rotation of savings and progressive funding by the banks. NRLM also plays an important role in conducting the weekly meetings. During COVID-19, the frequency of meetings has increased to 5 months. A few members do not come due to personal reasons, such as visiting their parents' town. The group creates a peer mechanism through which people who lack collateral by their social capital can access the capital to carry out the entrepreneurship venture. NRLM members helped us, trained us to save money as 1 rupee monthly. According to the interview, members of the group are counseled by the NRLM and are also given support in conducting trainings of the members of the group to help them earn their livelihood. Thus, Government agencies play an extremely important role in training the members and capacity building to facilitate self-sustainability of the groups and its members. NRLM also plays an important role in conducting the weekly meetings. NRLM members helped us, trained us to save money as 1 rupee monthly. We have also made internal rules of governance such as commission agent rates for manufacturers, gifts and donations, and bonuses. Thus, Government agencies play an extremely vital role in the sustainable development of the communities. It also helps to achieve the goal of financial inclusion.

Interview (Excerpts)

The SHPI plays a crucial role in identifying the specific art forms in which individual artists excel and the local community (Mohalla) they belong to. Based on these insights, we organize members into groups, establishing terms and conditions guiding their formation. Since all members share a common profession, they can effectively pool funds for collection and deposit. A qualified member within each group monitors financial activities and provides oversight. Over time, as these groups become more sustainable, SHPIs gradually withdraw support, allowing them to operate independently. This model thrives on familial and communal ties, enabling members to support each other both socially and financially. Given that most of these businesses are lineage-based, banks often find it challenging to provide individual loans. However, the established relationships among members, combined with their business correlations, facilitate timely repayments. Within each group, one literate member typically maintains the financial records, ensuring transparency and accountability. Members can reach out for assistance from our organization when needed. In instances where income declines, some may migrate for better opportunities. Notably, approximately 50% of the Karkhanas (workshops) are family-owned. Our NGO supports these initiatives, and in cases where a member struggles to repay, social pressure from fellow members often encourages discipline and timely loan repayments. This group-based approach proves to be an effective financing method for illiterate members, fostering both community support and financial responsibility.

Thus, *from the analysis of the interview, it becomes apparent that SHPIs or NGOs play an extremely important role in training the members of the community.*

Interview (Excerpts)

An interview was conducted with the head of the help promotion institute. In our village, we have established a service area where we engage with local artists to identify those with a foundational knowledge of various art forms. From this group, we select individuals to participate in our SHG initiative. Our team conducts individual visits to the village to gather data and subsequently holds two group meetings to explain the benefits offered by both the government and our organization. After these discussions, we formed the SHGs. A significant number of villagers are involved in traditional crafts such as weaving mats using banyan bait, which is in high demand. They also create coral mats, handicrafts, and hand-embroidered items. This craft is often a family tradition. Initially, we provide individuals with loans, and as they develop their skills, they transition to obtaining loans from banks. Currently, groups are proactive in conducting meetings to discuss various issues and maintain attendance and financial registers, including passbooks. Members receive their initial loans of ₹10,000 only after demonstrating a period of performance. In some cases, members may struggle to repay the loans; however, the group as a whole often assists in covering these payments temporarily. Although a few groups have encountered strategic default issues, we are addressing these challenges through closer interactions and decisive measures. Community Resource Persons (CRPs) conduct social audits, and banks evaluate SHG performance, typically only engaging with the groups in cases of loan defaults when we step in to provide support. We are part of an NGO committee that selects officers for field visits, providing them with ongoing training, auditing, and development programs. The NGO focuses exclusively on SHG loans rather than individual ones, ensuring that insurance is also provided. Our team conducts weekly visits to the SHGs to support them in resolving any challenges they face. Recently, we've initiated digital literacy training for SHG members, especially leaders, empowering them with skills to use WhatsApp and mobile technology effectively. Our training programs cover digital and financial literacy, helping members achieve independence over time. Their families have already begun to reap the benefits of these initiatives. The government facilitates support for attending marketing events, and funds from NABARD further bolster these efforts. We provide training on color and design strategies, aiming to enhance their artistic skills. During the initial joining phase, members receive tailored guidance and inspiration to engage with banking services.

Interview (Excerpts)

SHGs enable small and medium enterprises to get linked to the government agencies, which provide essential training and guidance to improve operational capacity. SHPI enables the community lending institutions to select the right kind of members. If the members are not rightly selected, this might lead to adverse selection and conflict among the members of the group. SHGs are mainly aimed at promoting entrepreneurship among the members of the group. Thus, the lack of knowledge about conducting meetings and maintaining records leads to the failure of groups. SHGs evaluate the internal dynamics to make decisions regarding the viability of the business plan.

Open Coding

The analysis of the qualitative data highlighted that in a group, the SHPIs play an important role in training the members of the group, providing the financial literacy training, promoting social objectives, promoting equity and inclusion, and training members of the SHGs.

Table 3 provides the detail of open coding.

Thus, from the analysis of the data, a SHPI or a NGO plays an important role in promoting various social objectives and a higher level of proficiency in the financial domain. It involves furtherance of social causes such as equity and financial inclusion. To ensure the operational sustainability of the groups, it's important to facilitate adherence to group norms. The SHG promoting institutions facilitate that the members of the group adhere to the group norms.

Theoretical Coding

Fig. 27 provides details of theoretical coding.

From the analysis of data, it is apparent that Governance is the main objective of any sort of activity undertaken by the SHPI. SHPI or an NGO plays an important role in providing the sustainability and livelihood training that includes training regarding the skills such as handloom manufacturing and textile manufacturing. Besides, the NGOs also provide the financial literacy which enables the members of the organization to get financially included and become self-sufficient. Thus, from a broader perspective, the SHG institution plays an important role in promoting good governance and the incubation of small and medium enterprises. SHPIs work on the principle of continuous innovation, which emphasizes community empowerment through collaboration and entrepreneurship.

Table 3. Open Coding.

Open Coding
Training members of group or self-help groups
Enable members to become self-sufficient
Providing financial literacy
Promoting social objectives
Promoting equity and financial inclusion
Promoting financial discipline
Facilitating adherence to group norms

Source: Author's creation.

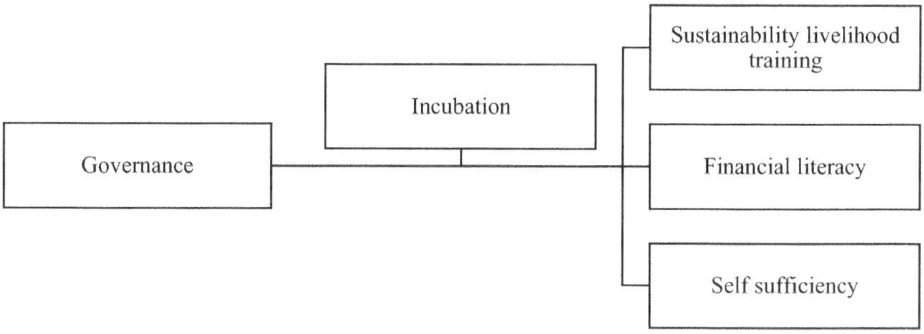

Fig. 27. Theoretical Coding. *Source:* Author's work.

Analysis of Communication and PR Strategies to Promote NRLM

Public relations is an important area in the public policy and of importance to the field of microfinance as well. Financial markets are imperfect, and supply for microfinance does not always match the demand for microfinance. In this scenario, public relations play an extremely important role in promoting the reputation of public organizations. Storytelling is a powerful technique and a widely used tool to influence and engage an audience. Without narratives, visual images cannot lead to the achievement of any objective, but the narratives help to solicit emotional responses from the audience. Storytelling helps to build credibility and trust among the audience. Through sharing the stories and the case in point is the video training modules designed by GOI, SHG bank linkage NRLM. The training module opens with a heartwarming narrative featuring a young girl diligently revising her mathematics lessons under a tree in the center of her village. As she studies, a woman named Ram Dulari approaches and asks what she is learning. Curiously, the girl inquires about Ram Dulari's destination. Ram Dulari shares that she is heading to the nearby village to sell papads. The girl then asks whether she has begun making them. Ram Dulari beams with pride, explaining that she is a member of a SHG, which has empowered her to start this endeavor. Suddenly, a man named Vande joins the conversation, expressing his admiration for Ram Dulari's early morning venture. He mentions that everyone, including his mother, raves about the quality of her papads. Ram Dulari proudly highlights the impact of the NRLM, noting that it has provided women with sustainable livelihoods through SHGs that leverage government schemes. Vande echoes the sentiment, recalling how his mother appreciates NRLM's role in supporting women's economic empowerment. Intrigued, the girl asks Vande about the DAY NRLM scheme and how it creates job opportunities for rural women. While Vande admits he doesn't know much, he shares that his mother told him about numerous women benefiting from NRLM. Ram Dulari chimes in, explaining how groups of 10–20 women are formed and registered, with one woman elected as Adhyaksh (President) and another as Kosh Adhyaksh

(Treasurer). Through this organization, they are successfully generating profits from selling their papads. Encouraged by Vande, Ram Dulari smiles and takes this opportunity to elaborate on the significance of the NRLM program, asserting that it has truly transformed the landscape of their village. Her testimonial serves as a powerful reminder of the collective strength that comes from community empowerment and the critical role of SHGs in fostering sustainable livelihoods. After providing a brief introduction to the rural economy of Jammu and Kashmir, the Government representative, Vande, further questions Ram Dulari Chachi about the success of DAY-NRLM. Ram Dulari Chachi gives an example of the Vimla Chachi in a nearby village, who was extremely poor, so much so that her mud hut had collapsed in last monsoon, and how she had no means of livelihood. The girl further replies that Vimal Chachi could get her home rebuilt under the PM Gramin Awas Yojana, but to run the household, the livelihood was facilitated through SHGs. The girl further asserts that Vimla Chachi is earning a lot of revenue through poultry under the DAY NRLM, and both her children have also started going to school. The video goes on to highlight the facts about the contribution of DAY NRLM to the reduction of poverty in villages. It further details that under DAY NRLM, rural women can form groups to pursue handicrafts, Mache making, Anar dana, jeera, and bunai, to name a few. Then the video highlights the importance of the DAY NRLM by referring to real-life of examples of various rural women who have become successful by joining Umeed SHG linkage. Further, the little girl named Nanhe and Vande decide to meet Rajeshwari Didi, who is conducting regular meetings to financially discipline the rural women. The video highlights the importance of DAY NRLM in the form of mass communication, bank credit linkage, savings, market linkages, and women empowerment, along with the promotion of handicrafts and small and medium enterprises. This engaging narrative not only informs but also inspires, showcasing the profound change that can arise when communities unite through initiatives like NRLM. Empowerment through collaboration is the key to a brighter future! The video is highly engaging as it highlights the core values of DAY NRLM, such as (1) Inclusion of extremely poor sections of rural India, (2) creating opportunities for financial and social development of the rural women, (3) skill development, (4) women empowerment, (5) development of small and medium enterprises, (6) improving self-efficacy of rural women in form of social capital of group, (7) development of leadership skills, and (9) promoting make in India products. This program is a scheme to promote the democratic participation of the people from the bottom of the pyramid and marginalized sections of society. The video beautifully articulates the demand and supply factors that impact the success of DAY NRLM program. On the demand side, there is financial literacy and demand for credit by the groups. And on the supply side the SHG bank linkage program enables access to bank credit for the poor people below the bottom of the pyramid through social intermediation and trainings.

Analysis of Narrative as a Communication Strategy Adopted by DAY NRLM

The State Government has effectively used the narratives to communicate the program values, vision, and mission of the DAY NRLM program by narrating strong narratives about the successful SHG and sustainable footprints of their age-old handicrafts and craftsmanship. Through highlighting the women empowerment stories and reformation, communication creates sensitization through building a unique identity for the program. The narratives play an important role in engaging the stakeholders, building, and attitude formation through demonstration. The narratives also highlight the benefits that the communities reap by having a strong artisan community. The stories and narratives also help rural women to build strong social capital and network of artisans. By engaging the audience emotionally, storytelling also helps to create trust and credibility among the members of the society. The art of storytelling can increase the impact of your message and retention with the audience. Psychologically, storytelling helps the audience to connect with the emotions of real people. Various studies highlight that business incubators provide various support services, which include working space, management training, and strategic linkages and networking opportunities.

Public–Private Partnership as a Tool to Facilitate Incubation

Within the domain of microfinance and incubation for small and medium enterprises, public–private partnerships are fast emerging as the tool for facilitating mentoring and capacity building. Many of the academic institutions and research organizations are coming forward to facilitate incubation and hand-holding for the people at the bottom of the pyramid. The private players have expert knowledge in their respective domain of handicraft.

Conclusion

The people at the bottom of the pyramid do not have access to finance due to the lack of physical collateral and because the banks do not have any information about their creditworthiness. In this regard, the SHPIs and NGOs have come to play an important role in hand-holding and providing training and financial intermediation to facilitate the financial inclusion of the poor through early-stage incubation and counseling. These intermediaries have come to play an important role in ensuring cohesion and solidarity among the members of the group. They also play an important role in the financial inclusion of the poor and marginalized by providing them necessary training to impart financial literacy and skills required for bookkeeping and conducting meetings. With the advent of various incubators such as academic institutions, NGOs, the sustainability of SHGs has increased manifold.

References

Baag, P. (2014). *Predicting the probability of default using asset correlation of a loan portfolio*. Working paper series. IIMK.

Bruche, M., & Gonzalez Aguado, C. (2010). Recovery rates, default probabilities and the credit cycle. *Journal of Banking and Finance*, *34*(4), 754–764.

Cochran, W. G. (1986). *Sampling techniques* (3rd ed.). New York: John Wiley & Sons.

Evans, M. D. D., & Lyons, R. K. (1999). Order flow and exchange rate dynamics. *Journal of Political Economy*, *110*(1), 170–180.

Haugh, T. (2021). Leading a healthier company: Advancing a public health model of ethics and compliance. *American Business Law Journal*, *58*(4), 799–848. https://doi.org/10.1111/ablj.12195

Herbane, B. (2010). The evolution of business continuity management: A historical review of practices and drivers. *Business History*, *52*(6), 978–1002. https://doi.org/10.1080/00076791.2010.511185

Mukul, K., & Sheeri, G. (2024). Social entrepreneurship: Distinct dimensions leading to inclusive growth and sustainable development. *Journal of Entrepreneurship & Management*, *13*(1).

Volk, T., Rednak, M., & Erjavec, E. (2012). Western Balkans agriculture and European integration: Unused potential and policy failures? *Post-Communist Economies*, *24*(1), 111–123.

Walsh, J. P., & Ungson, G. R. (1988). Organizational memory. *Academy of Management Review*, *14*(1), 57–91. https://doi.org/10.5465/amr.1988.4306775

Chapter 8

Technology and Its Impact on Microfinance

Abstract

With the advent of technology like blockchains, artificial intelligence, and mobile banking, the domain of microfinance has changed completely. More and more peer-to-peer (P2P) lending and community-based crowdfunding lending programs are making their inroads in microfinancing. Besides that, technology can also be used to improve the coordination and monitoring the microfinance operations in India. This chapter will cite the important case studies such as Drone Didi and Bank Sakhis present in digital gains of Akodara, Jhattipur, and Surakhpur and their role in promoting financial inclusion through microfinance. The theory of technological change and acceptance will be used to highlight the impact of technology in improving the supervision and monitoring of microfinance institutions and community lending programs. This chapter will use the qualitative method of case study to discuss the impact of technology on microfinance. The primary data will be collected by using the semi-structured interview. The secondary data will be collected using the existing published literature. For data collection, the samples will be selected using purposive random sampling. This chapter will explore case studies from Bangladesh, China, India, and European countries of Germany, United Kingdom, Ireland, and Belgium.

Keywords: Microfinance; group lending; peer-to-peer lending; mobile banking; monitoring

Introduction

The financial inclusion for the people at the bottom of the pyramid remains a distant dream. Because the marginalized members do not have physical collateral and hence the banks are not willing to provide loans to the people. In this regard, NABARD launched the Self-Help Group–Bank Linkage Programme (SBLP) to facilitate access to loans and credit based on social capital. Similarly, the

Development and Conflict in Community Lending Programs, 149–159

doi:10.1108/978-1-83708-290-220251023

Government of India has introduced various microfinance initiatives, including loan provisions through Microfinance Institutions (MFIs). Besides microfinance, various alternative modes of finance such as peer-to-peer lending and community lending are enabling the people at the bottom of the pyramid to access finance. Not only are there alternate modes of financing, but there are diverse channels of finance, which include Drone Didi, and Bank Sakhi, which are enabling the people in the hinterlands and at the bottom of the pyramid to access finance. The people in the hinterlands find it extremely difficult to access finance, due to the lack of bank and bank branches. In this regard, the digitization program is initiated by the Government of India under the aegis of the E Shakti. *Digital Smart Village and Digital India* program is aimed at technological transformation through digital interfaces and providing access to citizen-centric services using the mobile application. However, there are several challenges in achieving the goal of financial inclusion which include the lack of financial and digital literacy and the lack of necessary skills to achieve the goal of sustainable development. In this regard, the Government of India has undertaken various initiatives, including the technological transformation of citizen-centric services. For analysis, in this study, the theoretical lens of technology acceptance is to analyze the impact of digitization on the intention to use technology. Various state agencies have undertaken intermediation initiatives such as digital literacy and financial literacy to promote the adoption of technology. However, still, there are many challenges, and the use of technology to ensure access to finance remains a distant dream in rural India. Using the case and semi-structured interview method of data collection, the study aims to explore how technology is improving the financial sustainability of the members at the bottom of the pyramid. And most importantly what are the various factors that impact the adoption of technology for banking.

Research Gap

The risk and deterioration in the financial health of MFIs is a well-accepted notion. Many case studies cite the importance of digital technology in promoting the financial sustainability of these MFIs through access to diverse business opportunities. Often studies highlight that technology helps improve the monitoring and supervision of financial performance. The objective of this study is to explore how technology enables the members of the community lending groups to monitor and supervise the performance of the members in the group.

> *RQ*. How does the technology enable the members to monitor and investigate the performance of community lending groups?

Literature Review

As per the literature digitization is the process of creating a digital product (Hopp et al., 2018), and the use of digital technology as part of the process of developing new products (Marion & Fixson, 2021). The literature further defines fintech revolution as application of innovative technology to financial sector. This technological transformation of citizen centric services help to lower the cost of production and improve the convenience in delivery of services (Schueffel, 2016) and provide better access to services at the door step (The Fintech revolution, 2015). Moreover, now artificial intelligence is also making inroads into the financial sector aimed at simplifying operations of financial management (Ashta & Herrmann, 2021). Various studies highlight that use of technology and IT (Information and Technology) help to offer faster operational connectivity, at low cost (Davamanirajan et al., 2006). Digital transformation helps in making the business processes leaner and more efficient. Binaluyo et al. (2024) in their research study highlight that digitization leads to increased operational efficiency, positive client experience, and quality delivery. Though, there are various issues with digital delivery of services, which include data security, lack of infrastructure and lack of digital and financial literacy. The research study further highlights the need to carry out initiatives for the development of the financial services. Alam (2024) in his research study highlights that digitization of microfinance leads to poverty alleviation and economic empowerment among the marginalized communities. Further literature highlights the importance of various technological drivers to combat the barriers to the technological transformation in the form of lack of technology infrastructure, lack of knowledge in reaping the benefits of technological transformation. Fishbein and Ajzen (1975) in their research study highlight that the human behavior is impacted by the attitude, which refers to the feelings of an individual, social norms or social influence. These two factors namely social norms and attitude impact the intention to use technology. Lastly, the intention to use technology motivates the actual usage of the technology for transactions. Ajzen (1991) in his study propounded that in addition to the subjective norms and attitude, perceived behavioral control also impacts the intention to use technology. The subjective norms and attitude are individual factors, while perceived behavioral control refers to the availability of resources, opportunities and skills and perceived significance of these resources to achieve the outcome. Theory of reasoned behavior highlights that the behavior is impacted by the habit, facilitating conditions and intentions, where intentions are impacted by the social factors and attitude. Triandis (1977) in his study highlighted that the habit and facilitating conditions in addition to the affective factors, social factors and subjective norms impact intentions, which impact the behavior to use technology. Davis (1986) in his research study highlighted that the technology acceptance depends on the perceived ease of use, perceived usefulness of that technology. Rogers (1962) in his research study highlights that the new ideas, products, and practices generally spread through the social system. The key concepts of diffusion of innovation theory include innovation, communication channels, time, and social system. According to the author, in the adoption of technology, an individual goes through the stages of knowledge, persuasion, decision, implementation, and confirmation. As per the theory the adoption of technology has various stages: innovators, early adopters, early majority, late majority, and laggards.

Epistemological Stance

In this paper, the epistemological stance adopted is that of critical realism. Financial inclusion through Digipay sakhi is seen as contingent upon the existing structures, that include the relationship that exist between the villagers and Digipay Sakhi. Social structures that exist in hinterlands among the people at the bottom of pyramid, is a part of an open system, that is dependent on various extrinsic and intrinsic contingencies. Thus, the order and stratification in the social system of rural hinterlands lead to interactions of various factors such as gender, education, and livelihood that leads to grave situations like poverty. These inequities and generative mechanisms lead to observable states and events like penury and poverty. Digipay SAKHI program provides solution to the social reality of rural poverty due to the financial exclusion, by dismantling the structures of informal finance, bank monopolies through access and social support. Social contexts in rural India are determined by the dynamics of how resources are allocated among the individuals, in the given structure. In the absence of access to formal banking, wealthy moneylenders often exploit people at the bottom of the pyramid. Thus, within the rural social structure, and informal financial system, the human agency in form of Digisakhi through their communications, personal interactions ensure social change. Many a times commercial banks are also wary of lending money to these people, due to their lack of credit history and lack of physical collateral. Thus, the social context of rural hinterlands with lack of financial infrastructure and structure of power and monopolies leads to financial exclusion and penury among poor people.

Theoretical Framework

Digital transformation helps the corporations to achieve competitive advantage and realize their strategic visions through goal alignment. Technology implementation for transformation is a strategic choice that is extremely feasible to implement due to low cost, but throws various challenges in terms of the acceptability. Digital transformation requires adapting the existing structure of the community lending groups through new form of trainings, social intermediations, and devising newer systems. If the strategy formulation is strong, but strategy implementation is low, the corporation will not be successful. Undoubtedly digitization helps to improve the efficiency of corporation through cost cutting and improves efficiency of management. Transformation, helps to improve effectiveness of organization by facilitating coordination and linkage between the external environment and the organization. As a strategy, digitization enables the organizations to thrive and not just survive. However, to reap the efficiency gains from digital transformation there is a need for change management and capacity building.

Fig. 28 provides details of strategy formulation and implementation.

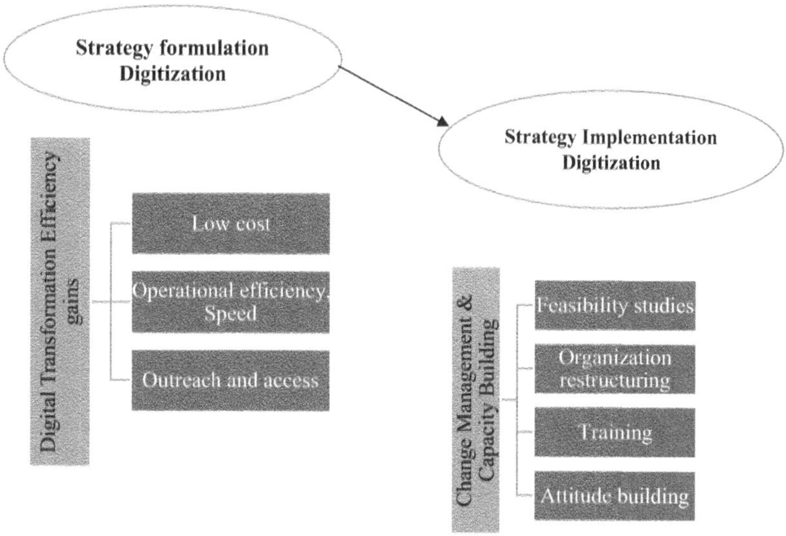

Fig. 28. Strategy Formulation and Implementation.
Source: Author's own work.

Excerpts From Interview

Strategic intervention—1 Gram Panchayat One Bank Sakhi
Strategic objective—Financial inclusion

The Government of India has Implemented 1 Gram Panchayat and 1 Bank Sakhi to Realize the Dream of Financial Inclusion

As part of the Azadi ka Mahotsav, 50,000 women self-help group members were enrolled as Bank Sakhis. The villagers find it extremely difficult to travel to the banks located at 10–12 km. In this regard, appointed banking correspondents called as Digi pay Sakhi will help to provide financial and banking services at the door step. Digi pay Sakhi is engagement of the self-help group members as banking agents. These banking agents are provided with a Digi pay application, through which the members can do banking transactions using the Aadhar Enabled Payment System (AEPS). The state envisages to deploy at least 1 bank Sakhi in each rural region or village. The objective of this program is not only financial inclusion, but also to promote the use of digital technology to coordinate activities of different banks including Regional Rural Banks (RRBs) to engage self-help group members.

This strategic intervention is aimed at providing banking services to the rural people at (1) Low cost (2) Efficiently at high speed (3) Wide outreach and access.

Case Study of Efficiency Gains From Digi Pay Initiative

An officer with state level banking committee highlighted that a 1 Gram Panchayat 1 Business Correspondent Sakhi Mission is being undertaken under the aegis of Deen Dayal Antyodaya Yojana - National Rural Livelihood Mission (DAY-NRLM) by the Ministry of Rural Development. This program, according to him facilitates ease of banking in remote locations. This program aims to provide banking services in every Gram Panchayat in rural India. It aims to boost digital transactions among self-help groups and their members. Under the aegis of this program is enshrined the concept of DigiPay Sakhis. Common Services Center (CSC) has emerged as a major channel to facilitate the local delivery of citizen-centric services. Under the DAY-NRLM, the Government has signed a Memorandum of Understanding with CSC e-Governance India limited to engage women members as "Digi Pay Sakhis." These Digi Pay Sakhis empower the members of the self-help groups by providing them access to local citizen-centric services, including senior citizen pension services. Digi pay Sakhis also enable village women to get access to bank loans. This channel also allows the delivery of the pension to senior citizens and subsidy dissemination to the disabled and the disadvantaged at the doorsteps. It also enables the member working under the aegis of MNREGA to access monetary compensation at their doorsteps. The CSC-enabled AEPS services were initiated in 2016 with the help of National Payment Corporation of India (NPCI). This mechanism is channelized through the State and the Central Government agencies to provide services such as Social Security Pension, Vikalang, and Vridhawastha Pension to the beneficiaries directly through the AEPS and biometrics. In July 2018, the Ministry of Rural Development signed a Memorandum of Understanding under the aegis of DAY NRLM and CSC SPV to facilitate banking and delivery of citizen-centric services through the Digi Sakhi, Business Correspondent (BC) Sakhi, CSC Sakhi to the members of the self-help groups. This program aims to empower the members of the self-help groups to work as the Village Level Entrepreneur (VLE), Digi Sakhi, BC Sakhi. These services provide new avenues of earning for the members of the self-help groups. The Common Services Center has issued approximately 62,000 Common Services identity numbers to the members. The executive stated that the members of the self-help groups use the services of Digi Pay Sakhi to deposit their savings and pay for loans. This way, the members need not travel to the remote banks, which are approximately 18–20 Km from the villages. The members can download the Digi Application from the Mantra on their mobile phones. This initiative has made depositing, withdrawing, and accessing the mini-statement easy. DIGI Pay Sakhis are local women proficient in the local language, so they can easily mix up with rural women and promote citizen-centric services. Thus, they can create a market for themselves. In a woman-enabled center, the women feel incredibly convenient and easy to visit. According to the executive, this facility has enabled the delivery of bank services at their doorsteps.

Strategy Implementation

Challenges to Implementation of 1 Gram Panchayat and 1 Bank Sakhi

This strategic initiative of 1 Bank Sakhi and 1 Gram Panchayat is being implemented by selecting women from the self-help groups as the Bank Sakhis. The major challenge in implanting this strategic initiative is the lack of digital financial literacy. In order to ensure effective implementation of this scheme, the self-help group members are being provided one week's residential training at Rural Self Employment Training Institutes (RSETIs) established by the Lead bank of the district and they have to pass an online examination conducted by the Indian Institute of Banking and Finance (IIBF), Mumbai for getting the certification as per the guidelines issued by Reserve Bank of India (RBI) that each business correspondent should be IIBF certified. Ninety-six per cent of the women SHG members in the rural areas who have appeared for this examination have cleared it. More than 54,000 Women SHG members have been trained and certified by IIBF as Business Correspondent so far. The cost of training and IIBF Certification is borne by the Ministry of Rural Development.

Excerpts From Interview: Effectiveness in Implementation of Digisakhi Program

Digi Pay Sakhis are provided the training in digital banking; moreover, according to the respondent, there is a concept of Champion Didi. Champion Didi uses peer influence to sensitize women regarding net banking. These Didi's, who work as VLEs, are provided the commission and transaction charges. These Didi also peer monitor the working of Digi pay. Under the Saksham program, financial literacy training is offered to the members of the SHGs covered under Digi pay. As part of Azadi ka Amrit Mahotsav, several Center for Financial Literacy and Service Delivery (SAKSHAM Centers) are launched under DAY-NRLM of the Ministry of Rural Development. SAKSHAM Centers are managed by the SHG network, mainly at the Cluster Level Federations (CLFs) level, with the help of trained Community Resource Persons (CRPs). Ministry of Rural Development and the National Academy of Rural Development and Self Employment Training Institute (RUDSETI) (NAR) organize financial literacy sessions for the members of the self-help groups in six domains—personal investment, savings, insurance credit, etc., to name a few. In order to be eligible for this scheme, the woman should be a member of the self-help group, should be between 18 and 35 years of age, should know how to operate an android phone and should be a high school pass. A 7-day residential training is provided to these members by Indian Institute of Banking and Finance. Aadhar Enabled Payment Services (AEPS) is a kit that comprises of payment system linked with bank account, which is provided to the members of self-help groups to facilitate banking services. This scheme, when linked with Rural Livelihood Mission is aimed at ensuring basic income to the people at the bottom of the pyramid. Digi Sakhis are aimed at providing only banking services to the villagers. Some monetary benefits and commission are provided to these Digi pay sakhis in exchange of their services. Digi pay Sakhis provide various services such as opening of Jan Dhan Accounts, scholarships for children, pension for senior citizen under Kisan Samman Nidhi, Ayushman Bharat Card, and other government benefits and schemes for the welfare of the villagers.

Digi Pay Sakhi: Story of Suniti Sahu

Suniti Sahu, the Digi pay Sakhi living in a remote village was moved by the plight of many villagers, who had to travel around 12 Km, to the bank. There are hardly one or two bank branches within a radius of 10–12 Km, and there is no alternative option for the villagers. By becoming a Digi pay Sakhi, Suniti Sahu helps deliver banking services at the doorsteps of the villagers. As a Digi pay Sakhi, she has transacted around 34 Lakhs and she is also extremely well regarded among the villagers (Digital India, 2022). Similarly, there are other Digi Pay Sakhis who use their vehicles to reach remote locations and collect monthly roughly around 1 Crore and help the villagers do commerce and exchange money. The initiative is enabling the villagers to get access to digital banking services at their doorsteps and realize the dream of financial inclusion.

Case Study of ONDC, EmpowHER Biz, and SHE COHORT 3.0

Digital payments and digital ecosystem have changed the way commerce takes place in the hinterlands and in the rest of the world. As compared to the rest of the world, India has made large leaps in digital transactions. In comparison to 2013, when India recorded 127 crore digital transactions, the number rose dramatically to 12,700 crore transactions in 2023. Government of India through Unified Payment Initiative (UPI). To achieve economies of online e-commerce, the government introduced Open Network for Digital Commerce (ONDC). Various tech players have committed to joining ONDC and providing access to e-commerce to the retailers. On the demand side, E-commerce has a potential of more than 120 billion and India has hardly tapped 10% of this potential. And hardly 6% of the retailers have ever come online. This is the rationale behind the ONDC, which is going to impact all the domains. The pilot was launched in 2022, and by 2023 it had expanded to around 85 merchants. By 2024, the ONDC was present in more than 500 cities with more than 3.3 lakh merchants onboard and doing more than 90 lakh transactions a month. It is a growth of more than 4,500 times and the reason behind this success is the network effect. As compared to retailers like Amazon and Flipkart, there is no monopolization, less commission, and more options to sell. ONDC enables reduction of the cost of customer acquisition and provides more visibility. However, the ONDC through the supply chain integration and use of blockchain is aiming to improve the customer experience. Through blockchain confidex, ONDC is soliciting feedback and customer reviews and feedback to improve customer experience. Blockchain is aimed to segment the sellers into various categories and through blockchain it can become an e-commerce disruptor. The marketing strategy used by ONDC is very customized, targeting advertisements according to the needs of the customers. Still, there is a need for more emphasis on customer care and ONDC is promoting various hackathons and seed funding for startups to create higher impact.

EmpowHER Biz: Sapno ki Udan by Niti Aayog

EmpowHER Biz is an online retail ecosystem provided by Niti Aayog for women entrepreneurs. As part of this scheme, 50 participants, between the ages of 15 and 35 years will be selected through an online application process based on specific criteria. The top 20 of these participants will receive a 100% waiver on a new shop franchise and this will empower them to own and operate the retail shops. This scheme will offer mentorship and comprehensive training, covering retail management, digital tools, and financial literacy. This initiative provides various services such as community and networking, funding and financial assistance, incubation, compliance, entrepreneur skilling, and marketing. From 2023, the Government will also introduce an award for the program.

PM Street Vendor Atamanirbhar Nidhi

PMSVANidhi is aimed at providing micro-credit to street vendors, who sell products through temporary establishments called khoka, and thela. These loans are provided without any guarantee. The honorable PM has introduced various schemes for the upliftment of the poor. PMSVANidhi provides access to microcredit for the financial inclusion of these vendors to facilitate an increment in income. Under these schemes, loans are provided in three installments at extremely low rates of interest. And on timely repayment and digital transactions, they are also offered cashback and subsidies. This scheme offers transparency through mobile apps, dashboards, and grievance redressal through customer care. PMSVANidhi has benefited 62 lakh street vendors, out of which 45% are women and these vendors and their families are also provided access to eight different schemes. More than 82 lakh loans are provided under this scheme, amounting to Rs 11,000 crores. This scheme is providing wings to the dreams of millions of street vendors.

Loan Guarantee for Micro, Small and Medium Enterprises (MSME)

PM Vishwakarma scheme is aimed at providing the free credit guarantee to millions of handicraft makers. CG (Credit Guarantee Fund Trust for Micro and Small Medium Enterprises) scheme is aimed at providing the credit guarantee for the credit and loan taken by the various handicraft makers and craftsmen. This scheme came into effect on August 1, 2000 and was aimed at providing the various credit facilities to the borrower, by undertaking the guarantee for the repayment of the loan. Credit Guarantee Fund Trust for Micro and Small Enterprise (CGMTSE) has inked various memorandum of understanding with various entities such as Open Credit Enablement Network (OCEN) to empower the entrepreneurs in various states including Manipur, Rajasthan, Orissa, and Assam to facilitate the flow of credit to the marginalized poor. CGTMSE is a scheme where credit to an applicant is not backed by any collateral or third-party guarantee. CGMTSE acts as a protective layer for the people who are providing loans to the micro and small enterprise.

She Cohort 3.0

She Cohort 3.0 is the scheme that is aimed at empowering the women startups and students to create the high-tech growth firms and contribute to the vision of Vikshit Bharat by 2047. The aim of the project or the program is to provide support to the early-stage tech ventures run by the women entrepreneurs. The objective of the SHE Cohort 3.0 is aimed at nurturing business leaders and entrepreneurs by providing them the necessary training, mentorship, and support for the necessary resources. This initiative aims to give push to the entrepreneurial ecosystem to facilitate networking and learning opportunities for the women. Incubators and entrepreneurial ecosystem provide the growth opportunities in the form of necessary infrastructure and human capital for the growth of the high-tech firms. This scheme is particularly beneficial for the citizens aged above 18 years and cover sectors such as trading, manufacturing, and services. Based on loan, CGTMSE scheme deploys a fixed fees-based system with varying interest rates and different credit lines. Borrowers and financial institutions significantly influence the cost of borrowing for the small and medium enterprises from the marginalized section of society.

Conclusion

Government of India has introduced various schemes for the upliftment of marginalized sections of society. These schemes include the PMSVA Yojana, PM Vishwakarma scheme, She Cohort 3.0, and EmpowHER Biz. Recently, the Government of India has introduced the CGMTSE scheme to provide guarantee for the credit facilities availed by the various rural women entrepreneurs. These schemes will give a further push to the several different initiatives that are aimed at providing push to the livelihood activities undertaken by the entrepreneurs.

References

Ajzen, I. (1991). The theory of planned behavior. *Organizational Behavior and Human Decision Processes*, *50*(2), 179–211.

Alam, M. S. (2024). *A study of digital transformation in the microfinance landscape of Bangladesh*. s.l.:s.n.

Ashta, A., & Herrmann, H. (2021). Artificial intelligence and fintech: An overview of opportunities and risks for banking, investments, and microfinance. *Special Issue: Artificial Intelligence in Finance*, *30*(3), 211–222.

Binaluyo, J. P., Santos, A. R., & Agustin, N. B. (2024). Challenges and opportunities for digital transformation in Philippine microfinance institutions. *International Journal of Economics and Financial Issues*, *14*(5), 269–278.

Davamanirajan, P., Kauffman, R. J., Kriebel, C. H., & Mukhopadhyay, T. (2006). System design, process performance and economic outcomes in international banking. *Journal of Management Information Systems*, *23*(2), 67–92.

Davis, F. D. (1986). *A technology acceptance model for empirically testing new end-user information systems: Theory and results*. Sloan School of Management, Massachusetts Institute of Technology.

Digital India. (2022). *Digital India*. https://www.facebook.com/OfficialDigitalIndia/posts/amritmahotsav-becoming-digipay-sakhi-with-cscgovin-the-women-of-rural-india-are-/4962627087106727/. Accessed on March 18, 2025

Fishbein, M., & Ajzen, I. (1975). *Belief, attitude, intention and behavior: An introduction to theory and research*. Addison-Wesley. s.l.:s.n.

Hopp, C., Antons, D., Kaminski, J., & Salge, T. O. (2018). Disrup-tive innovation: Conceptual foundations, empirical evidence, and research opportunities in the digital age. *Journal of Product Innovation Management*, *65*(8), 446–457.

Marion, T. J., & Fixson, S. K. (2021). The transformation of the innovation process: How digital tools are changing work, collaboration, and organizations in new product development. *Journal of Product Innovation Management*, *38*(1), 192–215.

Rogers, E. M. (1962). *Diffusion of innovations*. Free Press.

Schueffel, P. (2016). Taming the beast: A scientific. *Journal of Innovation Management*, *4*(4), 32–54.

The Fintech revolution. (2015). A wave of startups is changing finance—For the better. *The Economist*, *13*, 8937.

Triandis, H. C. (1977). *Interpersonal behaviour*. Brooks/Cole Pub. Co.

Chapter 9

Role of State Intervention in Development Through Community Lending and Recommendations for Various Stakeholders

Abstract

The self-help group bank linkage initiative is aimed at providing access to microfinance to people at the bottom of the pyramid. These people lack collateral, and formal financial institutions are wary of lending to them due to lack of collateral and information asymmetry. Group lending through social capital provides a panacea to the issue of lack of physical collateral. Despite all assertions, group lending is fraught with issues of institutional unsustainability, lack of financial literacy, and lack of theory and understanding on peer mechanisms of selection and monitoring. This study will explore the importance of state intervention in ensuring sustainable development and provide recommendations for various other stakeholders. It will also explore the role of various factors, such as peer monitoring and social intermediation in ensuring the financial sustainability of these groups.

Keywords: Microfinance; Joint Liability Groups; peer monitoring; information asymmetry; collateral

Introduction

The need for microfinance for the rural unbanked and underbanked, who lack physical collateral and face information asymmetry, prompted the establishment of Joint Liability Groups (JLGs). Due to a lack of collateral and financial returns, banks are unwilling to lend to the unbanked and underbanked (Ghatak & Guinnane, 1999). Lenders also lack information about these people and their creditworthiness, resulting in moral hazard and adverse selection. Due to these

Development and Conflict in Community Lending Programs, 161–179

Published under exclusive licence by Emerald Publishing Limited
doi:10.1108/978-1-83708-290-220251026

reasons, till 1992, the financial inclusion of the poor was the responsibility of the state. The state, by providing financial subsidy and financial support, enabled the people at the bottom of the pyramid to get financially included. In 1992, NABARD created a self-help group (SHG) linkage to provide financial services to the poorest of the poor by leveraging social capital and social collateral. In SHGs, the availability of social capital compensates for the lack of physical collateral (Sanae, 2003). According to various sources, providing credit to the poor or unbanked and underbanked is costly due to the high cost of monitoring, selection, and enforcement. When left solely to experiential learning, the outcomes of SHGs remain uncertain, and within fragile contexts marked by poverty and gender bias, the objective of achieving financial inclusion becomes highly challenging. Financial exclusion, an age-old problem, is not only an attitude issue but it's about affiliation and the right associations. It is not only conditioning or state of mind but also accreditation and affiliation that lead to lifelong learning, membership, social status, and behavior change. Thus, state intervention and affiliations in a group build a bridge between where the financially excluded are and where they want to go. Formal financial institutions do not find it viable to lend to the microborrowers due to high transaction costs, financial illiteracy, and higher cost of monitoring the poor people. From a realist perspective and positivist paradigm, the banks find it unviable to lend to the poor living in fragility contexts. Thus, the phenomenon of financial inclusion is a very intense process that involves facing the odds and starting from a fragile context and building it into a house of aspirations. This process is not only psychologically daunting but also involves a lot of time and effort. However, for people with fragility context, it can be a very painful process even though it might have a pleasant ending. Indeed, in this sojourn of financial inclusion, there is a need for hand-holding and state intervention to ensure that it acts as a beacon of hope and lighting lamp that guides through the pathways that bridge the gap between financial exclusion and inclusion. The state intervention provides necessary morale support and intermediation while motivating the members to coordinate and work relentlessly toward the achievement of group goals. Thus, the existing results show that the group members with higher social ties and state interventions can generate better loan repayments and savings with greater income generation from the livelihood activities. The Self-Help Group Bank Linkage Programme (SBLP) has achieved remarkable success, reflected in repayment rates of around 95%, along with significant growth in savings and thrift. It has also facilitated credit generation, thereby promoting micro-financialization and advancing the financial inclusion of the poor (Kropp & Suran, 2006). JLCs facilitate reduction of the transaction costs involved in lending to the poor (Puhazhendi, 2002). Due to moral hazard and adverse selection, it is important to monitor the functioning of these JLCs. Peer monitoring and social capital, according to a study of current research performed through the lens of agency theory, serve to resolve the issue of moral hazard and adverse selection (J. E. Stiglitz, 1990; Varian, 1990). Yet, given the fragility contexts, the members in a group are not rational to operationalize the social contract of SHGs with joint group liability and limited individual liability. It is the state intervention and hand-holding for the initial six months under the aegis of Deen Dayal Antodaya National Rural Livelihood Mission (DAY NRLM) that enables the success of this initiative. Left to themselves, the poor people or the bottom of the pyramid do not understand that the cost of sacrifice today and financial discipline implies a good sound sleep, free of anxiety in the future. Given the natural settings of fragile contexts like villages or hinterlands, the poor fraught with depression and anxiety are much overwhelmed with given state to spare any resources to overcome their plight. With state intervention, the poor feel much at home and find community lending and saving as an expression of themselves. A little bit of state aid provides a voice to their anxieties, depression, and penury. This empathy helps them transform from their given state to a newer world free from anxieties, depression and exclusions. The state intervention helps the members from poor backgrounds to see the light at the end of the tunnel. It helps with appreciating the power of wisdom that they can come to possess through the vehicle of SHGs. Through the process of learning with government aid and hand-holding, the group scheme DAY NRLM enables the members to achieve harmony in their lives. To ensure ending up in the finishing line, the state intervention helps to overcome the resistance to learning and initiate the creative process of self-discovery and writing a will for oneself. How can we call self-help group a will for self? Once the state has helped the group of people to initiate the creative process of community lending and overcome the resistance to cooperate for mutual good, the process of mutual financial planning through self-groups is self-sustainable. Let's dwell into the process of how self-help groups' work after initiation. In a Joint Liability Group (JLG) with limited liability, members are able to assess each other's risk profile or repayment propensity, and in the event of default, they are generally unwilling to cross-subsidize high-risk borrowers. Through peer monitoring, they are able to exert social pressure to enforce repayment of loans (Coate & Loury, 1995; Conning, 2005; Ghatak & Guinnane, 1999). It truly plays the role of an enabler in improving the operational performance of these groups (Jensen & Meckling, 1976). Social capital or social collateral is used by the members to enforce social sanctions and make it costly for the borrowers to default (Leathers, 2006). JLGs enable the members to identify the defaulting individuals to be punished (Rai & Bhatia, 2004). However, despite a rationale for the members to cooperate, research highlights that without state intervention, these groups might suffer from adverse selection and moral hazard, leading to the breaking up of the groups and nonrepayment of bank loans. There is a gap in existing research in what makes members choose the members of the same risk profile or join the SHG in the first place. Moreover, how state intervention facilitates the members to enter into a mutually beneficial social contract that maximizes the welfare of all the members is not a well-researched area. Thus, although there is a lot of research on SHGs, there isn't much on what is the role of state intervention in ensuring the success of this scheme. While a few key research studies stress the importance of peer or self-selection, as well as risk homogeneity (Armendáriz & Morduch, 2005; Ghatak & Guinnane, 1999), in mitigating the adverse selection problem, other research emphasizes the need of state interventions. As a result, a gap persists in existing research concerning the role of state intervention and how peer mechanisms, when complemented by state support to mitigate risk, can enhance financial and institutional sustainability. There is room for more study in the domains of peer monitoring, moral hazard (J. E. Stiglitz, 1990), and adverse selection (Van Tassel, 1999) due to a lack of clarity on the impact of borrowers' riskiness on operational performance. Furthermore, in these groups, financial and institutional sustainability is a major concern (Christen, 2007). Most JLCs have issues with institutional sustainability, such as poor bookkeeping, record keeping, meeting minutes preparation, and adherence to group norms (Ackerly, 1995). As a result, there is a lack of institutional sustainability, which causes loan and credit repayment to be delayed. Financial literacy and expertise may help organizations acquire a competitive edge and become financially self-sufficient. This study will provide a discussion of the literature pertaining the role of state intervention in promoting financial and institutional sustainability of the JLCs. It will also explore the importance of various factors such as financial.

Objective of Study

In fragility contexts of penury, the poor people find themselves holed up in the rut and falling back again and again into the same financial misery. This research seeks to provide a comprehensive assessment of how the state enables the members to change their habitual dispositions and habits through expression of right self that is motivated to achieve freedom from penury and exhibit capabilities through right behavior. Indeed, the goal of a self-help group is to operationalize peer-to-peer monitoring in lowering costs and making group lending a feasible and financially sustainable proposition. Banks are hesitant to lend to unbanked and underbanked people due to a lack of information about their creditworthiness and a lack of physical collateral. This social position of the poor leads to a lot of anxieties and rigidity in their financial behavior. There are instances where people join the group but are unwilling to overcome their bad habits due to their compromise with their fates and fragility contexts. Financial inclusion is an unknown territory and a deep sea where they are drowning without any aid. These fears are also not unfounded given what the attitude of bankers does to the financial dispositions of these poor people. However, it is also true that to attain financial freedom, these people need to risk entering into the unknown territory of the complex financial world and dismantle the existing social structures and habits surrounding them. They need to undergo metamorphosis and integrate with the new world order. Indeed, SHGs enable better loan repayment by facilitating the utilization of social capital and social relationships, as well as trust among individual members. The goal of this research is to see how state intervention enables the members of the group to get access to finance through community lending and how it makes banking accessible to the poorest members of society who lack the resources to satisfy their fundamental needs. The specific objectives are:

- Identify the role of state intervention in facilitating access to finance to the poor by bridging the gap between where they are and where they want to go.

- Identify the various factors that lead to the financial sustainability and viability of the JLCs.
- Identifying the role of various factors such as social intermediation and financial training to promote sustainability of groups.

Methodology

A comprehensive literature study is used to assess the breadth and length of literature in the subject of microfinance. Evidence from organizations, experiments, and stakeholder views were used to supplement the data. To further validate the study's conclusions, evidence data were gathered from academic journals, articles, books, reports, monographs, and dissertations, as well as an internet search using numerous databases. The PRISMA framework was used to conduct the research. A total of 50 articles were chosen from 1,200 entries. Back referencing from well-known literature and the highest citation served as an additional screening criterion. Throughout the literature on SHG bank linkage scheme, common themes were identified using the following keywords:

With a view to gain insights into challenges facing SHG bank linkage, articles across the year were shortlisted as per the citation (See Table 4).

Table 4. List of Online Databases.

S.NO	**Databases**
(1)	SCOPUS
(2)	EBSCO
(3)	ABI/Inform
(4)	ERIC
(5)	Web of Knowledge
(6)	JGATE
(7)	Google Scholar

Throughout the literature on SHG (Self-help bank linkage) scheme, common themes can be identified as:

Keywords
Adverse selection, Credit, Demand and Supply factors, Financial Inclusion, Financial sustainability, Impact investing, Information asymmetries, Moral hazard, Monitoring, Savings, Social finance, Technology, Transaction costs, Types of SHG Linkages, Women Empowerment, Social Finance

Previous Research: Discussion and Analysis

Background of SHG Bank Linkage Program

SHGs are self-organized groups of individuals. These groups were formed to achieve a shared goal. People of similar social origins, castes, and vocations join forces to achieve a common objective. The goal of these organizations is to raise funds and manage resources to assist their members (Jerinabi, 2016). In 1972, SHGs were introduced in India (Jerinabi, 2016). The groups, they claim, aim to provide rural women with a source of income and encourage self-sufficiency. These organizations are based on the idea that a substantial portion of the Indian population still does not have formal credit and must rely on informal sources such as moneylenders or family members (Coopers, 2019). According to the report, these groups achieve self-sufficiency by providing self-help organizations with access to and use of money. Self-help organizations provide rural women with a stable income solely via peer pressure, with no financial collateral or oversight. In 1992, NABARD introduced an SHG bank linkage program to provide financial services to rural women in India. According to Tankha, (2012), research on financial inclusion indicates that SHG bank savings contribute significantly to improved financial outcomes. One of the sustainable development targets has been identified as self-help bank linkage. Financial inclusion, financial intermediation, financial sustainability, and women empowerment are all indicators of the SHG bank linking scheme's effectiveness. Although financial inclusion is a significant driver for SHGs to linkage with banks, other characteristics such as financial knowledge, sensitivity, and access to financial services also play a role. One of the most frustrating aspects of group lending's financial competence is that these players do not follow accounting rules and maintain books of accounts, do not have physical collateral, and do not formalize loans through documentation (Schmidt & Krahnen, 2004). According to the research, a large percentage of Indian rural women are financially disadvantaged. The most frequent method for determining the reasons for financial exclusion is to measure account ownership; however, this has proven to be ineffective. In summary, the data suggest that if the Indian rural population is not self-regulating and financially disciplined, it may be managed by a financial intermediary or network that is more closely linked to the Indian rural diaspora. This theory was widely applicable, and it resulted in the creation of a financial intermediary, the SHG Bank Linkage program. Later, Sinha (2010) argued that SHGs, according to the study, provide a unique approach to financial intermediation since they integrate access to low-cost financial services with a process of self-management and women empowerment. Despite this progress, many self-help organizations have had high dropout rates, poor loan repayments, and financial instability (Ledgerwood, 1998). Existing research shows that members of these groups' financial behavior are influenced by the availability of additional financing options and financial knowledge. Due to a lack of numerous factors such as financial literacy, rural women are more likely to use informal sources of money such as borrowing from family, friends, and stores, according to the research available in this subject. Many scholars such as Chakravarty (2014), Nair (2005), and Puhazhendi (2002) argued that SHG federations play an important role in improving the sustainability of the SHGs by increasing the value of assets and saving rates, providing access to institutional loans and eliminating the informal loans. Despite all claims, many scholars argue that to achieve financial sustainability, there is a need for a good business model that incentivizes the members through a share in the revenue generated. Although the literature recognizes the importance of SHGs in poverty reduction, the role of SHG bank linkage in promoting women empowerment is misunderstood. Confusion persists surrounding the economic impact of SHGs in promoting well-being of their members. Also, there is a lack of research in credit creation through the SHG bank linkage program. Various studies show that women members from SHGs in certain areas rely more on informal sources of finance than traditional sources of finance. The contribution of informal sources to the cause of financial Inclusion through financial intermediation is negative (Akmal, 2016). In the newer context, the group members generally receive informal assistance, provided by the family and friends, and legal assistance professionally provided. Most of the members who took informal assistance from family and friends were women. These members do not have much say in decision-making and depend on their family members and husbands. The difference between men and women is primarily due to some societal factors and cultural norms. Perhaps, in rural India, households regard maintaining independence as a lower priority, and consequently, women try to rely more on friends and family. In an emerging economy like India, large banks tend to confine their business to the wealthier bank's potential customers. Considering, poverty alleviation as one of the Sustainable Development Goals (SDGs), the interest of emerging economies like India lies in the financing of small businesses or microenterprises. So economic growth is likely to occur if specialized financial institutions, like Regional Rural Banks, take on this portion in the financial services market since microenterprises contribute to economic growth if they obtain adequate investment capital. Under the SHG Bank Linkage scheme, the Commercial, Rural Regional Banks, and Cooperative banks provide credit to the members of SHGs for consumption and production purpose. However, as per the available literature, the large banks tend not to strive as much as other microfinance entities to diversify their investments. The major reasons banks do not lend the poor borrowers are Moral Hazard and Adverse Selection (Armendáriz de Aghion & Gollier, 2000). Various studies highlighted the lack of studies in the domain of financial sustainability. Financial sustainability depends on Repayment Capacity, Loan Outstanding and awareness about the objectives of the SHG. There is a lack of studies in the area of sustainability of the SHGs. The main reasons for the lack of sustainability are mismanagement of borrowed funds and lack of accountability and commitment toward group activities (Sinha, 2010). The local moneylender with local orientation and knowledge of the customer and appropriate intermediation and local consultation profitably expanded the business to the microenterprises or the members of SHGs (Rosenberg, 2009). Microenterprises' existing demand for microfinance is constrained by the lack of financial literacy, stereotyping, and lack of digital literacy. Lack of empathy on the part of bank officials has led to the loss of clientele to informal lenders and requiring the Government to fund the livelihood activities of micro enterprises partially. The overriding principle behind SHG Bank Linkage is Social Finance, which aims at creating a positive impact through banking. Contrary to the financial perspective, SHG Bank Linkage aims at providing financial sustainability and social capital with financial returns (Weber & Ahmad, 2014). Graduating to the next stage, there is a need for robust standards and measures to quantify the social impact of the SHG Bank linkage scheme (Rozas, 2011). Intervention that has touched the lives of millions of poor and marginalized Indians has achieved the distinction of being the world's largest microfinance scheme (Morduch & Cull, 2017). Massive social capital embedded in the institutional framework of community networks, the SHG bank linkage scheme represents intervention with the potential to draw capital from diverse sources, including quasi-equity and private equity investors. Despite its outreach, the research question that remains unanswered is what will be the next breakthrough model that can be adopted and replicated to benefit the low-income communities (Sudewa, 2020). Impact investing has been flowing into SHGs for years, through the Indian microfinance ecosystem, as a sustainable solution to economic issues such as poverty and lack of economic growth has emerged only recently.

Mission Drift and Shift From Welfare Economics to Financial Sustainability

The perspectives on microfinance follow two diverse paths, namely financial perspective and poverty lending perspective (Robinson, 2001). The successful journey of microfinance that has permeated into the lives of millions of poor people has been made possible by a shift from the donor-based model of the 1980s to the institutional perspective based on the market principle of 1992. The latter approach of the early 1990s is referred to as the financial perspective, which emphasizes large-scale outreach to the economically poor. The test of progress is whether more added to the kitty of those who have in abundance is at the expense of those who have very little. Most of the literature discusses the paradox of mission drift to choose between helping the poor and making money for investors. In the new market-driven world order, the future of the financial institutions in the rural areas hinged upon financial viability. Dismal growth of the regional rural banks and lack of motivation among the commercial banks due to the high interest cost and information asymmetry led to a major investment gap, which was detrimental to the growth of the microenterprises (Ashta, 2018). Though SHG bank linkage is a powerful tool, it is not impactful without the initial hand-holding by the state. It's a natural human instinct to escape the burden of financial discipline and drudgery of cooperating with other members to achieve financial wisdom that leads to financial autonomy. What motivates the members to take that first step to change is an unexplored territory? Despite being a great initiative, the SHG in itself does operationalize to channelize the synergies of group. Who is interested in the welfare of these people? Indeed, no one. Many studies highlighted that from the Hawthorne effect perspective, which says that other people watching you improve the performance, the concept of monitoring becomes important (Conning, 2005). But the banks are wary of lending or monitoring the poor due to high costs of monitoring. The cultural dispositions embedded within fragile contexts such as poverty often suppress even the most capable individuals, thereby undermining the transformative potential of the unique innovation of Self-Help Groups (SHGs).

The further assertion was that JLGs are successful because of (1) Peer pressure, (2) social capital, and (3) reduced transaction costs (Ghatak & Guinnane, 1999). Innovative peer-to-peer lending and group monitoring did not work for these group lending institutions (SHGs) (Christen, 2007). However, most of the studies do not provide a viable Business Model for Monitoring by the Financial Intermediary (Morduch & Armendáriz de Aghion, 2003). To take the movement further, bank linkages were introduced, but the concern that attracted the attention of most of the policymakers was that the actions of the agent were unobservable (J. Stiglitz, 1990). Within the paradigm of peer-to-peer lending, it was presumed that due to the Hawthorne effect, the SHGs would be able to pay. However, the major reason for nonpayment was an unwillingness to pay (Diagne, 2000). Concerns that Moneylenders could earn far higher profits by private information led to tensions in the financial systems existing in rural India. Moneylender had lower costs due to access to private information about the borrower and was able to charge higher interest rates (Rosenberg, 2009). This drew the attention of the policymakers, and the SHG Bank Linkage scheme was introduced as a milestone to bridge the investment gap and give impetus to entrepreneurship (Beaman & Karlan, 2014). Many scholars have lauded the role of state in reducing the gap and showing concern for cause of the poor. Through hand-holding, access to initial seed funding and social intermediation, this scheme has paved way for the emancipation of the poor. Due to the lack of enough resources banks and other agencies do not have to contribute toward the emancipation of a chunk of people are disadvantaged and are indeed the boundaries and borders in the panorama of a rich society. At the center of this society are the rich, and they are hardly concerned about the peripheries. As per the literature, in India, SHGs represent a unique approach to financial intermediation. The state intervention through DAY NRLM acts as a bridge between the peripheries and the center. With hand-holding the SHG linkage program provides access to low-cost financial services with a process of self-management and development for the women who join as members of an SHG (Sinha, 2010). Recognizing the importance of seed funding by the Government, the scholars argued that the financial intermediation role of state in MFI/SHGs deposit-taking leads to positive financial outcomes driven by the upward accountability factors and the downward beneficiary economic empowerment (Tang et al., 2009).

Initially, till the 1980s, social capital and donor funds pushed the growth of these SHGs. This led to the debate whether commercial investments are viable in these social institutions like SHGs. One of the fundamental poverty/ sustainability questions was whether services could be delivered at an affordable cost to clients. Answering this question required looking carefully at the cost structures and the delivery methodologies of financial institutions (Rhyne, 2009). The journey that started with the setting up of SEWA, a women's group, had achieved a milestone that inspired the setting up of numerous Microfinance institutions. But what came to the fore was that hardly 2% of the microfinance institutions were sustainable (Banerjee et al., 2015). Many studies raised the question of whether microfinance at subsidized rates was a miracle for the microenterprises or were microenterprises lacking financial management and personal finance acumen. Financial literacy and personal finance management emerged as a significant gap (Basu & Srivastava, 2005; Kempson & Whyley, 1999; National Institute of Rural Development and Panchayati Raj, 2019). It is proven that microenterprises hold promise, and SHGs are miracles that bring homogenous entities together for business. But this miracle of SHG can wane in case there is not enough hand-holding by the state to ensure financial inclusion of the poor. Regarding the financial sustainability and social impact of these entities, the scholars started suggesting that saver graduation and built-in tendency toward membership expansion led to sustainability, and elimination of informal sources led to impressive social empowerment (Badatya & Puhazhendi, 2002). The process of saver graduating from a fragile context to somebody who has fire in his belly to beat the odds and undergo the drudgery of financial transformation. The idea of sustainability, which touted the nonreliance of the SHGs on external sources, started gaining prominence but at the cost of widening of these margins and borders called as fragility contexts of penury, lower caste discrimination, marginalization and exclusion. Thus, slowly and it was slowly realized that saver graduation was much important than mere financial sustainability. The academicians started looking at financial inclusion as a gradual process of graduation that leads to financial sustainability and not the other way round. Now, the definition of financial sustainability of a community has broadened. Sustainability now implied financial sustainability and organizational sustainability (Bhuiya, 2016). An essential consideration in the success of group lending-based models is the basic tenets underlying their existence (Armendáriz & Morduch, 2005). These principles include social relations and proximity, inclusion, social and peer monitoring, discipline, and refrain. If we look at some of the modern theorists who compare community lending to technology that ensures access to finance for all, these theorists do not take into account the process of graduation that needs to be operationalized and is not a crystalized concept. Let's look at some examples of financial inclusion. In other parts of the world and geographies, microfinance lending institutions have been thriving. The CGAP study covers the experience of microfinance institutes worldwide on interest rates charged, and the study exhibits that median interest rates have fallen and differs from continent to continent. Probably, a new technology that ensures access to information and interest rates is the panacea (Narain, 2009). Of particular interest is the finding that the new model relies on high volumes, not high margins. And it uses private benefit limits, holistic performance standards, and third-party certification to ensure that MFIs meet the bottom lines with social impact (Karlan, 2014). Financial technology is touted to be the panacea for sustainable growth with desired social impact (Tamhane & Pandit, 2017). There is no conclusive evidence on whether SHGs have a transformative impact on the financial behavior of SHGs. Further, there is a need for research in the domain of how state intervention under a unique innovation such as DAY is enabling the poor to commit their time and resources toward cause of financial inclusion. SHGs help in financial attitude or behavior change and how this behavior change drives more transformative outcomes such as higher incomes and savings.

Self Help Group Bank Linkage and Financial Intermediation

SHG bank linkage holds great promise for its users. The deposit-taking function plays a pivotal role in the economic empowerment of the members at the bottom of the pyramid. This model has also been lauded for ensuring accountability through peer-to-peer monitoring, and due to lack of incentive and high transaction costs, members do not find any utility in operations where marginal benefit is not equal to marginal cost (Sinha, 2010). Though outreach of SHG bank linkage is impressive, the intervention has little impact on poverty reduction. To corroborate, hardly one-third of the poor SHG households have access to formal credit under SHG bank linkage (Tankha, 2012). Related to this question is the issue of the viable financial model for SHG bank linkage. There are concerns from the bank's client on lack of empathy and credit rationing by the bankers who, in the wake of information asymmetry, are unwilling to provide solvency to the insolvent members of SHGs. A homegrown movement initiated to create sustainable livelihood has been heralded as a landmark in the history of microfinance. The dominant force behind this movement is the premise of self-sustainability. SHG Federations, a cluster of many SHGs, play an essential role in improving sustainability through per capita savings, recovery of loans, better access to loans, and elimination of the informal sources of finance (Sinha, 2010). Not only repeat loans but also the reduction in transaction cost is the panacea to the problems of SHGs (Rhyne, 2009). The Deendayal Antyodaya Yojana – National Rural Livelihoods Mission (DAY-NRLM), also known as Aajeevika, was launched by the Ministry of Rural Development (MoRD), Government of India, in June 2011. DAY-NRLM is the flagship program of the Ministry of Rural Development (MoRD) for promoting poverty reduction through building strong institutions for the poor, particularly women, and enabling these institutions to access a range of financial services and livelihoods. DAY-NRLM adopts a demand-driven approach, enabling the States to formulate their own State-specific poverty reduction action plans. The blocks and districts in which all the components of DAY-NRLM are implemented, either through the SRLMs or partner institutions or NGOs, would be the intensive blocks and districts whereas the remaining would be nonintensive blocks and districts. The National Rural Livelihood Mission (NRLM) is a restructured version of restructuring Swarnajayanti Gram Swarojgar Yojana (SGSY). The NRLM was renamed as DAY-NRLM w.e.f. March 29, 2016. All rural households with at least one deprivation, as identified by the Socio-Economic Caste Census (SECC-2011), form the target group of DAY-NRLM. In addition, households identified as poor through the process of Participatory Identification of the Poor (PIP) and duly validated by the Gram Sabha are also included as the DAY-NRLM target group. The Mission has a special focus on the early inclusion of the Scheduled Castes, Scheduled Tribes, persons with disability, elderly, poorest of the poor, and other vulnerable sections of community into SHGs fold under DAY-NRLM through participatory vulnerability assessment processes as part of social mobilization in the States/UTs. The Vulnerability Reduction Fund (VRF) provides a grant of up to Rs. 150,000 to each Village Organization (VO). This corpus fund is given to VO/Primary Level Federation at Village level to address vulnerabilities faced by the individuals or household(s) or communities. Special projects have been sanctioned for inclusion and comprehensive development of Particularly Vulnerable Tribal Group (PVTG) communities of Kerala, Jharkhand, and Chhattisgarh and for socioeconomic development of Vantangiya and Banwariya marginalized communities in UP. RSETIs are district-level Rural Self Employment Training Institutes managed by the Banks with active cooperation from the MoRD, the Government of India, and the State Government. These institutions are dedicated to ensuring necessary skill training of the rural youth to mitigate the unemployment problem. The lead bank in the district takes responsibility for creating and managing the RSETIs. The MoRD is providing one-time building grants up to a maximum of Rs. 2.0 crore per RSETI for meeting the expenditure on the construction of the building and other infrastructure. The State Government provides land for the construction of the RSETI building. At present, 591 RSETIs are functioning across 577 districts.

SHG Sustainability

A journey that began in 1972 with the setting up of SEWA has traversed various changes. Sustainability is at the core of this financial intermediation initiative. It has been defined as the ability to recover loans, per capita savings, and market linkages (Sinha, 2010). Intervention that has touched the lives of millions of Indians has social capital embedded, which is to be preserved through better access to institutional loans, higher rates of repayment, and elimination of informal loans. Related to this question is whether providing bank accounts, credit cards, and other financial products helps reduce poverty and is the financial model sustainable. The initiative that holds promise for solving the financial problem of marginalized poor is fraught with various obstacles such as high transaction costs and repayment discipline by use of social and peer pressure. The SHG bank linkage program has achieved a massive scale and reaches to meet the needs of millions of Indian poor with low-cost credit (Rhyne, 2009). However, there is need to enhance financial discipline and to promote adherence to group norms among the member of the group.

Need for Monitoring

This essay aims to examine the function of Joint Liability Contracts in the selection of group members. Lenders have less information about borrowers in a formal financial institution setup. The existing Joint Liability models and the factors influencing their performance and financial sustainability were examined using the systematic, thorough review approach. The study indicates that JLCs enhance credit generation through social capital or social relationships in underbanked and unbanked persons for whom there is no information in the market. Thus JLGs help address the problem of adverse selection (Tassel, 1999). JLGs are mentioned in a few research papers to decrease transaction costs while the bulk of research studies cite social capital as a way to finance micro-borrowers. The bulk of research investigations have recognized the problem of information asymmetry as (1) applicant screening (adverse selection), (2) financial behavior and loan use (moral hazard), (3) penalties to guarantee loan payback (enforcement), and (4) auditing or examining costs. Peer monitoring, peer enforcement, and peer penalty, according to financial models developed by (J. Stiglitz, 1990; Ghatak & Guinnane, 1999; Varian, 1990), assist in reducing the risk of loan default and assure improved loan payback.

Keeping in view the microfinance institutions' challenges, there was a need for appropriate monitoring frameworks. A perceptible shift in the financial sustainability paradigm is apparent by the need to put appropriate monitoring frameworks in place. However, despite the increased outreach, the SHG bank linkage is fraught with the high costs of monitoring. This problem is further exacerbated in Moral Hazard and Adverse Selection (Morduch & Armendáriz de Aghion, 2003). It is a misconceived notion that membership to the SHGs leads to free access to loans and credit. Instead, as per the SHG linkage, bank policy, if a member does not pay the loan, the entire group will be debarred from the future credit facilities. Many scholars argued that the overriding principle behind this issue is that safe borrower will have to subsidize the bad borrowers, which pushes the interest rate. Many scholars argue that the notion of joint liability in the group leads to the free-rider problem. This led to the emergence of two different contracts: one with a high level of Joint Liability and a lower level of interest costs and the other with a lower level of Joint Liability and a higher level of interest costs. An expansive view of the Free rider problem elucidates that the idea of the free-rider problem is unthinkable in a world with perfect information symmetry. This is because, in the case of SHG lending, there is a vast information asymmetry. Insolvent borrowers with no financial repayment capacity will have very different objectives (Ghatak & Guinnane, 1999). The idealized concept of peer-to-peer monitoring bears little resemblance to the actual work reality, which is fraught with information asymmetry and selfish motives and involves competing, deploying strategies to punish the defaulter, colluding for mutual gain, and ultimately acting cooperatively (Tirole & Holmstrom, 1997). Thus, in a group of borrowers, safe borrowers will be penalized if the risky borrower does not pay. Thus, the safe borrower will not be willing to subsidize the risky borrower.

Thus, clinging to the idealized concept of peer-to-peer monitoring did not bear fruits for the SHGs in rural India due to internal selection bias and social costs (Diagne, 2000). Further, the issue of failure of peer-to-peer monitoring is fraught with a free-rider problem. Any default in repayment of the group loans echoes back and leads to the chain reaction that can cause group default and grave damage to the economic rationale of these groups. This all leads to the rationale for compulsory monitoring of the operations of SHGs. At present, the monitoring initiative is not sufficient, and the NABARD run 3-tier governance structure is not sufficient for monitoring the activities of these financial groups (J. E. Stiglitz, 1990). Not only monitoring the behavior but also financial behavior and attitude change is the key to the financial viability of these groups.

It can be safely assumed that there is no satisfactory interpretation or study on the need for bank monitoring of activities of rural SHG bank linkage. Jensen and Meckling (1976)'s model of monitoring remains the most widely accepted model by the finance community. Generalizability, construct validity, and internal validity remain the significant challenges in replicating this model in the context of SHG bank linkage. Due to the lack of research, the monitoring of the SHG linkage domain is an experimental task that lacks external validity. Thus, there is apparent evidence of a lack of theory in the monitoring of group lending mechanism domains due to the lack of validity. From an epistemological view, the works of (Basu & Srivastava 2005) provides a valid justification for the need to undertake a qualitative study in the area of Monitoring of SHG bank linkage.

Barriers to SHG bank linkage

Barriers to SHG bank linkage are colloquially referred to as demand factors and supply-side factors. Demand-side factors are further classified as financial literacy, cost of transactions, livelihood profiles, and gender and age profiles, and supply-side factors are access to financial resources, and exclusion from the financial system could be access exclusion, condition exclusion, price exclusion, marketing exclusion, and self-exclusion, (Kempson & Whyley, 1999). Attitudes and dispositions are difficult to mold and are less malleable. There is a need for persistent observation and engagement to change the dispositions through the training. The nature of these interventions and the existing financial proficiency of the members underpins how the members respond to their financial obligations and debt liabilities. Just as access to finance leads to economic empowerment, access to credit with correct disposition leads to financial sustainability and coherence of these groups. With the increase in the viability of these groups, the member's permanent income changes, leading to an increase in marginal propensity to consume and save and hence leads to better welfare. Economic empowerment acts as an anchor or cognitive focal point and leads to psychological empowerment and better social dispositions (Reddy & Panda, 2019).

Financial inclusion

Financial inclusion is the process of making available the financial resources available to the women at the doorsteps of the citizen of India (Rangarajan, 2013). Persistent and institutionalized discrimination discouraged women from paid work, but the institution of SHG bank linkage and financial literacy led to women empowerment and increased per capita income. Through the SHG Bank linkage, gender barriers can be lowered by access to financial services (Coopers, 2019). Financial inclusion will act as a catalyst for economic growth and the eradication of poverty. And this will thus lead to the achievement of SDGs. The NRLM introduces financial Inclusion, loans from commercial banks, associations, and coordination with the bank and financial institutions. Despite moves toward financial inclusion, most rural India lacked basic skills leading to reduced or dismal usage of bank accounts and ownerships. More targeted and focused programs such as microfinance, microinsurance, and remittance helped promote financial Inclusion (Blaise, 2017).

Credit rationing. Collective women are difficult to engender. Most of the women belong to domestic and home-based workers, who are challenging to organize. Inequities and challenges notwithstanding, the SHG bank linkage is an initiative to reshape the work situation by providing women access to credit. But despite being an idealized concept, banks are wary of lending money to women due to a lack of economic resources, education, and credit. This leads to discrimination in access to credit and technology termed credit rationing. But despite all these odds, women workers should acquire financial literacy skills and personal finance management skills to reshape their social contexts. Moreover, the lenders model based on unbiased information sharing and capacity building among members of SHGs can be panacea financial exclusion (Banerjee et al., 2015).

Women empowerment

Various research studies highlight that the discrimination in valuing the work done by women in verticals such as handlooms and handicrafts could be handled only through collective bargaining and collective negotiation. Since the advent of the SHG SEWA, women empowerment has been a social concept much celebrated in India (Swain & Wallentin, 2009). But the research works remain inconclusive about the economic and social impact of the SHG bank linkage program (Datta, 2015). Although from a rationalist, perspective scholars argue that microcredit has a transformative impact on individual characteristics and women's empowerment, researchers remain inconclusive about the impact of SHG bank linkage on women's emancipation and empowerment. There is scope for rigorous research in the domain of Women empowerment through SHG linkage mediated by financial and accounting literacy (Gupta & Goetz, 1996; Mayoux, 1999)

Conclusion

Credit-deficient SHGs are finding it harder to sustain livelihood activities and social, financial support to their members. Financial illiteracy compounded by lack of financial discipline has led to an increase in nonperforming assets for banks. The existence of free enterprises system under SHG bank linkage is under financial constraint and is bound to collapse unless and until an institutional framework for monitoring and financial literacy and alternate technology is put in place.

References

Ackerly, B. A. (1995). Testing the tools of development: Credit programmes, loan involvement, and women's empowerment. *IDS Bulletin*, *26*(3), 56–68.

Akmal, R. (2016). Importance of the microfinance institutions in economy. *Ibrokhimov Ilkhomjon Shavkatjon ugli*, 94–96. https://euroasia-science.ru/ekonomicheskie-nauki/importance-of-the-microfinance-institutions-in-economy/

Armendáriz de Aghion, B., & Gollier, C. (2000). Peer group formation in an adverse selection model. *Economic Journal*, *110*(465), 632–643. http://www.jstor.org/stable/2565918

Armendáriz, B., & Morduch, J. (2005). *The economics of microfinance*. MIT Press.

Ashta, A. (2018). *Advanced technologies for microfinance—Solution and challenges*. Business Science Reference.

Badatya, K. C., & Puhazhendi, V. (2002). SHG-bank linkage programme for rural poor—An impact assessment. *SHG-Bank Linkage Programme Seminar*, New Delhi. https://www.findevgateway.org/paper/2002/11/shg-bank-linkage-programme-rural-poor-impact-assessment

Banerjee, A., Duflo, E., Glennerster, R., & Kinnan, C. (2015). The miracle of microfinance? Evidence from a randomized evaluation. *American Economic Journal: Applied Economics, American Economic Association*, 7(1), 22–53. https://economics.mit.edu/files/5993

Basu, P., & Srivastava, P. (2005). *Scaling-up microfinance for India's rural poor* (pp. 30–32). World Bank Policy Research Working Paper 3646. https://doi.org/10.1596/1813-9450-3646

Beaman, L., & Karlan, D. (2014). *Saving for a (not so) rainy day: A randomized evaluation of savings groups in Mali*. NBER Working Papers 20600. National Bureau of Economic Research, Inc. https://www.nber.org/system/files/working_papers/w20600/w20600.pdf

Bhuiya, M. M. (2016). Impact of microfinance on household income and consumption in Bangladesh: Empirical evidence from a quasi-experimental survey. *Journal of Developing Areas*, *50*(3), 305–318. https://research-repository.griffith.edu.au/bitstream/handle/10072/373435/BhuiyaPUB4899.pdf;jsessionid=2A6EFA184C0B25326CCDBD20C3DB5E2E?sequence=1

Blaise, G. B. (2017). Measures of financial inclusion – a central bank perspective, IFC Bulletins chapters. In Bank for International Settlements (Ed.), *The role of data in supporting financial inclusion policy* (Vol. 47). https://doi.org/10.1111/apce.12259

Chakravarty, S. (2014). Women empowerment through self-help groups: The role of information& communication technology—A case study of Jharkhand state in India. *International Journal of Applied Engineering Research*, *9*(24), 28631–28643.

Christen, R. P. (2007). Sustainability of self help groups in India: Two analyses. *Occasional Paper 12*. CGAP. https://www.cgap.org/sites/default/files/CGAP-Occasional-Paper-Sustainability-of-Self-Help-Groups-in-India-Two-Analyses-Aug-2007.pdf

Coate, S., & Loury, G. (1995). Antidiscrimination enforcement and the problem of patronization. *American Economic Review*, *85*(2), 122–126.

Conning, J. (2005). *Monitoring by peers or by delegates? Joint liability loans and moral hazard*. Economics Working Paper Archive Hunter College.

Coopers, P. (2019). *Price water house cooper SDG challenge*. Price Water House Coopers.

Datta, U. (2015). Socio-economic impacts of JEEViKA: A large-scale self-help group project in Bihar, India. *World Development*, *68*(C), 1–18. https://thedocs.worldbank.org/en/doc/715151459872408615-0050022016/original/SocioEconomicImpactsofJEEViKAALargeScaleSelfHelpGroupProjectinBiharIndia.pdf

Diagne, A. (2000). *Design and sustainability issues of rural credit and savings*. International Food Policy Research Institute (IFPRI). https://ebrary.ifpri.org/digital/collection/p15738coll2/id/92725/

Ghatak, M., & Guinnane, T. W. (1999). The economics of lending with joint liability: Theory and practice. *Journal of Development Economics*, *60*(1999), 195–228. https://doi.org/10.1016/S0304-3878(99)00041-3

Gupta, R. S., & Goetz, A. M. (1996). Who takes the credit? Gender, power, and control over loan use in rural credit programs in Bangladesh. *World Development*, *24*(1), 45–63. https://doi.org/10.1016/0305-750X(95)00124-U

Jensen, M. C., & Meckling, W. H. (1976). Theory of the firm: Managerial behavior, agency costs and ownership structure. *Journal of Financial Economics*, *3*(4), 305–360. https://doi.org/10.1016/0304-405X(76)90026-X

Jerinabi, U. (2016). *Micro credit management by women's self help groups*. Discovery Publication House.

Karlan, D. (2014). The next stage of financial Inclusion. *Stanford Social Innovation Review*, 42–49. https://ssir.org/articles/entry/the_next_stage_of_financial_inclusion

Kempson, H. E., & Whyley, C. M. (1999). Understanding and combating financial exclusion. *Insurance Trends*, *21*, 18–22. https://research-information.bris.ac.uk/en/publications/understanding-and-combating-financial-exclusion

Kropp, E. W., & Suran, B. S. (2006). *Linking banks and (financial) self-help groups in India: An assessment*. New Delhi: National Bank for Agriculture and Rural Development (NABARD).

Leathers, H. D. (2006). Are cooperatives efficient when membership is voluntary? *Journal of Agricultural and Resource Economics*, *31*(3), 1–10.

Ledgerwood, J. (1998). *Microfinance handbook: An institutional and financial perspective (sustainable banking with the poor)*. World Bank Publications.

Mayoux, L. (1999). *Micro-finance and the empowerment of women: A review of the key issues*. ILO Working Papers. International Labor Organization. https://www.ilo.org/wcmsp5/groups/public/—ed_emp/documents/publication/wcms_117993.pdf

Morduch, J., & Armendáriz de Aghion, B. (2003). Microfinance beyond group lending. *Economics of Transition and Institutional Change*, *8*(2), 401–420. https://onlinelibrary.wiley.com/doi/abs/10.1111/1468-0351.00049

Morduch, J., & Cull, R. (2017). *Microfinance and economic development*. Policy Research Working Paper; No. 8252. World Bank. https://openknowledge.worldbank.org/handle/10986/28913. License: CC BY 3.0 IGO.

NABARD. (2018, April). *Master circular on self help group bank linkage*. Reserve Bank of India. https://www.rbi.org.in/scripts/NotificationUser.aspx?Id=12063&Mode=0

Nair, A. (2005). *Sustainability of microfinance self help groups in India: Would federating help?* Policy Research Working Paper; No. 3516. World Bank. https://lccn.loc.gov/2005616661

Narain, R. G. (2009). *CGAP reflections on the compartamos initial public offerings* (pp. 145–181). CGAP. https://www.findevgateway.org/sites/default/files/publications/files/mfg-en-case-study-cgap-reflections-on-the-compartamos-initial-public-offering-jun-2007.pdf

National Institute of Rural Development and Panchayati Raj (2019). *An evaluation of SHG BLP with reference to loan portfolio & asset quality*. National Institute of Rural Development and Panchayati Raj. http://nirdpr.org.in/nird_docs/rss/rs070120.pdf

Parida, P. C., & Sinha, A. (2010). Performance and sustainability of self-help groups in India: A gender perspective. *Asian Development Review*, *27*(1), 80–103. https://think-asia.org/handle/11540/1671

Priya, F. (2006). Impact of self help group in economic empowerment of rural women-A study. *Journal of Advanced Research in Dynamical and Control Systems*, 401–414.

Puhazhendi, V. S. (2002). *Microfinance for rural people: An impact evaluation. Seminar on SHG-Bank Linkage Program at New Delhi*, New Delhi.

Rangarajan, C. (2013). *Committee on financial inclusion*. Reserve Bank of India.

Rai, S. C., & Bhatia, V. K. (2004). Dimensions of regional disparities in socio-economic development of Assam. *Journal of the Indian Society of Agricultural Statistics*, *57*(Special Volume), 178–190.

Reddy, S., & Panda, D. (2019). Predictors of microcredit default in Indian self-help groups. *Annals of Public and Cooperative Economics*, *91*(2), 303–318. https://doi.org/10.1111/apce.12259

Robinson, M. (2001). *The microfinance revolution sustainable finance for the poor*. The World Bank. https://openknowledge.worldbank.org/handle/10986/28956. License: CC BY 3.0 IGO.

Rosenberg, R. (2009). *The new moneylenders: Are the poor being exploited by high microcredit interest rates*. CGAP Ocassional Paper No. 145–181. https://www.cgap.org/sites/default/files/CGAP-Occasional-Paper-The-New-Moneylenders-Are-the-Poor-Being-Exploited-by-High-Microcredit-Interest-Rates-Feb-2009.pdf

Rozas, D. (2011). *Implementing client protection in microfinance the state of the practice*. Center for Financial Inclusion. https://responsiblefinanceforum.org/wp-content/uploads/2014/05/Smart-REPORT_Implementing-client-protection-in-microfinance-state-of-the-practice-2011_final.pdf

Rhyne, E. (2009). *Microfinance for bankers and investors: Understanding the opportunities and challenges of the market at the bottom of the pyramid*. McGraw-Hill Education.

Sanae, I. (2003). Microfinance and social capital: Does social capital help create good practice? *Development in Practice, Taylor & Francis Journals*, *13*(4), 322–332.

Schmidt, R. H., & Krahnen, J. P. (2004). *The German financial system*. Oxford University Press.

Sinha, F. (2010). *Microfinance self help groups in India: Living up to their promise?* Practical Action.

Sinha, F., & Wilson, K. (2006). *Light and shades*.

Sinton, J. (2014). An empirical investigation of the casual relationship between gold price, exchange rate changes and JCI. In *Proceedings of world conference* (pp. 1–10).

Stiglitz, J. E. (1990). Peer monitoring and credit markets. *The World Bank Economic Review*, *4*(3), 351–366. A symposium issue on imperfect information and rural credit. https://academic.oup.com/wber/article-abstract/4/3/351/1673313?redirectedFrom=fulltext

Sudewa, A. (2020, January 20). *Impact investing: Beyond microfinance business model*. Impact Investing. https://adisudewa.medium.com/impact-investing-beyond-microfinance-business-model-b40dcdfc6f1

Swain, R. B., & Wallentin, F. Y. (2009). Does microfinance empower women? Evidence from self-help groups in India. *International Review of Applied Economics*, *23*(5), 541–556. https://doi.org/10.1080/02692170903007540

Tamhane, T., & Pandit, V. (2017). *Impact investing: Purpose driven finance finds its place in India*. Mckinsey & Company. https://thegiin.org/assets/Impact-investing-finds-its-place-in-India.pdf

Tang, J. J., Quayes, S., & Joseph, G. (2009). Microfinance institutions, financial intermediation and the role of deposits. *Accounting and Finance*, *60*(2), 1635–1672. https://doi.org/10.1111/acfi.12506

Tankha, A. (2012). *Banking on self help groups twenty years on*. SAGE Publications Pvt. Ltd.

Tirole, J., & Holmstrom, B. (1997). Financial intermediation, loanable funds and real sector fund. *The Quarterly Journal of Economics*, 663–691. https://genderi.org/financial-intermediation-loanable-funds-and-the-real-sector.html

Varian, H. R. (1990). *Intermediate microeconomics: A modern approach* (2nd ed.). W. W. Norton & Company.

Van Tassel, E. (1999). Group lending under asymmetric information. *Journal of Development Economics*, *60*(1), 3–25.

Weber, O., & Ahmad, A. (2014). Empowerment through microfinance: The relation between loan cycle and level of empowerment. *World Development*, *62*, 75–87. https://doi.org/10.1016/j.worlddev.2014.05.012

Printed and bound by CPI Group (UK) Ltd, Croydon, CR0 4YY

13/09/2026

14961026-0001